The commodity options market

Dynamic trading strategies
for speculation and commercial hedging

The commodity options market

Dynamic trading strategies
· for speculation
and commercial hedging

Kermit C. Zieg, Jr.
William E. Nix

DOW JONES-IRWIN
Homewood, Illinois 60430

This publication is designed to provide accurate and
authoritative information in regard to the subject matter
covered. It is sold with the understanding that the
publisher is not engaged in rendering legal, accounting, or
other professional service. If legal advice or other expert
assistance is required, the services of a competent
professional person should be sought.

*From a Declaration of Principles jointly adopted by a Committee
of the American Bar Association and a Committee of Publishers.*

ISBN 0-87094-161-5
Library of Congress Catalog Card No. 78–449
Printed in the United States of America

2 3 4 5 6 7 8 9 0 K 5 4 3 2

Preface

This book is the first major presentation of the new domestic commodity options markets. Our purpose in writing this book is to present the reader with the necessary terminology, conceptual understanding, and tools of analysis to assist in developing a successful trading program.

This guide is written for new and experienced commodity dealers and traders, as well as stock option traders who wish to diversify into commodities. Securities and commodities brokers will find this book a valuable source of information on the domestic and London commodity options markets.

The chapters are structured to provide reference information on the basic concepts and mechanics of commodity futures and options trading, put and call trading strategies, methods of price forecasting, and the current interpretation of the tax treatment of commodity options transactions for commercial and speculative trading accounts. Practical advice is also included on how to select a broker or brokerage firm and how to utilize commodity research and other services available through a broker.

A general knowledge of the commodity futures markets would be helpful before an investor begins trading commodity options. We integrate substantial material about commodity futures markets in order to facilitate the understanding of the prospective options trader. As the reader will soon realize, several of the potentially most profitable trading strategies involve combinations of commodity futures and options. Although this book is primarily about the domestic commodity options market, a discussion of the futures markets is included (in Chapter 3) to help the reader understand the new domestic commodity options.

Commodity options trading is not for everyone. Even though the investor has limited risks in buying options, he stands to *lose his entire investment*. As is true of the commodity futures markets, there are two types of commodity options traders: the speculative trader who seeks substantial profits in return for taking substantial risks and commercial traders who desire to reduce risks associated with their business. Commercial and speculative traders each play essential roles in the vitality and effectiveness of international commodity markets.

Although the motives of the speculator and commercial commodity dealer (hedger) differ, the trading objectives are the same—*to make money!* In actuality, there is much common ground between the speculator and commercial dealer. Each must be familiar with the idiosyncrasies of the market; a workable trading program must be developed and employed; performance criteria for evaluating results must be established; and most important, each must acquire a methodology for controlling risks and managing risk capital. These are not easy tasks, but neither are they insurmountable. Careful planning, thorough study, the assistance of a good broker, and the development of a trading strategy for controlling risks and evaluating performance are the essential ingredients of successful commodity trading.

ACKNOWLEDGMENTS

We wish to thank Lisa Meadows and Cathy Like for their excellent secretarial skills in typing our manuscript. We also wish to thank Arthur F. Tubridy for his technical assistance in presenting some of the mathematical formulas and Susan Nix for her assistance in rewriting and proofreading sections of the manuscript.

We give special thanks to Stanley B. Block, chairman of the Department of Decision Sciences and Management for his part in reviewing our manuscript and making available all necessary resources at Texas Christian University, Fort Worth, and to Leonard R. Goldstein and Jeffrey S. Rosen, attorneys at law, for their assistance in reviewing the many new Commodity Futures Trading Commission regulations and in keeping us appraised of their impact.

Special appreciation goes to George Beardsley of Smith Barney Harris Upham & Co. for his painstakingly detailed review of the manuscript, guidance, and helpful suggestions.

March 1978

Kermit C. Zieg, Jr.
William E. Nix

Contents

Chapter 1

Introduction

LONDON GOLD PRICE HITS $200 DOLLARS PER OUNCE —SEVERE FROST KILLS COFFEE TREES IN BRAZIL—CIVIL WAR IN CHILE DRIVES UP COPPER PRICES: These are only a few examples of news-making events in the financial columns of newspapers and business weeklies. Whether up or down, commodity prices make news because they affect important areas of our daily living—what we eat, what we drink, and with what we build our homes. Whether commodity prices go up or down, someone is always making money and someone is always losing money. Unlike the securities markets, commodities are not an investment medium, but a speculative and commercial vehicle for high-risk capital. Commodities markets are channels of exchange that allow the free flow of risk capital to those sectors of the economy that are essential but entail a high degree of risk-capital financing by lending institutions.

Commodity futures markets have existed in the United States and other nations of the free world for over 100 years. Commodity options are relatively recent. Although London commodity options were traded prior to World War II, interest in options by U.S. traders did not become popular until 1972. An unfortunate turn of events in 1974 caused commodity option trading to be banned in the United States when government regulatory agencies uncovered large-scale fraud and abuse on the part of several commodity option firms operating in the United States. Loopholes in the laws governing unregulated commodity markets, inadequate registration procedures, and insufficient capitalization requirements for broker-dealers created a business climate conducive to widespread deception.

Unscrupulous option dealers sold uncovered commodity options (those not backed by positions in either the cash or futures markets) to unsuspecting buyers. These firms operated a Ponzi-like scheme in which funds paid in by new "investors" were used to pay off old "investors" with the net result being financial insolvency for the commodity option firms. When government investigation and private auditing firms discovered the fraud, these firms were closed down leaving their customers with large financial losses. Unethical commodity option firms initially got a foothold on American markets because of the untarnished reputation of London commodity option dealers, who backed their option positions by inventory or futures positions and thus remained financially solvent to meet their financial obligations.

Concurrent with these events, trading stock options on the Chicago Board Options Exchange (CBOE) and the American Stock Exchange (AMEX) swelled to unanticipated heights. The concept of options trading caught the imagination of both neophyte and experienced investors. The volume of stock options trading mush-

2

roomed during the bull market of 1975 to 1976. Initially, only call options contracts were traded on the major securities options exchanges; however, in June 1977, put options contracts were approved for trading on certain listed securities.

Stock option trading proved to be a viable investment and a speculative vehicle to attract investors and their risk capital back to the securities markets. Investors became familiar with a new and exciting vocabulary of market terms. Brokers devised new trading strategies to make money for their customers. In essence, the securities markets have seen an unprecedented growth and revitalized interest not witnessed since the long-term bull market of the 1960s.

After the success of stock option markets had been demonstrated, brokerage firms as well as commodity and securities exchanges revived their interests in commodity options. The Commodity Futures Trading Commission (CFTC) proceeded cautiously and judiciously in establishing the proper regulatory environment for commodity options trading in light of the scandalous and fraudulent activities that several commodity options firms had previously practiced. The proposed three-year pilot program for commodity options trading will either result in the dynamic growth of commodity options business or will result in its termination. One of the primary objectives of this book is to inform new and experienced traders on the merits and pitfalls of trading options.

WHAT ARE THE NEW DOMESTIC COMMODITY OPTIONS?

Domestic commodity options are the most recent vehicle for participating in the dynamic, volatile commodity markets with unlimited profit potential but with limited risk. Wide swings in world commodity prices in the last decade have attracted risk capital of both small and large traders who have sought opportunities for unusual profits and who are willing to take commensurately higher risks. These traders, however, were for the most part limited to trading commodity futures because the U.S. commodities markets were prohibited from offering trading in commodity options by the U.S. government. In 1978 these restrictions should be lifted. This will allow the trading of commodity options to commence on the U.S. commodities exchanges under a proposed three-year pilot program to determine the viability and economic justification of the commodity options concept. The introduction of domestic commodity options into the U.S. markets should not diminish the volume of commodity futures trading—as some have feared—but will probably stimulate new speculative and commercial activities by traders who have feared the extreme volatility of the commodity futures market.

The entry of new speculative and commercial traders will provide additional liquidity, thus making the free market system for buying, selling, and distributing world commodities more competitive and effective in meeting the needs of producers and consumers.

Commodity options trading is not for everyone. Even though investors have limited risks in buying options, they stand to LOSE THEIR ENTIRE INVESTMENT. As is true of the commodity futures markets, there are two types of commodity options traders: (1) speculative traders who seek substantial profits in return for taking substantial risks and (2) commercial traders who desire to reduce risks associated with their business in return for reasonable profit margins. Commercial and speculative traders each play essential roles in the vitality and effectiveness of international commodity markets.

Although the conceptual basis of the speculator and commercial commodity dealer (hedger) differ, the trading objectives are the same—to make money! In actuality, there is much common ground between the speculator and commercial dealer. Each must be familiar with the idiosyncracies of the market; each must develop and employ a workable trading program; each must establish performance criteria for evaluating results; and most important, each must acquire a methodology for controlling risks and managing risk capital. These are not easy tasks, but neither are they insurmountable. Careful planning, thorough study, the assistance of a good broker, and the development of a trading strategy for controlling risks and evaluating performance are the essential ingredients of successful commodity trading.

This book is written for both new and experienced commodity traders as well as stock option traders who wish to diversify into commodities. Certain chapters of the book are relevant to business executives and commercial commodity dealers who may or may not have had experience in trading commodity futures. Securities and commodities brokers will find this book a valuable source of information on the domestic and London commodity options markets.

The chapters of the book are structured to provide reference information on the basic concepts and mechanics of commodity futures and options trading, put and call trading strategies, methods of price forecasting, and the current interpretation of the tax treatment of commodity options transactions for commercial and speculative trading accounts. Practical advice is also included on how to select a broker or brokerage firm and how to utilize commodity research and other services available through a broker.

A general knowledge of the commodity futures markets would be helpful before an investor begins trading commodity options. This book integrates substantial material about commodity futures markets in order to facilitate the understanding of the prospective options trader. As the reader will soon realize, several of the most potentially profitable trading strategies involve combinations of commodity futures and options. Although this book is primarily about the domestic commodity options market, a thorough discussion of the futures markets will benefit the reader in understanding the new domestic commodity options.

This book is the first major presentation of the new domestic commodity options markets. Our purpose in writing this book is to present the readers with the necessary terminology, conceptual understanding, and tools of analysis to assist them in developing a successful trading program. Commodity options will become one of the most exciting and dynamic investment vehicles ever made available to the general public.

Chapter 2

How to get started trading options

In way of review, some background material should be covered before getting into the more interesting aspects of commodity options trading. Commodity option contracts are traded on U.S. exchanges and are standardized with respect to the specific commodity, contract size, strike price, and expiration dates. Although commodity option contracts can be exercised for the underlying commodity futures, the majority of option contracts will either expire worthless, or will be offset (liquidated) by a purchase or sale transaction.

Option contracts are paper transactions representing an underlying commodity that is bought and sold on a continuous auction market. Option contracts will rarely materialize into the demand for the actual commodity. This may sound unusual to readers not familiar with the mechanics of commodity futures markets. If readers can imagine their bank accounts as being somewhat similar to the mechanics of the commodity markets, they will find commodity markets easier to understand. For example, if a bank customer has a checking account, a savings account, and a personal loan account each held in different banks, actual money is not moved from one account to another but is credited and debited as bookkeeping entries through a central clearing house.

This way of handling customers' money is more efficient and eliminates the need to physically move funds from one account to another. Commodity futures and options transactions work the same way in that the customer's purchases and sales are credited and debited between accounts and processed through a central clearing house. Figure 2–1 illustrates how customers' orders are executed and processed.

A commodity option is the right, but not the obligation, to buy or sell a commodity at a specified price prior to its expiration date. Call options are the right to buy a specific commodity. Put options are the right to sell a commodity. Even though commodity options can be exercised into futures contracts, options have specific characteristics that distinguish them from futures contracts. A commodity futures contract is an agreement to buy and receive or to sell and deliver a commodity at a future date for a specified price. Commodity futures are margined contracts and are thus highly leveraged trading vehicles with the potential for unlimited profits as well as for unlimited losses.

The value of buying commodity options is that traders can participate in the highly volatile commodity markets with a predetermined risk. Volatility is synonymous with price risk. Owning a commodity option can afford traders the opportunity to make substantial profits with predetermined risks. Traders purchase this right

8

FIGURE 2-1

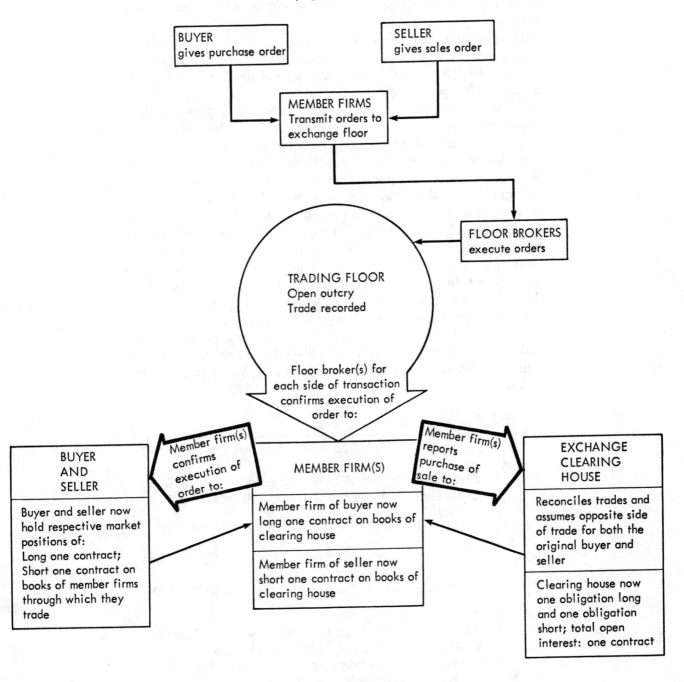

A. Commodity option order execution process

| BUYER gives purchase order | SELLER gives sales order |

MEMBER FIRMS
Transmit orders to exchange floor

FLOOR BROKERS execute orders

TRADING FLOOR
Open outcry
Trade recorded

Floor broker(s) for each side of transaction confirms execution of order to:

Member firm(s) confirms execution of order to:

Member firm(s) reports purchase of sale to:

BUYER AND SELLER

Buyer and seller now hold respective market positions of:
Long one contract;
Short one contract on books of member firms through which they trade

MEMBER FIRM(S)

Member firm of buyer now long one contract on books of clearing house

Member firm of seller now short one contract on books of clearing house

EXCHANGE CLEARING HOUSE

Reconciles trades and assumes opposite side of trade for both the original buyer and seller

Clearing house now one obligation long and one obligation short; total open interest: one contract

B. Option exercise procedures

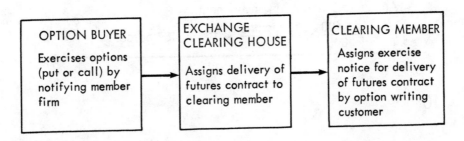

OPTION BUYER

Exercises options (put or call) by notifying member firm

EXCHANGE CLEARING HOUSE

Assigns delivery of futures contract to clearing member

CLEARING MEMBER

Assigns exercise notice for delivery of futures contract by option writing customer

when they pay a fixed premium to buy put or call options from a broker.

The premium charged for owning a put or call is a function of several factors: (1) time to expiration, (2) volatility of the underlying futures price, (3) buyers'/sellers' expectations about what a particular commodity price will do in the future, and (4) supply and demand of a particular option contract series. The premium is a consideration paid to the option writer, who either has access to an inventory as part of a commercial operation, or is holder of a long or short futures contract. For example, John Smith, a gold bullion dealer, who carries a surplus inventory of 1,000 troy oz. of a deliverable grade of gold bullion, may want to hedge himself against an anticipated decline in gold prices for the next three months. He may then write (sell) ten options at a current December gold price of $140 per troy oz. for a premium of $6 per oz., or $6 × 100 oz. per contract × 10 contracts = $6,000 total premium. The call buyer, Bob Jones, who believes that gold will be selling for $170 per oz. within the next three months readily purchases these ten options because he believes he can make a handsome profit of $24 per oz. for a limited-risk investment of only $6 per oz. If the call buyer is correct, he will make $2,400 per contract profit on a $600 investment for an annual return of 1,200 percent. (See Table 2–1 for complete details of transaction).

TABLE 2–1

Opening transaction (July):   December gold futures price = $140 per oz.
    Gold bullion dealer sells 10 December gold 140 calls at $600.
    Gold speculator buys 10 December gold 140 calls at $600.

Closing transaction (December):   December gold futures price = $170 per oz.
    Gold bullion dealer tenders delivery of 1,000 oz. of gold bullion to commodity exchange at $140 per oz.
    Gold speculator sells 10 December gold 140 calls at $2,000.

Net results
    Gold bullion dealer in effect sold inventory for $146 per troy oz.: $140 (Strike Price) + $6 (Premium) = $146.
    Additional return on inventory capital was 100 oz. × $6 per oz. premium × 10 contracts = $6,000.
    Gold speculator netted out $1,400 profit per call option: $2,000 − $600 = $1,400 profit per contract for six-month period.
    Annualized return on investment =

$$\frac{\$1,400}{\$600} \times \frac{12 \text{ months}}{6 \text{ months}} \times 100 = 467 \text{ percent.}$$

10

On the other hand, John Smith, the option writer, accomplished two objectives when selling these calls. He achieved price protection of $6 per oz. against a decline in gold prices for a three-month period as well as potentially liquidating surplus inventory at a selling price of $146 per oz. If John had originally acquired this surplus inventory at a cost basis of $135 per oz., he will make a handsome profit of $11 per oz. If the call options have not been exercised or sold by the option buyer at the expiration date, the call writer may then write a new series of ten calls at the same or different striking price to receive more premium income from his surplus inventory. This brief example illustrates the rationale and some of the mechanics of option buying and writing in gold bullion.

Before prospective investors try trading commodity options, they should ask several pertinent questions.

How much risk am I willing to take?

How much money could I afford to lose without affecting my standard of living?

How should I select a broker?

How can I obtain all the necessary information from available sources to make intelligent trading decisions?

What type of trading strategy should I employ? One based upon fundamentals or one based upon technical conditions of the market?

Commodity trading is not for everyone. Successful commodity traders are characterized by a dispassionate interest in the emotions of the marketplace. They can evaluate and assume large financial risks with a disciplined temperament and equanimity. They quickly admit when they are in a wrong position and begin to look for other potentially profitable trades. They are savy to risk/reward ratios—most successful traders look to make a minimum of $3 for every $1 at risk. They cut losses quickly and ride out profitable price trends until their positions reverse. They have studied the fundamental and technical conditions of the market before taking a position. They will add to (pyramid) winning positions with profits generated by the appreciating equity in their accounts. They diversify their positions so that risk capital is not concentrated in one or two large positions that could wipe out trading capital if those positions have sharp reversals.

For readers unfamiliar with the concepts and operations of commodity trading, several questions can be asked to help in understanding the new commodity options markets.

WHAT ARE THE TYPES OF OPTION CONTRACTS?

Option contracts are simply the right, but not the obligation, to buy or sell a commodity prior to an expiration date. There are, however, two types of option contracts that differ considerably:

Exchange option contracts are traded on national exchanges. The premiums are determined by the competitive forces of supply and demand through a continuous auction market on an exchange floor. Exchange options can be exercised to futures contracts, which can be then margined, bought, or sold.

Dealer option contracts are negotiated through broker-dealers. They are referred to as "off-exchange" options because the option writers determine premiums based upon actuarial calculations, and not by the competitive forces of a free market. Off-exchange options are usually granted by commercial dealers in the commodity.

WHAT ARE OPTION CONTRACTS?

Option contracts (put and calls) are the right, but not the obligation, to buy or sell a specific quantity, grade, and type of commodity at a future date. Option contracts traded on U.S. exchanges can be exercised prior to the expiration date to an underlying futures contract, which then can be bought or sold on the exchange. Puts and calls are exercisable only on the exchange they were purchased.

WHERE ARE OPTIONS TRADED?

Commodity options are traded in a continuous auction market on several major U.S. and London commodity exchanges. Each option contract represents a buyer and seller transaction. U.S. exchange option contracts are transferrable; that is, they can be bought or sold several times prior to the expiration date of the option. Appendixes A and B list the trading facts for commodities on which options are traded. The major contract markets for options are located in Chicago, New York, and London.

HOW ARE OPTION CONTRACTS DESIGNATED?

Option contracts are designated by the specific commodity, strike price, class of option (put or call), exchange where traded, and the month and year in which the option expires. Several examples will clarify how an option contract series is designated.

July 79 copper 70 calls on the Commodity Exchange
December 79 silver 450 calls on the Commodity Exchange
October 79 sugar 9.00 puts on the N.Y. Coffee and Sugar Exchange

HOW ARE OPTION PRICES QUOTED?

Option prices are quoted as cents or dollars per unit size; for example, 5.00 cents per pound for copper, $7.00 per troy oz. for gold, 9.00 cents per troy oz. for silver. To calculate the option premium (consideration paid to the option writer), the option price quote is multiplied times the size of the contract as specified in pounds, ounces, or board feet. Using the above examples to illustrate these calculations, we can compute option premiums as follows:

Commodity	Size of contract	Price quote	Premium
Copper	25,000 lb.	5.00¢	$1,250
Silver	5,000 troy oz.	9.00¢	450
Gold	100 troy oz.	$7.00	700

WHAT ARE THE ADVANTAGES AND DISADVANTAGES OF TRADING OPTIONS?

Unlike buying or selling commodity futures contracts, option contracts have limited risk with an unlimited profit potential. Traders who buy a put or call option for a $800 premium know from the outset that their maximum risk (loss) is limited to an $800 investment. If commodity prices move in their favor during the life of the option, the traders have the potential to double or triple the initial investment within a relatively short period of time. This is obviously a distinct advantage over meeting margin calls, fear of limit moves, and being stopped out of potentially profitable positions due to capricious reversals in the futures market.

The primary disadvantage of options trading is that investors stand to lose their entire investment if the option is not offset (liquidated) or exercised prior to the expiration date. An experienced futures trader could show a significantly higher rate of return than an option buyer because less money is required to initiate a position in the futures market compared to an option purchase. Many other advantages and disadvantages of trading options will be covered throughout the book.

CAN OPTIONS BE TRADED ON ALL COMMODITIES?

Not all commodity contract markets will be permitted by the Commodity Futures Trading Commission (CFTC) to trade commodity options. The CFTC regulations specifically prohibit options trading on certain commodity contract markets. For example, live cattle, hogs, corn, wheat, soybeans, and soybean products are only some of the contract markets that are prohibited from trading options. Copper, silver, gold, cocoa, sugar, coffee, and plywood are some of the contract markets on which options trading may be permitted if the Board of Governors of the exchange approve.

If the growth in commodity options trading parallels that of securities options, the number of contract markets approved for options trading should expand significantly over the next five to ten years.

HOW CAN I DEVELOP A TRADING PLAN?

Before one develops a plan for trading commodity options, one should ask: Do I want to speculate or hedge using the options market? What is my attitude toward risk—am I a risk preferrer, risk neutral, or risk avoider? How much trading capital do I want to commit to a trading program? Do I have time to follow the markets to make my own decisions, or must I rely on a broker's recommendations? Am I a market fundamentalist or a technician?

The material covered in this book is presented to help both inexperienced and experienced traders formulate their own trading plans. There are many different approaches to market timing, market analysis, and risk-capital management. The structure of a trading plan must include the following elements:

1. A procedure for signalling entry into the market; that is, initiating new market positions.
2. A procedure for signalling exit from the market position; that is, liquidation of market positions.
3. A procedure for allocating and management of risk capital to minimize risk and yet optimize profit opportunities.
4. Satisfactory performance criteria for measuring the success (profitability) of a trading plan.
5. Procedures for obtaining reliable sources of market information, price quotes, necessary fundamental and technical information, and trading recommendations derived from research of the commodity markets.

WHAT IS THE SYSTEMS APPROACH TO TRADING COMMODITIES?

Commodity monies, especially large speculative and commercial trading accounts, can be managed using a computerized systems approach. Commodity trading systems using computer technology have been developed for timing entry and exits from commodity markets as well as managing risks associated with commodity positions. A systems approach to trading commodities, even though not guaranteed to be profitable, has many distinct advantages over other trading methods. Computerized trading systems can detect price trends,

14

give unemotional buy or sell signals, manage account equity so that risk capital is diversified and not concentrated in too few positions, and eliminate much of the market myopia caused by emotions and unverified beliefs.

The primary advantage of a computerized commodity trading systems approach is that the validity and reliability of its performance can be measured and tested on historical price data, and then cross-validated using current market price data to confirm the validity of its design.

SELECTION OF A BROKER AND BROKERAGE FIRM

Before opening a commodity trading account with a brokerage firm, a prospective customer should discern the following information:

1. How reputable is the brokerage firm in handling customers' funds?
2. How committed is the brokerage firm to commodity research, broker training and licensing, and providing good customer service?
3. How experienced and knowledgeable is the broker on managing commodity futures and option accounts?

There are a number of reputable brokerage firms that will meet their financial and moral obligations to their customers. In the area of commodity options, several brokers have defrauded their customers because the customers did not bother to check the firm's reputation and business practices. Recent legislation should create a less favorable climate for nonreputable brokers, but it is still imperative that prospective customers assure themselves that the brokerage firm they select is reputable and has the customers' interests in mind.

If in doubt about the reputation or business practices of a brokerage firm, a person can obtain information from the local Better Business Bureau, Securities and Exchange Commission, or the Commodities Futures Trading Commission. Before opening an account with a brokerage firm, a person should thoroughly check the firm's reputation, business practices, and the amount of experience their account representatives have had in handling commodity accounts. A reputable firm will provide full disclosure of its commission costs, mail written confirmations to its customers, be registered with the CFTC, and have licensed and well-trained account representatives.

Commodity research is a very important subject for the prospective commodity trader. Good fundamental and technical research reports with trading recommendations provided by a brokerage firm could substantially increase performance. Fundamental research is needed for developing a longer term perspective of the overall market potential to move decidedly up or down during a period of time. Technical research is needed for timing the entry and exit from the market once the move has begun or ended. Fundamental and technical research complement each other and are not in opposition for making profitable trading decisions. Many brokerage firms committed to commodity research provide excellent fundamental market reports and technical recommendations for both speculative and commercial customers.

HOW MUCH RISK CAPITAL SHOULD I INVEST IN COMMODITY TRADING?

The new commodity speculator is advised not to put more than 10 percent of his or her net worth into a commodity trading program as a rule of thumb. The net worth figure should be exclusive of home, car, and other personal assets. For example, if Peter Brown, a prospective commodity trader, had an estimated net worth of $100,000 composed of stocks, bonds, and real estate, he should probably not invest more than $10,000 in a commodity trading program. Another rule of thumb for commodity trading is to set a predetermined loss figure to terminate a trading program. As an example, Mary White, a speculative trader, would terminate a trading program if she incurred $5,000 in losses out of her original $10,000 investment. Of course, these trading rules for risk-capital management apply to the speculator, not to the commercial trader who uses the futures and options markets for price insurance.

HOW DO I OPEN AN OPTION TRADING ACCOUNT?

Commodity options trading accounts can be opened through any brokerage firm registered to do commodity business in the United States. Brokerage firms' representatives should be licensed to take orders and be knowledgeable regarding the rules and regulations governing commodity trading as required for registration by the Commodity Futures Trading Commission.

Many brokerage firms have minimum financial requirements for their customers to prevent an undercapitalized person from suffering disastrous financial consequences in the commodity markets. These minimum financial requirements differ among brokerage houses; however, they are instituted for the protection of the customer's and the firms' assets.

Opening an options trading account with a brokerage firm in-

16

volves filling out a customer's financial questionnaire, signing several forms required by the commodity exchanges, and making an initial deposit of funds. The broker will ask for the usual personal information, including references (personal and credit), type of trading account (speculative or commercial), instructions on sending notice statements, and any special requests the customer may have regarding the account; for example, setting up a limited or general power of attorney.

The type of account opened depends upon the customer's situation and trading objectives. The different types of accounts are speculative, commercial, sole ownership, partnership, and corporate. Commercial accounts are designated differently from speculative accounts. Usually a commodity broker will explain the risks and pitfalls of commodity trading to the prospective customer before opening an account in order to be certain that the customer understands and appreciates the risks and mechanics of commodity trading before placing an order.

Precise communication between broker and customer is essential for maintaining a long-lasting broker-customer relationship. Broker-customer communication should result in clear instructions for placing an order. Ambiguous instructions can only result in the broker placing a discretionary order, which generally spells trouble and costly mistakes for both broker and customer. Discretionary orders are usually undesirable and should be avoided.

HOW ORDERS ARE EXECUTED ON THE EXCHANGE

When a customer gives an order to the broker, the broker then transmits it to the exchange trading in that particular commodity. Orders are sent to a specified exchange for execution depending upon the customer's preference and the particular commodity. Once on the exchange floor, the floor broker attempts to fill the order by open outcry. If other floor brokers are willing to do business, the transaction is completed, and notification of the order is transmitted to the initiating broker. The broker then communicates the confirmation of the trade to the customer by phone, followed by a written confirmation from the brokerage firm. The entire process of entering an order and receiving notification of its execution might not take longer than five to ten minutes, if the order can be filled immediately.

The open outcry method of executing orders is probably one of the best methods of filling a customer's order because orders from a multitude of buyers and sellers are shouted out on the exchange floor to be filled at a free market price. London commodity options on the London Metal Exchange (LME) are not handled by open outcry but are negotiated through broker-dealers. Premiums on LME options are computed on a actuarial basis and not subject to the forces of free market competition.

WHERE CAN I FIND INFORMATION ON COMMODITY TRADING?

There are many excellent sources of information for educating oneself about the commodity markets. Brokerage firms will provide free literature to prospective customers. Public relations departments of commodity exchanges will mail free literature as well as movies, slide presentations, and other educational materials upon request. Local public and university libraries are excellent sources of reference information. The U.S. Government Printing Office has booklets, pamphlets, and statistical reports on commodities and commodities markets. There are many excellent daily, weekly, and monthly publications that contain timely and essential market information for making trading recommendations and decisions. The Bibliography lists some of the primary and secondary sources of information to help the reader get started in researching topics of interest.

MARKET AND BROKER TERMINOLOGY

Before prospective commodity traders begin trading, they should have a grasp of the following market terms so that they understand what they want or what their brokers want them to do. Improper understanding and communication between customer and broker can only result in hard feelings and financial losses.

The role of clear communication between broker and customer cannot be over-emphasized. Even experienced brokers and commodity traders become confused on occasion as to what the customers want to do. This miscommunication results in errors and unnecessary financial losses.

TYPES OF ORDERS

Brokers can enter many types of orders for their customers. Our discussion will be limited to the more commonly used orders. They will be defined so that readers will have a general knowledge of how to use them.

Market order Buy or sell orders filled at the prevailing market price; used to initiate or close out positions.

Limit order Buy or sell orders filled at specific **price** or better; that is, buy orders filled at limit price (or lower); sell orders filled at limit price (or higher).

Stop order   Buy or sell orders become market orders when a specific price is reached or penetrated; stop orders can be used to prevent excessive losses as a stop-loss order or can be used to initiate new positions.

Day order   The order is entered for one day only; it is cancelled if not filled by the close of the market.

Good-til-cancelled order   The GTC order remains a valid order until it is filled or cancelled.

Basis order   This order is entered as a price differential between two futures or options contract series; used for executing a spread or straddle order at a given basis; for example, Buy July copper and sell December copper with December 200 points over July (200 points is the basis between July and December copper).

DEFINITIONS AND TERMINOLOGY

The following is a list of important definitions and market terms that are essential for understanding commodity futures and options trading. The Glossary at the end of the book is provided to help clarify other concepts and terms presented throughout.

Call option   The right but not the obligation to buy. Call buyers anticipate a rise in market prices.

Put option   The right but not the obligation to sell. Put buyers anticipate a decline in market prices.

Exercise   Put and call options can be converted (exercised) to a futures contract at a given strike price prior to the expiration date of the option. Call options can be converted to long futures position. Put options can be converted to a short futures position.

Futures contract   An agreement to buy or sell a specific grade and quantity of a commodity at a given price at some future date. Futures contracts can be bought and sold at any time up to the last trading date specified by the commodity exchange on which it is traded. Less than 2 to 5 percent of all futures contracts traded result in delivery of the actual commodity. Most futures contracts require less than a 10 percent margin deposit of the initial value of the commodity.

Expiration date (also referred to as declaration date)   The date on which a put or call option expires worthless. Put and call options may be offset or exercised to a futures contract at any time prior to the expiration date by the option holder.

Premium   The monetary consideration, minus intrinsic value of the option, for buying or writing an option. Option buyers pay the consideration to the option writer. Option premiums are paid in full to the option writer and, therefore, are not marginable as futures contracts are.

Strike price (also referred to as the exercise price) The predetermined price at which an option can be exercised to a futures contract. Strike prices are listed at fixed intervals for each contract series.

Commission The fee charged by the brokerage firm for executing and handling customers orders. Referred to as Round-Turn Commission.

Straddle The combination of a put and call option. Straddle buyers would buy a put and call on the same contract series. Straddle writers would write (sell) a put and call on a contract series.

Option contract series The designation of the type of option, the contract month, and the strike price. For example, July 70 copper calls, October 10 sugar calls, December 500 silver puts.

Spread The combination of buying and selling either puts or calls at different contract series. Not to be confused with a straddle which is a combination of a put and a call. Buy July 70 copper calls versus sell December 70 calls, for example.

Speculator A trader who seeks optimum risk in return for optimum profit opportunities in the market.

Commercial trader (usually referred to as a hedger) Person who trades commodities as a means of taking price protection on actual commodities bought or sold from inventory. A commercial trader may be a producer, processor, or distributor who hedges inventory position in the futures or options markets.

Hedge The process of buying or selling futures and/or option contracts against an inventory of commodity materials similar to the specifications of the futures of options contract.

Confirmation The written communication between broker and customer notifying the customer of the transaction. The confirmation usually includes the quantity, price, contract month, and commodity exchange as details of the customer's transaction.

Commodity exchange The physical location of a contract market where customers' orders are transmitted for execution on the floor of the exchange by open outcry. Many different commodity futures and option contracts are traded at an exchange. Orders are executed by floor brokers who are members of the exchange.

Order The written or verbal communication between customer and broker to buy or sell a futures or option contract. An order must specify the quantity, type of commodity, contract month, commodity exchange, price, and time period that the order is to be kept in force. An example would be "Buy Five December 70 copper calls at 2 on the COMEX, day order."

Margin deposit   The amount of funds required by a brokerage firm to initiate and maintain a commodity futures position. Margin deposits are usually no more than 5 to 10 percent of the market value of the commodity bought or sold.

Option writer   A trader who sells (writes) puts or calls for a consideration (premium) that obligates the trader to deliver a long or short futures position to the option holder up to the expiration date of the option.

Intrinsic value   The option price minus the premium; if the option price for out-of-the-money puts and calls equals the premium, the intrinsic value equals zero; a call has intrinsic value only if the commodity futures price is above the option strike price, a put option has intrinsic value only if the commodity price is below the strike price.

In-the-money option   A call is in the money when the futures price is above the strike price; a put is in the money when the futures price is below the strike price.

Out-of-the-money option   A call is out of the money when the futures price is below the strike price; a put is out of the money when the futures price is above the strike price.

Offset   A closing out transaction of selling a put, call, a long futures position, or buying back a short futures position.

Dealer options   Puts and calls sold by commodity dealers, not traded on national commodity exchanges; commodity merchants granting options to buyers and guaranteeing the fulfillment of option contracts.

Option price   The price quote of the put or call that includes option premium and intrinsic value (if any). Option premium is often used interchangeably with option price but is not the same since an option premium *never* includes intrinsic value of the option.

Chapter 3

Futures
versus options

This chapter describes the similarities and differences between futures and options markets with respect to their roles in maintaining viable commercial and speculative trading activities. The introduction of U.S. exchange options markets is designed to complement, not compete with, the existing commercial role of futures markets. Trading strategies utilizing a combination of futures and option contracts are presented to show the considerable flexibility and profitability of combination futures-options trading programs. Let us first begin with a brief history of the development of futures markets in the United States.

HISTORY OF FUTURES MARKETS IN THE UNITED STATES

In the middle 1800s, American farmers and grain merchants were experiencing price volatility in corn, oats, and wheat crops that impeded their commercial utilization. Droughts, crop disease, and overproduction caused wide price swings between the time that crops were planted and harvested. Farmers were always uncertain how much they could sell their crops for at harvest. Grain merchants were not sure how much they should pay for the farmers' crops after harvest because prices could either rise or decline dramatically within short periods of time. The financial risks involved in buying, storing, and marketing grain crops prohibited merchants from buying and storing large inventories of grain for resale to millers and other processors.

Surplus inventories of corn, oats, and wheat stayed in farmers' hands and never entered the more efficient merchandising channels of distribution. There was much waste and spoilage of valuable foodstuffs due to improper storage and inefficient marketing methods. Grain merchants, farmers, and processors partially resolved these crucial problems through the creation of the "to arrive contracts." The implementation of the "to arrive contract" served as a forward pricing agreement that transferred some of the risk of ownership to those willing to assume it. The "to arrive contract" achieved several important objectives: (1) transferred some of the risks of ownership; (2) established a forward pricing agreement between producers, processors, and merchants; (3) made marketing and physical distribution of grains and foodstuffs more efficient and thus less costly to consumers.

Regardless if grain supplies were abundant or scarce, farmers, merchants, and processors could establish future prices for their crops, or inventory requirements. Farmers could contract future prices for their crops during the season of the year when prices were generally higher. Merchants and processors could forward contract their inventory needs for corn, oats, and wheat during the year when prices were favorable and their inventory requirements were more accurately known. This procedure of establishing future prices and inventory commitments provided a measure of stability and marketing efficiency during the formative years of American agribusiness.

The "to arrive contract" provided the commercial basis for the modern concept of futures trading. Central markets for futures trading were organized in Chicago in the 1870s. The volume of futures trading in corn, oats, and wheat contracts still contribute a large share of the revenues to the Chicago Board of Trade today. The creation of organized futures markets broadened the participation of producers, merchants, and processors considerably. The greater participation by speculative traders in the markets has enhanced the liquidity and viability of futures markets in achieving their fundamental purpose of offering price insurance to commercials, and providing for the transfer of ownership risks of commodity inventories.

Since the inception of futures trading in the United States, the number of futures markets and the dollar volume of trading have grown substantially. It is estimated that there are 500,000 commodity traders in the United States and that the commodity business is a $600 billion industry. Futures markets are now central market places for agricultural products, livestock, metals, forest products, coffee, cocoa, sugar, foreign currencies, and, most recently, financial instruments (T-bills, GNMA's, commercial paper).

For more than 50 years, futures trading was done by a relatively small group of professional traders located in Chicago and New York. They were responsible for maintaining active and orderly futures markets. Participation in the futures markets by the general public is a relatively recent phenomenon. Futures trading during the past 15 years has experienced an unprecedented rate of growth due to advertising and promotional efforts by commodity exchanges and brokerage firms. Brokerage houses and commodity exchanges have done a fairly good job at educating the investing public on the merits and pitfalls of futures trading. Because of the volatility of the futures markets and the high degree of financial leverage, futures trading is not a suitable investment for the undercapitalized or unknowledgeable investor.

WHERE ARE FUTURES MARKETS LOCATED?

Futures contracts are traded on commodity exchanges just as listed securities are traded on stock exchanges. Major U.S. commodity exchanges are located in Chicago and New York. Futures contracts also are traded on London, Paris, Sidney, and Winnipeg commodity exchanges. London commodity exchanges also trade option contracts on metals, cocoa, coffee, and other commodities. It is conceivable that commodity option trading will expand to other international markets after option trading has proven to be a viable commercial and speculative endeavor in the United States. Table 3–1 lists basic information on commodity futures contracts traded on U.S. exchanges that could have corresponding options contracts. Appendixes A and B provide more detailed information on optionable commodities traded on U.S. and London futures markets.

TABLE 3–1
FUTURES VERSUS OPTIONS

Commodity	Exchange	Trading hours	Contract unit	Value of 1¢ per $1 move	Minimum price change
Cocoa	N.Y. Cocoa	9:30–2:30	30,000 lb.	$ 300.00	1/100¢ lb.
Coffee "C"	N.Y. Coffee and Sugar	9:45–2:45	37,500 lb.	375.00	1/100¢ lb.
Deutsche Mark ..	IMM	8:45–1:10	125,000 DM	1,250.00	0.0001
Gold	CBT	8:25–1:30	3 kg. (96.45)	96.45	10¢ oz.
Gold	COMEX	9:25–2:30	100 troy oz.	100.00	10¢ oz.
Gold	IMM	8:25–1:30	100 troy oz.	100.00	10¢ oz.
Gold	NYME	9:25–2:30	1 kg.	32.15	20¢ oz.
GNMAs	CBT	8:50–1:30	$100,000	1,000.00	1/32 pt.
Lumber	CME	9:00–1:05	100,000 bd ft	100.00	10¢ mbf
Platinum	NYME	9:45–2:10	50 troy oz.	50.00	10¢ oz.
Plywood	CBT	10:00–1:00	76,032 sf	76.03	10¢ msf
Rubber	N.Y. Cocoa	9:45–2:45	33,000 lb.	330.00	5/100¢ lb.
Silver	COMEX	9:40–2:15	5,000 troy oz.	50.00	10/100¢ oz.
Silver	CBT	8:40–1:25	5,000 troy oz.	50.00	10/100¢ oz.
Silver coins	NYME	9:35–2:15	$10,000 face amount (10 bags)	10.00	$1 bag
Silver coins	IMM	8:50–1:25	$5,000 face amount (5 bags)	10.00	$2 bag
Sugar No. 11 ...	N.Y. Sugar	10:00–3:00	112,000 lb.	1,120.00	1/100¢ lb.
T-bills	IMM	8:35–1:35	$1,000,000 face value	100 basis pts. $2,500	1 basis pt. 0.0₁

WHAT IS FINANCIAL LEVERAGE?

The power of leverage is one of the most important differences of commodity trading compared with other forms of investment. Leverage is simply an investor's capability of controlling a large amount of capital with a small investment. For example, to buy or sell a futures contract requires a deposit from 5 percent to 10 percent of the market value of the commodity. Also there are no interest charges on the customer's debit balance since the deposit of funds to the broker represents earnest money (good faith deposit). Premiums paid for put or call options are generally higher than the initial margin requirements for futures contracts—usually ranging from 10 percent to 20 percent of the market value.

In contrast, marginable stocks traded on national stock exchanges currently require anywhere from a 50-percent to 75-percent deposit of funds on the market value of the security. Interest is charged on the customer's debit balance. A debit balance is the difference between purchase cost of a security and the amount of funds deposited with a broker.

A commodity trader can buy, or sell short, one contract of gold (100 troy oz.) for about $1,000 when the market value of the gold contract is at $14,500 ($145 per troy oz.). A trader deposits only 7 percent of the market value of the gold contract without being charged interest on the debit balance of $13,500 (that is, $14,500 — $1,000 = $13,500).

Unlike securities markets, a short sale can occur without an uptick in the price of the commodity. A short seller and a buyer are treated as equals in the market place. A buyer of a futures contract believes that commodity prices are going up; whereas a seller believes they will decline. For every buyer of a futures contract, there is a seller. The number of unliquidated contracts at the end of the day is known as the *open interest*. The number of contracts traded during the day is referred to as the *volume of trading*.

Commodity options, like futures contracts, are highly leveraged investments. An option buyer pays a premium to an option writer for the privilege of being able to exercise the option for a futures contract prior to its expiration. (Of course, an option buyer will usually offset the contract without exercising the option). Premiums paid to the writer usually represents no more than 20 percent of the market value of the futures contract. Unlike futures contracts, however, premiums paid for options represent the maximum financial risk for the buyer. For example, if a trader bought a December 80 gold 150 call (at $1,500 premium, the call buyer would have invested only 10 percent of the market value of the gold if December gold futures were $145 per oz. This is a *leverage ratio* of 10.3 to 1, compared to a ratio of 14.3 to 1 for the gold futures contract. Futures contracts will generally have higher leverage ratios—indicating greater risks as well as greater profit potential. See Figure 3–1, which illustrates the percentage profit/loss on a New York gold 150 call option over a wide range of gold futures prices.

Commodity options have been described as the ideal investment because they offer a profit potential much greater than the maximum loss possibility. In addition, the maximum loss of an option can be calculated to the exact dollar prior to committing funds. Unlike futures trading, the option buyer need not worry about placing stop-loss orders, about limit moves, about depositing additional margin funds to maintain a position, or about minor reversals "squeezing

FIGURE 3–1

PERCENTAGE PROFIT/LOSS ON N.Y. GOLD 150 CALL OPTION
OVER WIDE RANGE OF GOLD FUTURES PRICES

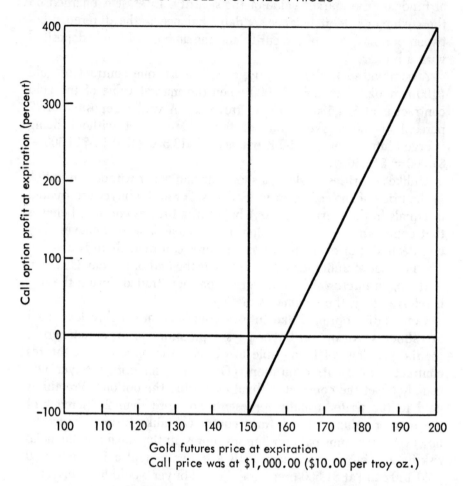

Gold futures price at expiration
Call price was at $1,000.00 ($10.00 per troy oz.)

him or her out of the market." The option buyer does not have to be as precise about when to initiate a position in the market as the futures trader does. In maximizing the return on investment through leverage, option buyers have only two primary concerns:

1. The formulation of long-term price forecast of the commodity underlying the option based upon sound fundamental and technical analysis of the market; that is, to what extent is the price of the commodity expected to rise or fall within a specified period?

2. Paying a fair-valued (or hopefully undervalued) premium for puts or calls. (Methods for valuing option premiums are discussed in later chapters; buying overpriced options greatly reduces the leverage of an option investment.)

WHY DO MOST COMMODITY SPECULATORS LOSE MONEY?

For most speculators, commodity futures trading proves to be traumatic—nearly 70 to 80 percent lose money year after year in the futures markets. The reasons that commodity speculators lose money are numerous. The principal ones are described as follows:

1. Failure to identify and follow the major price trend of the commodity.

2. Failure to cut losses early and to hold profitable positions until the price trend changes.

3. Failure to diversify commodity positions so that market risks can be spread over several situations and not concentrated on a few big "win or lose all" positions.

4. Not having sufficient risk capital to begin a diversified trading program.

5. Not following a systematic trading program that includes well-defined rules for money management and initiating and closing out market positions.

6. Trading in futures markets with a relatively low volume of trading and small open interest.

7. Overtrading to make small gains instead of initiating positions that afford the trader at least a one to three risk/reward ratio (that is, an opportunity to make at least $3 profit for every $1 at risk).

Naturally, put and call options do not eliminate all risks of trading commodities, but they do allow the speculative trader a great degree of flexibility which was not available before. Several categories of trading strategies can be developed to suit the individual preferences of the speculator. They are:

1. *Option buying strategies*
   Buy call options in anticipation of a price rise.
   Buy put options in anticipation of a price decline.

2. *Covered call option writing*
   Buy futures contracts versus writing (selling) call options against the futures contracts.

3. *Trading futures contracts against purchased puts or calls*
   (options are used as a form of "insurance")
   Selling short futures contracts against a call option.
   Buying futures contracts against a put option.

4. *Option spreads*

   Buying one contract series of an option versus the simultaneous sale of another contract series.

5. *Straddles and doubles*

   Buying a combination of a put and call in anticipation of a major either up or down during the life of the purchased straddle.

   Writing (selling) a combination of a put and call in anticipation of the underlying commodity price remaining relatively unchanged during the life of the written straddle.

The next section will discuss how futures contracts can be traded against puts, calls, and straddles.

TRADING FUTURES CONTRACTS AGAINST OPTIONS

Since the premium paid to the option writer represents a purchase of time, it would be unwise to cut short that time interval by exercising an option prior to the maturity date. The temptation to exercise a profitable put or call option presents itself when an anticipated price move occurs early in the life of the option. There is a way to have one's cake and eat it too. Rather than exercise the put or call option to an underlying futures contract, the option holder should trade against the option in the futures market. He or she would buy or sell the number of futures contracts not exceeding the number of contracts specified by the option. Several trading rules and suggestions will help clarify the situation:

1. With a call option, a short position in futures at a price above the strike price locks in the difference between the strike price and short sale price, but not necessarily a profit because the premium must be taken into account.

2. With a put option, a long futures position at a price below the strike price locks in the difference between the strike price and the long purchase price, but not necessarily a profit because the premium must be taken into account.

3. Buyers should not exercise the option until the maturity date, and on some occasions it may not be necessary or advisable to exercise it at all. With the premium, buyers merely have paid for time and should use the full life of the option to trade against it.

4. It is suggested that buyers purchase more than one option. Buying only one option makes trading against option less flexible. If option holders have several options they can trade against them on a scale-up or scale-down, as the case may be.

5. The total number of futures contracts traded against options should not exceed the quantity represented by options. If five

futures contracts were sold but only four calls were held, the option holder must deposit original and variation margins for the contract that he or she is net short.

The intriguing aspect of trading against an option is not "locking in" a profit but in taking advantage of interim price changes. To illustrate this point, as well as that of maintaining the underlying put or call option until its expiration date, Figures 3–2 and 3–3 should be helpful.

A straddle, as previously defined, is a combination of put and call options with the same strike price and expiration date. A straddle is even more interesting when considered in the context of trading against options. The strike price, in effect, becomes a springboard from which to trade when futures prices are above or below that price. As a general observation, a straddle has particular appeal in a market characterized by broad price fluctuations and an uncertain overall trend. Figure 3–4 illustrates this contention, with hypothetical data for December gold 150 call and December 150 put options.

WHAT IS THE COMMERCIAL ROLE OF COMMODITY OPTIONS?

Commodity futures exchanges allow commercial dealers in specific commodities to obtain price protection against highly volatile price moves by hedging their cash positions with futures contracts. Speculators, in hopes of making unusual profits, assume the price risks that commercial hedgers are unwilling to take. For example, John Jones, a plywood merchant, might want to hedge an inventory of plywood sheets in his warehouse because he believes that plywood prices could decline through the fall season. He calls his broker to place an order to sell ten contracts of January plywood futures to hedge against a possible price decline.

On the other hand, Mary Smith, a speculator, believes that plywood prices might rise during the fall in anticipation of expanding commercial and residential construction. She tells her broker to buy 10 contracts of January plywood futures. The plywood merchant has protected his profit margins on inventory regardless of whether plywood prices rise or fall. If prices decline, the speculator loses money. If plywood prices rise, the speculator makes tremendous profits on a small investment. So far so good, but what if the following situations happen?

1. What if plywood futures decline dramatically first and then rise sharply by late fall? The speculator is forced out of her long positions and then becomes afraid of entering the long side of the market when prices begin an upward trend.

FIGURE 3–2
ILLUSTRATION OF TRADING FUTURES CONTRACT AGAINST
CALL OPTIONS

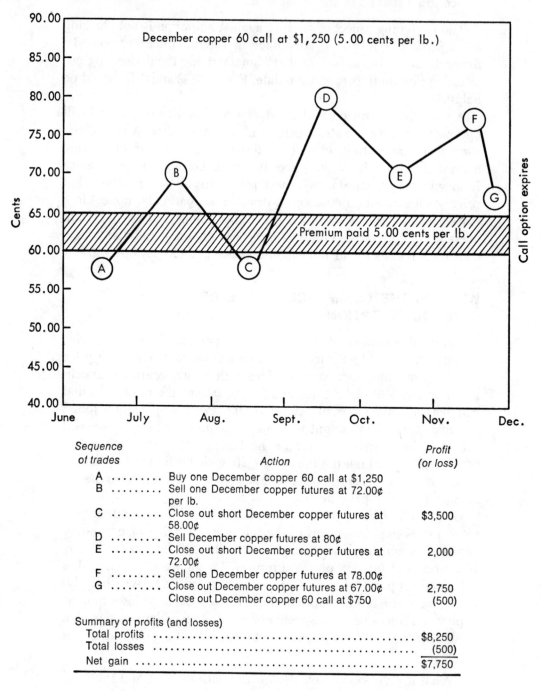

December copper 60 call at $1,250 (5.00 cents per lb.)

Premium paid 5.00 cents per lb.

Call option expires

Cents

June   July   Aug.   Sept.   Oct.   Nov.   Dec.

Sequence of trades	Action	Profit (or loss)
A	Buy one December copper 60 call at $1,250	
B	Sell one December copper futures at 72.00¢ per lb.	
C	Close out short December copper futures at 58.00¢	$3,500
D	Sell December copper futures at 80¢	
E	Close out short December copper futures at 72.00¢	2,000
F	Sell one December copper futures at 78.00¢	
G	Close out December copper futures at 67.00¢	2,750
	Close out December copper 60 call at $750	(500)

Summary of profits (and losses)
Total profits $8,250
Total losses .... (500)
Net gain $7,750

32

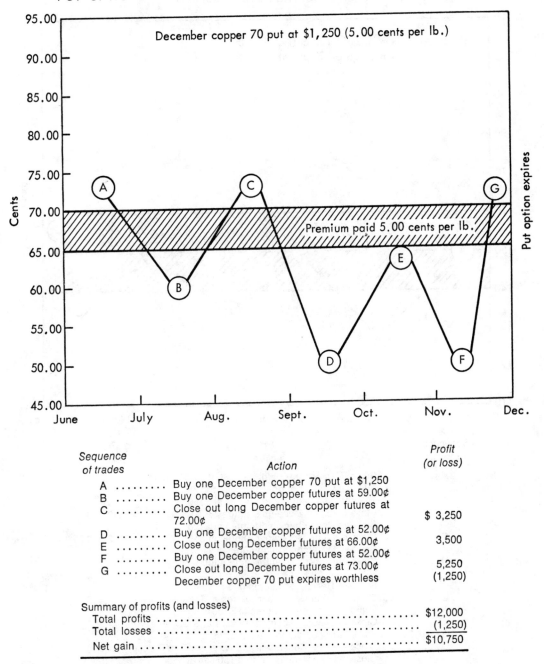

FIGURE 3–3
ILLUSTRATION OF TRADING FUTURES CONTRACTS AGAINST
PUT OPTIONS

December copper 70 put at $1,250 (5.00 cents per lb.)

Premium paid 5.00 cents per lb.

Put option expires

Sequence of trades	Action	Profit (or loss)
A	Buy one December copper 70 put at $1,250	
B	Buy one December copper futures at 59.00¢	
C	Close out long December copper futures at 72.00¢	$ 3,250
D	Buy one December copper futures at 52.00¢	
E	Close out long December copper futures at 66.00¢	3,500
F	Buy one December copper futures at 52.00¢	
G	Close out long December copper futures at 73.00¢	5,250
	December copper 70 put expires worthless	(1,250)

Summary of profits (and losses)	
Total profits	$12,000
Total losses	(1,250)
Net gain	$10,750

FIGURE 3–4
ILLUSTRATION OF TRADING FUTURES CONTRACTS AGAINST A
STRADDLE (combination of put and call options)

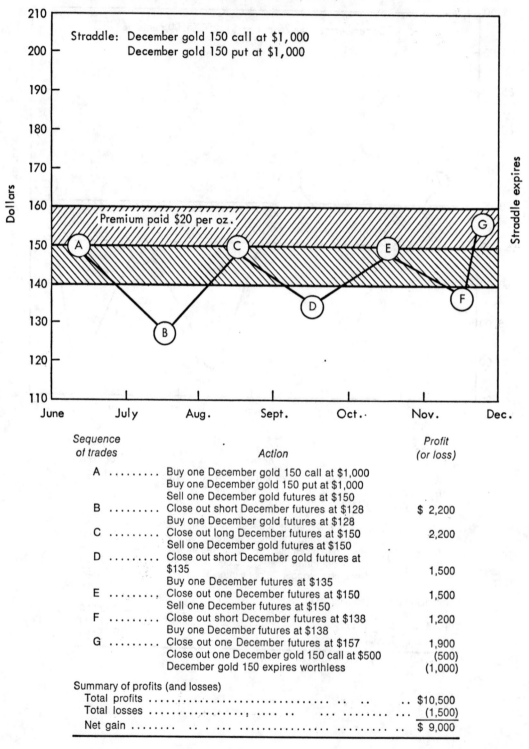

Sequence of trades	Action	Profit (or loss)
A	Buy one December gold 150 call at $1,000	
	Buy one December gold 150 put at $1,000	
	Sell one December gold futures at $150	
B	Close out short December futures at $128	$ 2,200
	Buy one December gold futures at $128	
C	Close out long December futures at $150	2,200
	Sell one December gold futures at $150	
D	Close out short December gold futures at $135	1,500
	Buy one December futures at $135	
E	Close out one December futures at $150	1,500
	Sell one December futures at $150	
F	Close out short December futures at $138	1,200
	Buy one December futures at $138	
G	Close out one December futures at $157	1,900
	Close out one December gold 150 call at $500	(500)
	December gold 150 expires worthless	(1,000)

Summary of profits (and losses)

Total profits	$10,500
Total losses ...., ...	(1,500)
Net gain	$ 9,000

34

2. Or what if plywood futures make a five-day nonstop limit move down before trading is permitted on the exchange floor? Unfavorable limit moves are frightening to even the most experienced commodity traders.

The situations described above are not uncommon in the futures markets. The extreme volatility and caprice of the futures market discourages speculation and thus reduces its liquidity. Speculators play an essential role in maintaining a viable market for commercials to obtain the necessary price insurance they need. Without continuous speculative trading, futures markets would probably not have the liquidity to permit large scale commercial hedging.

How does this relate to the commercial role of commodity options? Very simply, commodity options can afford speculators some price insurance of their own and allow them to "hedge" their futures positions without fear of limit moves, unexpected margin calls, and whipsaw markets. Commodity options incorporated into a well-designed trading program can offer speculators some peace of mind!

Commodity options will thus probably encourage greater speculative and commercial participation in futures markets to make them more efficient central market places for commodity pricing and physical distribution. Commercial dealers can benefit from increased flexibility in hedging programs by using a combination of futures and option contracts in achieving their marketing objectives. A greater volume of statistical information regarding production, consumption, and distribution of optionable commodities will become available. This information can assist both speculators and hedgers in making more accurate price forecasts. Commodity option markets should encourage business risks now associated with futures transactions to be transferred to speculators who are willing to assume these risks for profit. Thus commodity options should enhance the commercial role of futures markets, not reduce it!

Chapter 4

Option trading techniques

CALL OPTIONS

With the basics behind us, we can now proceed with the interesting subject of commodity option trading techniques. There are a tremendous number and variety of uses for calls, but most are only slight modifications of a basic group. Each of these primary uses is discussed in depth in this chapter, and simple examples that actually could have taken place are provided.

1. Purchase calls—anticipating a price rise

One of the most basic of all trading techniques is the purchase of a call when a major upward move is anticipated. Assume that in August, July sugar is at 9.20 cents (point A on Chart 1). At this level it is giving a technical buy signal, and fundamental analysis indicates we are running into a period of tight supply due to major weather damage of world crops. Based on this information, a strong upward move is anticipated which should carry the price to 12.00 cents. Although all indicators are pointing to higher sugar prices, the contract has been in a major downtrend. Since the July contract has been under liquidation for more than five months, it is difficult to predict the exact timing of the big upside move. Therefore, the sophisticated futures buyer going long at the channel breakout at point A would place a stop at 8.50. The risk would thus be 70 points, or $784 plus commissions. An alternative to buying the future for $1,500 margin, and risking over $800 if stopped out, would be to purchase one six-month call option on July sugar at a premium cost of $1,120 with a declaration date of February 9. Since options are struck at the market price, the call would have a 9.20 strike price. Purchasing this call position means that the buyer (taker) is now potentially long 112,000 pounds of July sugar at 10.20, calculated by adding the striking price of 9.20 to the premium cost of $1,120, expressed as 100 points. Dollar premium costs are converted to trading or market points by dividing the dollar premium cost by the dollar value of one market point. The answer from this calculation will be the premium cost in market points. (All charts used in this chapter are hypothetical in order that they do not become dated, yet price scaling and volatility have some relationship to the price levels and movements existing at the time of writing.) Premium costs are approximately equal to London premiums with minimal markups. For example, the dollar premium cost of the six-month sugar call was $1,120, and the value of one point is $11.20.

$$\frac{\text{Dollar premium cost}}{\text{Value of one point}} = \text{Point of value of premium cost}$$

$$\frac{\$1,120}{11.20} = 100 \text{ points}$$

If the option had cost $1,904 the call in points would be

$$\frac{\$1,904}{11.20} = 170 \text{ points}$$

The maximum loss to the call buyer (taker) can never exceed the premium cost. The maximum loss will occur only if the option is not exercised or converted because the market does not move above the 9.20 level. On the other hand, if the market does move above the strike price, as Chart 1 shows, the size of the loss decreases as the price rises until the breakeven point is reached. As the price rises above the breakeven point, the option becomes profitable, and the profit increases as the price continues to advance. Once the price has reached the 12.40 level, the taker decides to exercise the call option and thus will be long one contract of July sugar at 9.20. Simulta-

CHART 1
SUGAR—JULY (hypothetical chart)

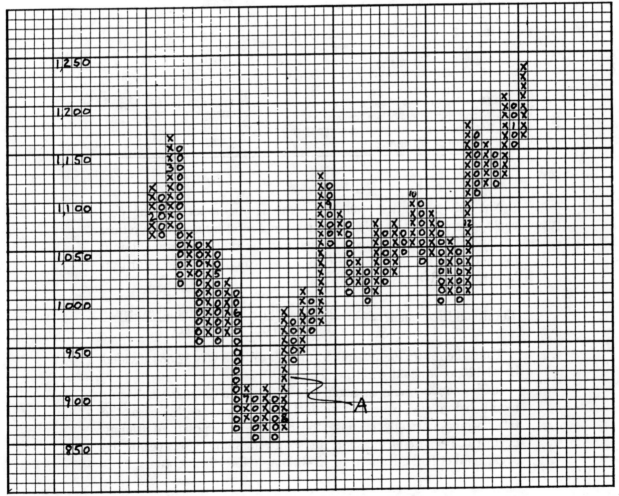

neously, one contract of July sugar will be sold at the market price of 12.40. The net profit on the trade after deducting commissions is assumed to total $100, and the cost of the call is $2,364. Two alternative methods of calculating the net profit are shown in Table 4–1.

TABLE 4–1
TWO PROFIT CALCULATION METHODS

Method 1

Sell one future contract at	12.40¢
Exercise call going long one future contract at	9.20¢
Gross profit in points	3.20¢ = 320 points
Gross profit in points	320
Multiplied by value of one point	$ 11.20
Gross profit in dollars	$3,584
Less dealer exercise commission	100
Net profit on exercise transaction	$3,484
Net profit on exercise transaction	$3,484
Less premium cost of call	1,120
Net profit on call investment	$2,364

Method 2

Sell one future contract at	12.40¢
Call striking price plus premium in points (9.20 + 1.00)	10.20¢
Net profit in points	2.20¢ = 220 points
Net profit in points	220
Multiplied by value of one point	$ 11.20
Net profit in dollars before commission	$2,464
Less standard dealer exercise commission	100
Net profit on call investment	$2,364

Not only is the net profit on a transaction important, the percentage return on the investment is also of vital interest. The return on investment is calculated by dividing the dollar investment into the net profit before tax. The formula for calculating the return on investment (ROI) is shown below.

$$\text{Return on Investment} = \frac{\text{Net income before tax but after all expenses}}{\text{Total dollar investment}}$$

Thus, the return on investment in the example was $2,364 divided by $1,120, or a healthy 211 percent.

In the above example, sugar hits its peak in January, only one month before the expiration or declaration date. In this case, the taker would normally exercise the option, as opposed to trading against it, because of the short life span remaining. However, if the sugar market had advanced to 12.40 long before the February 9 ex-

40

piration date, the taker would have several additional courses of action open.

2. Calls—trading against profitable options

So far we have discussed only the primary benefit of trading options—the unlimited opportunity for gains with a fixed, relatively moderate risk. Another distinct advantage offered by options is their flexibility—the fact that they can be traded against.

If takers have a profitable option position, they can trade against it in several ways and draw many more possible benefits from the option than simply its exercise.

The following examples show how this can be done.

Example A

If John Smith, the call buyer, believes the July sugar market (Chart 1) has advanced as far as it will and that it may decline and not advance again to the 12.40 level before the declaration date, he can "lock in" his profit by making a short sale of one July contract at 12.40. On the declaration date, Carol Williams, the call taker, exercises her option, thus establishing a long position at 10.20 (strike price of 9.20 plus premium of 100 points) and liquidates this long position against the short sale at 12.40, thus realizing the same profit as in the earlier example. The advantage of this technique over an immediate exercise is that the option is kept alive until the declaration date in case the taker may decide at a later date to trade against it.

Example B

If, instead of believing the commodity has topped out and will not again reach the 12.40 area before the declaration date, the taker, Carol Williams, feels the market may move lower and then rally again before the declaration date, she will trade against her option by selling short one July contract at the current level of 12.40. When the market moves lower, the short will be covered with a buy order. This transaction will generate a profit and leave the original option unchanged. If on the declaration date, the market is above the striking price, the call is declared, thus going long at 9.20, and simultaneously the position is liquidated in the market. Thus, she has made a profit on her option and also on her trade against the option. If on the declaration date, the market is below the original strike price, the option is abandoned causing a loss of the premium. The premium loss is, of course, offset by the profit made on trading against the option.

In order to clarify the concept of trading against the option, let us run through Example B again, this time using some numbers.

The July sugar contract is at the 12.40 level and Carol believes a decline is imminent, to be followed by a rally. She, therefore, shorts one July sugar against the call at the current price of 12.40. The decline does occur and carries July sugar to 11.00. Believing 11.00 represents the bottom of the decline, she covers the short position at 11.00. This transaction generates a profit of 1.40 cents, or $1,568 before commissions, or $1,468 after the $100 commission charged by the option underwriter on the short sale, and leaves the call intact. Following the decline, sugar does generate additional strength and rallies to 12.40 on the declaration date. Since the profitable short sale transaction now affects the call in no way, the option is declared. Declaring the call results in a long position at 9.20 which is simultaneously sold in the market at 12.40. The exercise of the call realizes a net profit of $2,364 after deducting commissions, and the premium cost of the option is calculated exactly as shown earlier in Table 4–1. Trading against the option resulted in an additional net profit of $1,468 not otherwise possible. Thus the total net profit attributable to the call is the sum of the $1,468 profit made trading against the call and the $2,364 profit resulting from the exercise.

But what if sugar did not decline below 12.40, the point which Carol went short against the option? In this case, on the last day of the option's life, she would declare the call, thus going long one contract of July sugar at 9.20. Since she is now long one contract at 9.20 and short one contract at 12.40, the long position covers the short position leaving a zero net position, and a net profit of $2,364 results after deducting all commissions and the premium cost of the call.

Although it would never be truly possible to always trade at all of the major peaks and troughs during the option life, the purchaser of the July sugar call could theoretically have made the transactions shown by letters in Table 4–2 and on Chart 2.

Example C

What happens if, after July sugar reaches its peak (12.40 in our example) and Carol has gone short, sugar declines below the call striking price and remains below the striking price on the declaration date? Should this occur, the call would be abandoned and the short covered at the market on the declaration date. The short could, of course, be kept open after the declaration date of the call as a regular future trade, but since we are only concerned here with options and their use, and because holding an unhedged futures position creates an additional risk, we will assume that all trading positions are closed on the declaration date.

For the arithmetic results of Example C, let us assume July sugar to be 8.40 on the declaration date, and the short is covered at that price. (See accompanying table.)

Shorted one July sugar at		12.40
Covered one July sugar at		8.40
Gross transaction profit in points		4.00 = 400 points
Gross transaction profit in points		400
Multiplied by point value in dollars	$	11.20
Gross transaction profit before commissions		$4,480
Gross transaction profit before commissions		$4,480
Less option dealer commissions		100
Net transaction profit		$4,380

CHART 2
SUGAR—JULY

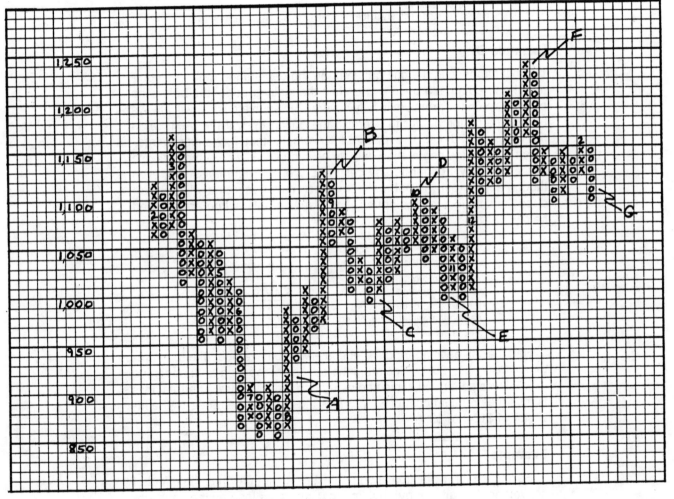

Net transaction profit		$4,380
Less premium cost of call		1,120
Net profit		$3,260

$$\text{Return on investment} = \frac{\$3,260}{\$1,120} = 291 \text{ percent}$$

TABLE 4–2

POSSIBLE TRADES AGAINST CALL ON JULY SUGAR

One call was purchased on August 3, Basis July sugar, struck at 9.20 to expire February 9, for a premium cost of $1,120. Trade points indicated as letters are shown in Chart 2.

Signal-entry point	Transaction		Close out point	Transaction gain (loss)		Accumulated gain (loss) in points*
	Price	Type		Price	Points*	
B	1,130	Short	C	1,000	130	130
D	1,110	Short	E	1,000	110	240
F	1,240	Short	G	1,116†	124	364
A	920	Purchased call	G	1,116†	196	560

* Commissions excluded.
† Closing market price on February 9, the declaration date.

Example D

What happens to the call option if, on the declaration date, the commodity is trading at a price higher than the striking price, but below the price at which the premium is fully covered? In such a case, it will always benefit the option holder to exercise the option even if the premium is not fully covered. Let us suppose, for example, that July sugar is trading at 9.40 on the declaration date. In all such cases where the exercise of the option will generate any cash after covering commissions, even though a net profit will not result, the cash thus generated will help reduce the total loss on the option. The results of this action are outlined below.

Sell sugar future at	9.40
Declare call at	9.20
Gross transaction profit in points	0.20 = 20 points
Transaction profit in points	20
Multiply by point value	$ 11.20
Transaction profit in dollars	$224
Less option dealers commission	100
Net transaction profit	$124

Had the call been abandoned, the loss would have been the total premium cost of $1,120. By declaring the option as opposed to abandoning it, $124 was generated, which helps reduce the total loss. The total loss is thus the premium cost of $1,120 less the net cash returned to the investor of $124, or $996.

Example E

Selling a futures position short against a call not only has the effect of converting the call to a put, but, in most cases, as long as the short position is held open, the present profit (the difference between the striking price of the call and the price of the short) is maintained, and no further profits will be generated. This is because as long as the future is selling at a price above the call striking price, the profit resulting when the option is declared must be the difference between the strike price

44

of the call and the price at which a future was shorted. For example, if the call was struck at 9.20 and a future was shorted at 12.40, the protected profit is 12.40 − 9.20 = 3.20 cents, or 320 points. A decline in the futures price to 9.20 would mean the abandonment of the call, but the same profit (short at 12.40 less cover price in the market at 9.20). If the future declined to 11.00, the same profit would result, as shown below.

Short in market at	12.40
Cover in market at	11.00
Profit on short sale	1.40
Sell long in market at	11.00
Declare call at	9.20
Profit on call	1.80
Profit on short sale	1.40
Plus profit on call	1.80
Total profit	3.20 = 320 points

Even if sugar rose to 16.00, the profit would be the same 3.20 (short at 12.40 less long position resulting from declaring the call at 9.20).

But there is one exception to the statement "while a short is protecting a profit on a call, no further profits can be generated." This exception occurs when the price declines below the striking price of the call. For example, assume a short is entered at 12.40 against a call struck at 9.20, locking in a profit of 320 points through all commodity price levels above the 9.20 striking price of the call. But additional profits are made as soon as the market price declines below the strike price of the call. When the market price is below the strike price of the call, the total profit is larger than the protected, or hedged, profit on the call, and the larger profit is a function of the difference between the short sale price (12.40) and the market price.

Thus, when the market price is 8.00, the profit is the difference between the short sale price of 12.40 and the market price of 8.00, or 4.40. At a futures price of 7.00, the profit is 12.40 − 7.00, or 5.40. In other words, when the market price is below the strike price of the call, the short has a profit value calculated as if no call existed.

In order to better clarify this concept, let us look at the protected profit calculations in another way. The profit being protected is the difference between the price of the short sale and the strike price of the call. Thus, the profit being protected is 12.40 − 9.20, or 3.20. The short will always be covered by the lowest priced long position available which will always be the 9.20 strike price whenever the market is above 9.20. But whenever the market declines below 9.20, the long position can be purchased at a price below the strike price, and the profit will thus be increased. And since the sale (short sale) price remains constant, the lower the cost of the long position used to cover the sale, the greater the profit.

45

In all of the examples cited above, it should be noted that the buyer of the option will not be called for original or variation margins on his trading against his option, provided it is clearly stated at the time of the trade that this is what he wishes to do.

To summarize the concept of trading against a profitable option, it should be remembered that selling futures against a call has the effect of converting it to a put. As long as the short futures position is maintained, no further profits will be yielded, except as in Example E where the futures price declines below the strike price of the call. But in all cases, the present profit, the difference between the striking price of the call and the price at which futures are shorted, is protected.

Trading against an option prevents having to exercise it in an instance where the option is profitable, yet a temporary setback seems imminent. As long as the market moves and the option remains open, the trading process as outlined in the above examples can be repeated any number of times, allowing the speculator to make a profit on the futures position even if the option ultimately proves unprofitable and is abandoned. Trading against the option, as opposed to exercising it prematurely, permits the option taker to keep the option in force until it expires. This is important for the following reason: When an option is purchased, the taker is buying time, and this trading gives the taker the opportunity to take advantage of all the time paid for rather than exercising the option prematurely.

3. Purchase calls—a stop order substitute

Example F

Calls can also be used quite advantageously as substitutes for stop-loss orders in the futures. Let us take another example. Assume in April, March copper is at 72.00 (point A on Chart 3). It has given a point-and-figure sell signal, it has broken its moving average, and the near-term fundamental outlook is bearish. At this point, the futures trader decides to short one March copper at 72.00. But being uncertain of the exact timing of the continuation of the decline and believing a stop could be executed by a short-term technical reaction before the major decline, a six-month call is purchased in lieu of a stop. The call costs $1,500 and has a striking price of 72.00. This call provides a permanent stop for all single shorts for six months, meaning the maximum possible loss, regardless of how high copper rises, is the $1,500 cost of the call. The call also has the advantage in that it places no limit on the potential profits able to be earned on the short side.

To recap, the call has the following advantages over the stop-loss order.

1. The price is guaranteed, whereas a futures stop order in a fast moving market might not be exercised at the stop price, but at a much less desirable price.

2. Even if the call were carried unprofitably, it could be traded against, as will be discussed in a later section.

3. There is no limit to the number of times the call can be used during its life as an alternative to a stop.

4. A call option precludes a whipsaw in the event that a rally did not constitute an actual breakout but was only another and slightly extended move in the congestion area before the major decline.

CHART 3
COPPER—MARCH (hypothetical chart)

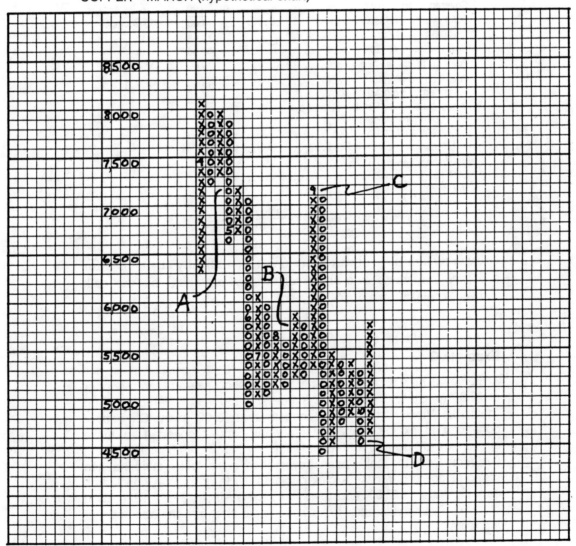

As Chart 3 shows, the call was not needed, for March copper declined to 50.00. After a period of consolidation, copper appears to have bottomed, and the short is covered in July on a point-and-figure buy signal at 58.00 (point B) for a gross profit on the short of 14 cents or $3,500. Next, March copper rallies to 72.00, and since it appears to be overpriced, a short is entered at 72.00 (point C). With the original call at 72.00 against being used in lieu of a stop, the short is covered at 46.00 (point D) because the call's declaration date has been reached. This second short transaction generated a gross profit of 26.00, or $6,500, and the call is abandoned. The total profits from the shorts using the original call as a stop protection are in the accompanying table.

Short at (A)	72.00
Covered short at (B)	58.00
Point profit on transaction no. 1	14.00 = 1,400 points
Short at (C)	72.00
Covered short at (D)	46.00
Point profit on transaction no. 2	26.00 = 2,600 points
Total point profit (1,400–2,600)	4,000
Multiplied by point value	$ 2.50
Gross dollar profit before commissions	$10,000
Less option dealer commission (two transactions × $100)	200
Net transaction profit	$ 9,800
Net transaction profit	$ 9,800
Less call premium cost	1,500
Net profit	$ 8,300

$$\text{Return on investment} = \frac{\$8,300}{\$1,500} = 553 \text{ percent}$$

Even though the call was never needed and finally abandoned for a $1,500 loss, these two short sales, fully protected by the call, showed a total return of 553 percent.

Example G

But let us now assume that only the first short sale in March copper at 72.00 (point A, Chart 4) was successful and was covered at 58.00 (point B). After shorting the second time at 72.00 (point C), copper continued to exhibit tremendous strength and proceeded to move almost straight up to the 95-cent range. By the declaration date (point D), John Doe, the call option buyer, thanks his lucky stars he had the foresight to purchase a call, declares it. He goes long one March copper future at 72.00, and uses the long position to offset the short at 72.00. The resulting profit calculations are shown in the accompanying table.

48

Short at (A)	72.00	
Cover at (B)	58.00	
Point profit on transaction no. 1	14.00	= 1,400 points
Short at (C)	72.00	
Cover by declaring call at	72.00	
Point profit on transaction no. 2	.00	= 0 points
Total point profit (1,400 + 0)	1,400	
Multiplied by point value	$ 2.50	
Gross dollar profit before commissions	$3,500	
Less option dealer commission (two transactions × $100)	200	
Net transaction profit	$3,300	
Net transaction profit	$3,300	
Less call premium cost	1,500	
Net profit	$1,800	

CHART 4
COPPER—MARCH (hypothetical chart)

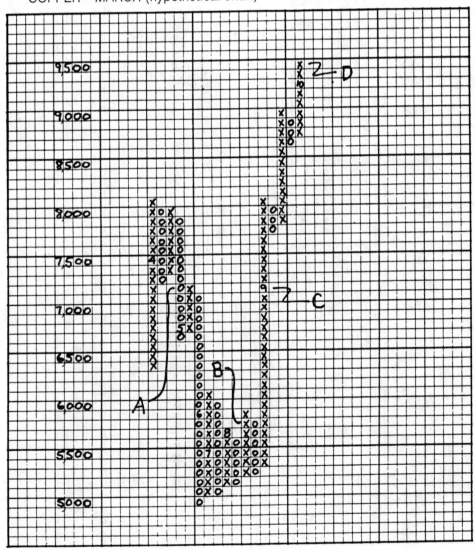

Example H

As in the two prior examples, the first short sale at 72.00 was successfully covered at 58.00. And as in Example B, copper rose rapidly to 95 cents after the second short sale at 72.00. But in this example, after reaching 95, a severe reversal occurred, carrying the price by limit moves to 46.00 (see Chart 5) by the declaration date of the call option. Because the second short, like the first, was totally protected by the call, the height of the rise was totally irrelevant. The maximum loss on the short, even if copper had risen to 125 by the declaration date, would

CHART 5
COPPER—MARCH (hypothetical chart)

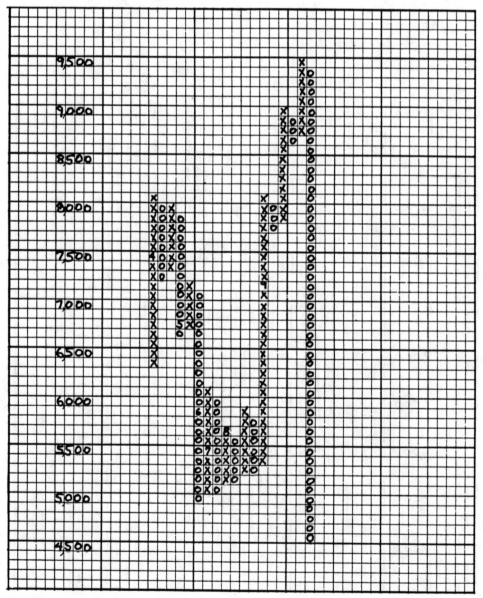

have been the premium cost of the call. The height of the rally and its length were also unimportant as long as there was the possibility of again having the futures price decline below the short price of 72.00 prior to the declaration date.

Since the futures did decline to 46.00 by the declaration date, the profit calculations will be exactly the same as in Example F. The profit calculations are repeated in the accompanying table.

Transaction no. 1
Short at 72.00
Cover short at 58.00
Point profit on transaction no. 1 .... $\overline{14.00}$ = 1,400 points

Transaction no. 2
Short at 72.00
Cover short at 46.00
Point profit on transaction no. 2 .... $\overline{26.00}$ = 2,600 points

Total point profit (1,400 + 2,600) 4,000
Multiplied by point value .... $ 2.50
Gross dollar profit before commission $10,000
Less option dealer commission
(two transactions × $100) 200
Net transaction profit .... $ 9,800

Net transaction profit .... $ 9,800
Less call premium cost 1,500
Net profit .... $ 8,300

$$\text{Return on investment} = \frac{\$8,300}{\$1,500} = 553 \text{ percent}$$

4. Calls—trading against unprofitable options

In nearly all of the examples used so far, the call has been profitable at one time during its life. Yet even if the option was never profitable in its own right, profits could be generated by trading against the unprofitable option. A single example should clarify this trading technique.

Suppose an option buyer, being bullish on silver, purchased a three-month call in August, on July silver at 532.00 (point A in Chart 6) for a premium of $1,000, or 2,000 points. The bullish move anticipated failed to materialize and silver started heading down. At 522.00 silver gave a sell signal and looked bearish over the near-term, so a futures contract is sold short against the call (point B). If the market continues down, as the chart shows it actually did, the short futures position can be covered profitably at the 494.00 buy signal (point C), and the call can be abandoned on its declaration date since the price never reached the strike price. The profit would be $300, calculated by taking the short sale price of 522.00 less the cover price of 494.00, or 2,800 points ($1,400), less the round trip commission paid to the option dealer of $100 and the premium cost of the call ($1,000). The return on the $1,000 investment is 30 per-

CHART 6
SILVER—JULY (hypothetical chart)

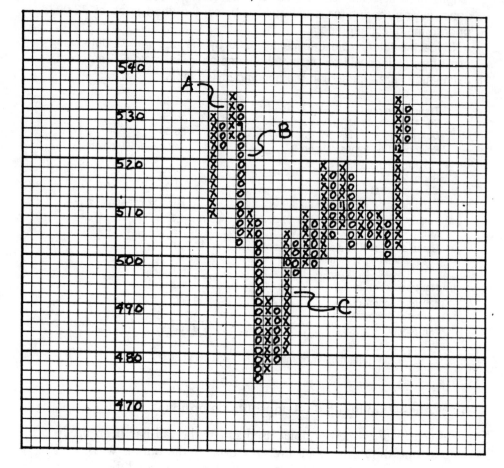

cent—not a bad dollar profit or percentage return for a situation which could have caused a $1,000 loss or a loss of 100 percent of invested capital had trades not been made against the unprofitable call.

However, if the market turns up after the futures had been shorted at 522.00, the option taker would be subject to a loss equal to the range from where the futures were shorted to the basis, or strike price, of the call. Thus, in this example of trading against an unprofitable call, the maximum additional risk exposure incurred by such trading, regardless of the height of the rally, would be the difference between the price at which the silver futures contract was shorted (522.00) and the strike price of the call (532.00), or 1,000 points ($500). Should silver, in fact, rise, additional margin generally would need to be placed with the dealer up to the maximum of the additional risk exposure, or $500.

5. Calls—hedges on profitable futures

A number of our earlier examples have shown how option profits could be protected through futures, how futures trading could increase the option's profitability, how options could be used in place of stops to keep a newly entered futures position from deteriorating into a substantial loss situation, and how futures could be used to profit from an unprofitable option.

In all of these examples, options were purchased at, or before, the time at which the futures position was taken as a trade against the option. But the process can be quite successfully reversed by entering into a futures position and then, at a later time, purchasing the option. Under this trading concept, the object is to use an option to protect, or lock in, the present profits of a profitable futures contract to show still further profits.

This concept can better be understood through an example. Paul Jones, the speculator, being short a July silver futures contract at 522.00, is in a highly profitable position when July silver is trading at 476.00. At this level he can protect the profit with a call. Should the market continue to decline, he can still benefit to the full extent, less the premium cost of the call, and the call will be insurance against a loss should the market rise. If numbers are important to your understanding, this example would have a gross profit of 4,600 points, or $2,300, locked in by the call (the gross profit being calculated as the difference between the price of the short sale at 522.00 and the strike price of the call at 476.00). Should silver decline to 400.00 by the declaration date of the call, the gross profit increases to 12,200 points, or $6,100, again calculated by the difference of the short sale price of 522.00 less the market price of 400.00. The net profit is obtained by taking the gross profit of $6,100 less the sum of the $1,000 premium cost of the one-month call and commission on the transaction, assumed to be $100. The net profit would be $6,100 − ($1,000 + $100), or $5,000.

If silver rallied back to 522.00 by the declaration date, the gross profit would still be the difference between the price of the short (522.00) and the strike price of the call (476.00), used to create a long position at 476.00 to offset against the short. The net profit would be the gross profit less the premium cost and the commission.

From both the verbal and the mathematical discussion, it is easy to see that having the opportunity to profit on the futures position from further price weakness, while at the same time locking in the current profits, easily justifies the relatively low premium cost of the call.

6. Calls—a hedge on profitable puts

This is the last of the normally used option trading procedures. Since this procedure requires a little more background than has been presented on the use and trading of puts, further discussions will be postponed until the next section.

Although there are six common uses of call options, as discussed in this chapter, many of the six can be used in combination or others can be created. The maximum possible use of calls and the techniques of trading against them are truly limited only by the imagination of the speculator. But no matter which technique or combination of trading methods is used at any point in time, one should never lose sight of the principal advantage of calls—the substantial leverage or protection they provide for a very small dollar risk exposure.

The next section delves into the mysteries of puts, a subject which must never be ignored by option buyers who want to be fully versed in the use of their tools.

PUT OPTIONS

As a review, a put option gives the buyer the right to sell a futures contract to the giver of the option at the basis, or strike price, at any time between his date of purchase of the option and its expiration, or declaration date. Let us now proceed with examples showing the use of puts.

1. Purchase puts—anticipating price decline

The most basic of reasons for the purchase of a put commodity option is because a major price decline is anticipated. Assume that in March, September sugar appears to have rallied too far and too fast. Based on this information, a major price reversal is anticipated which should carry the price lower by several cents, possibly even as low as 8.00. But since sugar has been in a major uptrend for months, the timing of the big downside move is uncertain. Instead of selling short futures for $1,500 margin and risking a loss of 50 or 60 points on a stop, a six-month put option is purchased at the point of the first three-box downside reversal after the 13.00 cent area has been penetrated in March. Premium cost is 100 points, or $1,120. The reversal occurs and the put is struck at 12.80 (point A on Chart 7). Taking a put option position means that the option buyer (taker) is now potentially short 112,000 pounds of September sugar at 11.80, calculated by subtracting the premium cost in market points (100 points) from the strike price 12.80.

54

CHART 7
SUGAR—SEPTEMBER (hypothetical chart)

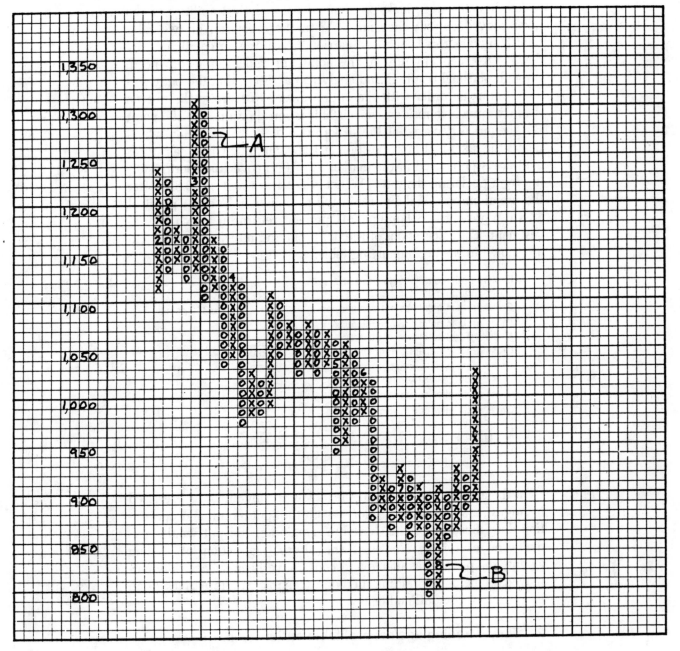

If September sugar fails during the life of the put to move below the strike price (12.80), the put will be abandoned for a maximum loss to the buyer (taker) of $1,120, the premium cost. This loss is not much larger than the loss sustained had a short future position been stopped out in the market. On the other hand, if the market does move lower, as Chart 8 indicates, a healthy profit could have been generated.

The hunch, guess, luck, or tremendous analytical abilities of the taker proved correct once more. With the exception of two false bullish signals, this bear move carries the futures price all the way down to 8.00 cents by July. At this point, our trader being convinced, through personal readings and analytical abilities, that the bottom is near, enters an order with the option dealer to exercise the put on the first three-box upside reversal. This reversal occurs at 8.30 (point B); the put is declared at the strike price of 12.80, an action which places the taker in a short position at 12.80. Simultaneously, a futures contract is purchased in the market at 8.30 to cover the short resulting from declaring the put. The net result is a profit of $3,820 after the premium cost of the put and the commission. The net profit of $3,820 represents a whopping 341 percent return on the $1,120 investment. The calculations of the net profit and return on investment are shown in the accompanying table.

Declare option and thus go short at	12.80
Cover short in market at	8.30
Gross profit in points before commission	4.50 = 450 points
Gross profit in points before commission	450
Multiplied by point value in dollars	$ 11.20
Gross profit in dollars before commission	$5,040
Gross profit in dollars before commission	$5,040
Less option dealer exercise commission	100
Gross profit after commission	$4,940
Gross profit after commission	$4,940
Less premium cost of put	1,120
Net profit	$3,820

$$\text{Return on investment} = \frac{\$3,820}{\$1,120} = 341 \text{ percent}$$

In the above example, sugar hit its low in July and was exercised in August, only one month prior to both the spot month and declaration date. Because of the short life remaining, the put would normally be exercised. However, the alternative action of trading against the put was available and could have been successfully employed. Some of the trading methods available as alternatives to an early exercise are outlined below.

2. Puts—trading against profitable options

The most basic use of puts is to allow the taker an almost unlimited opportunity for gains from a price decline with a fixed and relatively moderate risk. This simple method of exercising a put after a substantial price decline is a perfectly satisfactory use of the option. Substantial returns can be made by simply exercising the profitable put, and thus it is never necessary for the option holder to attempt even the simplest of trades against the put. But because there will always be some option buyers not satisfied with a 341 percent return, as shown in the exercise example, and because such trading can greatly enhance the profit potential, a number of trading techniques will be discussed.

The following are examples of trading against a profitable put.

Example I

If Bob White, the put buyer believes the September sugar market at 8.00 is bottoming and the next move will be on the upside, with 8.00 holding as the support level on any future weakness following the rally, he can lock in his profit by going long one September sugar future contract against the put at the first upside price reversal to occur. The reversal occurs at 8.30, and the long position is purchased at the same price. On the declaration date, Bob declares his option, becomes short one September contract at 12.80, and liquidates this short position against the long position at 8.30. The resulting profit from trading against the put was exactly the same as in the exercise example above because the execution prices in both cases were identical.

Even though in this case the profits from trading against the option are identical to those made from exercising, the trading technique has the advantage of keeping the option alive in case the taker decides to make additional trades against it.

Example J

To really highlight the advantage of trading against the put versus exercising it prior to the declaration date, as discussed in Example I, let us modify the price action of September sugar to reflect a slight rally to 9.10 cents after going long at 8.00, followed by a continuation of the downtrend which carries the price to 7.00 by the declaration date. (This modified hypothetical price action is reflected in Chart 8.) Had the put been exercised at 8.30, the option would no longer exist and the taker could not have participated in the further decline. But by trading long against the put at 8.30, the profits are perfectly protected against price rallies, yet the put remains intact to participate in any further declines once the long position is closed out.

The put trader expected a rally, or he would not have taken on the long position at 8.30 (point B). But realizing he could be wrong about a rally, he keeps a watchful eye for further signs of continued downward pressure. The price does decline, and wanting to profit from this further decline, he liquidates the long position at the point-and-figure sell signal at 7.90 (point C). By the declaration date, sugar is 7.00 (point D), the put is declared at 12.80, and the resulting short is covered in the market at 7.00.

By trading against the put at 8.30 instead of exercising it at that price, the taker was able to participate in the additional 130-point decline, and

CHART 8
SUGAR—SEPTEMBER (hypothetical chart)

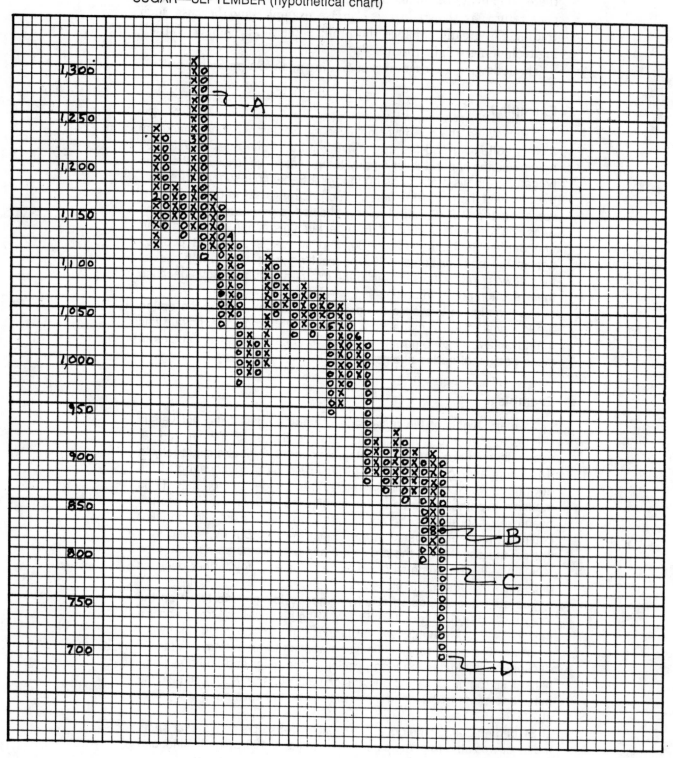

58

his addition profit was the difference between 130 points of gain from the further price decline and the 40 points lost in the trade of the long position, or a net of 90 points before commissions. The complete profit calculations are shown in the accompanying table.

Declared put thus going short at (A)	12.80
Covered short in market at (D)	7.00
Gross profit in put position before commission	5.80 = 580 points
Went long against put at (B)	8.30
Closed long in market at (C)	7.90
Loss on long trade against put	−0.40 = −40 points
Gross profit on put in points before commission	580
Less loss on long trade	−40
Gross profit in points on entire transaction	540
Gross profit in points on entire transaction	540
Multiplied by point value	$ 11.20
Gross profit in dollars on entire transaction	$6,048
Gross profit in dollars on entire transaction	$6,048
Less dealer commission (two transactions × $100)	200
Gross profit after commission	$5,848
Less premium cost of put	−1,120
Net profit	$4,728

$$\text{Return on investment} = \frac{\$4,728}{\$1,120} = 422 \text{ percent}$$

The long position taken at 8.30 would not need to have been a loss if the trader had been able to sense weakness and liquidate at the 9.10 resistance level before the downtrend resumed. Such action would have generated a very healthy additional profit.

Example K

What happens if after sugar bottoms and the put buyer goes long a futures contract against the put, the market rallies well above the striking price of the put, where it remains until the declaration date? Should this occur, the put would be abandoned on the declaration date. Of course, it is not necessary to liquidate the long position on the declaration date of the option. But, choosing to carry the futures position after the declaration date of the option creates three potential hazards. First, the trader is losing the protection of the option and must, therefore, assume the risk of adverse market movement. Second, carrying a naked or unhedged futures position creates the liability of margin calls during periods of adverse market action. And third, if the futures position is held to maturity, there is the problem of taking delivery. Generally, the best procedure is to liquidate the trading position on or before the declaration date of the option, an action which both avoids the problems mentioned above and also frees the cash proceeds for use in other investments.

Let us go through this example again, this time using some numbers and the price movement of March sugar. Early in February, an 11-month put is purchased for a premium of 150 points, or $1,680, at a strike price of 11.80 to expire January 15 (point A on Chart 9). Sugar does exactly as expected by declining to 8.50 by July. Believing this may be the bottom, the put taker decides to go long against the put on the next buy signal which occurs in August (point B) at 9.20. This process of going long against a put, in effect, converts the put into a call and locks in the gross profit of 2.60 cents (strike price of the put at 11.80 less price of

CHART 9
SUGAR—MARCH (hypothetical chart)

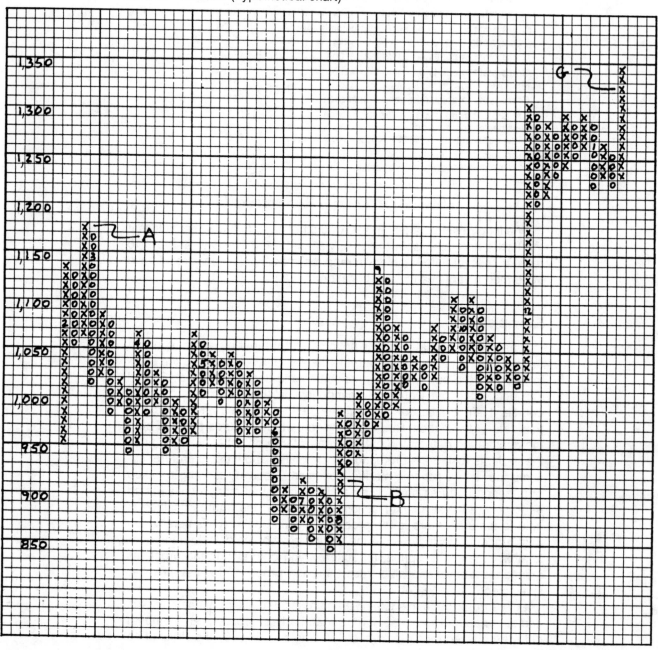

long position at 9.20). Sugar does rise to 11.40, consolidates for two months in the 10.00 to 11.40 range, and then takes a substantial upward thrust to 13.00 in the December–January period. Once sugar rose above the 11.80 striking price of the put, it remained about the strike until the declaration date. On the declaration date, January 15, the put is abandoned and the long position is liquidated at the market at 13.30 (point G). The resulting net profit is $2,812, and the calculations showing how it was derived are given in the accompanying table.

Market sale of long future position at	13.30	
Market purchase of long position at	9.20	
Gross profit in points before commission	4.10 = 410 points	
Gross profit in points	410	
Multiplied by dollar point value	$ 11.20	
Gross profit in dollars before commission	$4,592	
Gross profit in dollars before commission	$4,592	
Less dealer commission on one trade	100	
Gross profit after commission	$4,492	
Gross profit after commission	$4,492	
Less premium cost of abandoned put	1,680	
Net profit	$2,812	

Example L

Let us now create a fairly complicated chain of trades against a profitable put. Based on the price pattern as shown on the chart of March sugar, an 11-month put is purchased in February (point A on Chart 10) at a striking price of 11.80 and at a premium cost of $1,680. After the second decline to 9.50 (point B), the 9.50 level is assumed to be a support level, and thus a long position is taken which is subsequently sold at the resistance level of 10.70 (point C). A new long position is taken at the 9.20 point-and-figure buy signal (point D) with the close out sell at the reversal level of 11.10 (point E). A final purchase is made at the point-and-figure signal at 10.60 (point F) and held until the declaration date, at which time it is liquidated at the market at 13.30 (point G).

Do not try to understand the logic of the above transactions. The object is to show how a number of riskless trades could be made against a profitable put with a resulting gross profit of 580 points. This creates a greater profit than would have been possible by exercising the put at the 850 low or by abandoning the option on the declaration date. The net profit from the chain of trades is calculated in the accompanying table.

Sell long position in market at (C)	10.70	
Purchase of long position in market at (B)	9.50	
Gross profit in points on transaction no. 1	1.20 = 120 points	
Sell long position in market at (E)	11.10	
Purchases of long position in market at (D)	9.20	
Gross profit in points of transaction no. 2	1.90 = 190 points	
Sell long position in market at (G)	13.30	
Purchase of long position in market at (F)	10.60	
Gross profit in points on transaction no. 3	2.70 = 270 points	

CHART 10
SUGAR—MARCH (hypothetical chart)

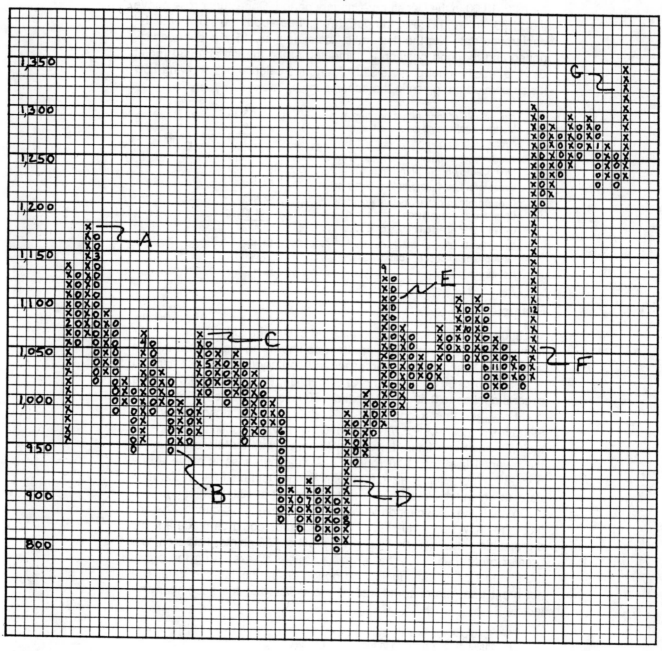

62

Gross profit in points on transaction no. 1	120
Gross profit in points on transaction no. 2	190
Gross profit in points on transaction no. 3	270
Total gross profit in points for transaction	580
Total gross profits in points for transactions	580
Multiplied by dollar point value	$ 11.20
Gross profits in dollars before commissions	$6,496
Gross profits in dollars before commissions	$6,496
Less dealers commissions (three × $100)	300
Gross profit in dollars after commissions	$6,196
Gross profit in dollars after commissions	$6,196
Less premium cost of put	1,680
Net profit	$4,516

$$\text{Return on investment} = \frac{\$4,516}{\$1,680} = 269 \text{ percent}$$

Example M

A put should always be declared, even if such declaration will not prove totally profitable, as long as the exercise generates more dollars than the commission cost to exercise. Therefore a put on March sugar at 11.80, which cost $1,680, would never be abandoned on the declaration date for a full loss if even $5 to $10 could be made by declaring. But before declaring, make sure that the price in the market would more than cover the commission cost to exercise a sugar put. Therefore, assuming a $100 commission of nine points, the put would not be exercised unless the market price of sugar is 11.71 or lower (striking price of put at 11.80 less commissions to exercise of 0.09). When working with a market price extremely close to the minimum exercise figure, execute the market side first before declaring the option. Only in this way can a "dollar throw off," defined as the cash generated from the transaction less commissions, be assured. If, for example, sugar is trading at 11.75 the last day before the declaration, place a limit order to buy at 11.71 or lower. If the purchase is made, then declare the put. If sugar fails to decline, and thus the purchase is not executed, the option is abandoned.

If this trading hint is ignored and the option declared when the tape shows sugar to be trading at 11.71 or slightly lower, by the time the purchase order reaches the floor, sugar may have rallied causing a loss in a transaction meant to have a "dollar throw off." Thus, always remember to make the market transaction before declaring.

Example N

Taking a long futures position against a put has the effect of converting the put to a call. During the period that the long position is kept open, the profit existing on the put at the time a long position is purchased, defined as the difference between the striking price of the put and the price of the long position, is protected. But under most circumstances, no further profits can be made until the long position is liquidated in the market and the put is left unhedged. This is true for as long as the futures contract is selling at a price below the striking price of the put. The profit resulting when the put is declared must be the difference between the strike price of the put and the price at which a future was purchased. For example, a sugar put struck at 11.80 and a long position taken on at 9.80 would lock in (protect) a 200-point gross profit before deducting commissions and the premium cost of the put regardless of the current market price. If the current market price of sugar or the market price on the declaration date is 11.80, the put is ignored and the long is liquidated in the market generating a 200-point gross profit. If sugar is 10.80 on the declaration date, the put is declared, creating a short at 11.80 which is offset by the long at 9.80 for a gross profit of 200 points. The put would also be declared at 11.80 and the short offset by the long at 9.80, generating 200 points of gross profit if the sugar price on the last day of the put life was 9.80 or even 2.80. As soon as the price rallies above the strike price of the put and the price of the long position, the put serves only as a potential stop, and the resulting profits will be the difference between the price of the long position and the current market price. Thus, if the long position were at 9.80 and the current price is 13.80, a price above the strike price of the put, the gross profit is the difference between the price of the long position and the current market price of 13.80. Therefore, in this case, the gross profit would be 13.80 − 9.80, or 400 points.

Let us now summarize some of the concepts in this section. First, note that buyers of the put will never be called for either original or variation margins on their long positions traded against and protected by the put option, assuming the put is in the money at the time a long position is taken. Second, it should be remembered that purchasing a futures contract against the put has the effect of converting the put into a call. As long as the long position is maintained, the profit is defined as the difference between the strike price of the put and the price at which a long future contract was purchased. This profit is totally protected, and in addition, there is a very real possibility, as shown in Example M, of having the futures rise above the strike price of the put and thus provide the opportunity to earn additional profits.

The third point to keep in mind is the idea that trading against the put prevents having to exercise it in an instance where the put is profitable yet a temporary price rally is imminent. As long as the market has volatility or movement and the option remains open (meaning that it has not been declared), the trading process can be repeated time and time again.

3. Purchase puts—a stop order substitute

A cardinal rule in commodity trading is that a futures position should always be protected against huge losses from adverse price movements, beginning at the time the initial position is taken. This may be done either through the use of a stop-loss order or an option. The stop has the advantage of having cost nothing unless exercised or, stated differently, will not cause a loss unless triggered. Thus, if sugar is shorted at 10.00 with a stop placed at 10.50, and sugar declines directly to 9.00, the stop was not exercised and thus no loss was incurred. The property of an initial stop causing a loss only if triggered is about the only advantage of the stop. Yet an option has a great many more advantages as shown below. First, an option provides protection at a guaranteed price. Second, there is no limit to the number of times an option can be used as a stop. Third, an option can be reversed, meaning a put can become a call and a call turned into a put. And fourth, an option provides protection against whipsaws.

Example O

Let us now see exactly how a put can be used in lieu of a stop on a long position. Because a put allows the taker to sell a future contract against it at the strike price through its entire life, it offers much the same protection as a stop. So when a long position is purchased in July silver of the following year at the point-and-figure buy signal at 470.00 (point A on Chart 11), the trader has two alternatives. The first is to place a stop below the recent low or support level of 454.00 (point B) to protect the position should silver fail to hold support at the bottom of the channel and break to the downside. The second choice is to purchase a put. Based on the fact that a six-month put would cost 2,500 points, or $1,250, and the stop, if executed, would cost 1,600 points, or $800 (470.00–454.00), the put seems a better buy.

Silver did not decline after the purchase, so the protection offered by the put was not necessary, but such protection was still vital, for few traders are wealthy enough or have the fortitude to totally ignore any type of protection. The protection offered by the put was appreciated but not used because silver became quite bullish and by late August was selling at 534.00. At this level, silver began to appear a little top heavy, and an order was placed to liquidate the long position at 522.00 (point C), which represented the next chart sell point.

After liquidating the long position for a gross profit of 5,200 points (sale price of 522.00 less purchase price of 470.00), the trader is left with a put at 470.00 having four remaining months of life. When silver is trading thousands of dollars above the strike price, the put has relatively little value. Yet on the same major price break which triggered the liquidation of the long at 522.00, silver is knocked all of the way back to 476.00. Still being bullish over the long term, a new long position is taken on the first upside reversal occurring near the protective strike price of the put (470.00). The reversal occurred, and a long position was taken at 482.00 (point D). Going long at 482.00 means a maximum potential loss of 1,200 points, or $600, should silver decline substantially and need to be protected through the declaration of the put at 470.00. Again the put protection is not needed, for silver is trading at 552.00 (point E) by the put's declaration date in early January. On the declara-

CHART 11
SILVER—JULY (hypothetical chart)

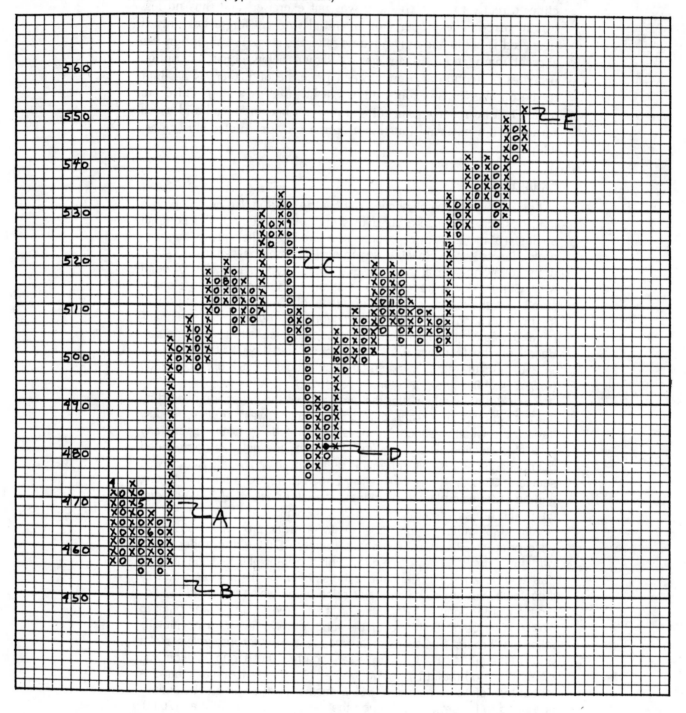

tion date, the put is abandoned, and the long position is liquidated in the market at 552.00 for a gross profit of 7,000 points, or $3,500 (552.00–482.00).

Even though silver never traded below the strike price of the put and, in the end, the put was abandoned, the put must be said to have served its purpose of protecting the trader against huge potential losses while in no way restricting profit opportunities. Was the premium cost of the put a wasted expenditure? Absolutely not. The premium expenditure of $1,250 seems a small cash outlay for the opportunity of making thousands of dollars under nearly riskless circumstances.

The calculations of the profits made from these two long positions using the put in lieu of a stop order are shown in the accompanying table.

Sell long position in the market at (C)	522.00	
Purchase long position in market at (A)	470.00	
Gross profit in points on transaction no. 1	52.00 = 5,200 points	
Sell long position in market at (E)	552.00	
Purchase long position in market at (D)	482.00	
Gross profit in points on transaction no. 2	70.00 = 7,000 points	
Gross profit in points on transaction no. 1	5,200	
Gross profit in points on transaction no. 2	7,000	
Total gross profit in points	12,200	
Total gross profit in points	12,200	
Multiplied by dollar point value	$ 0.50	
Total gross profit in dollars before commission	$6,100	
Total gross profit in dollars before commission	$6,100	
Less dealer commissions (two × $100)	200	
Total gross profit after commissions	$5,900	
Total gross profit after commissions	$5,900	
Less premium cost of abandoned put	1,250	
Net profit	$4,650	

Example P

Let us modify the last example to show the effect of one good trade and one trade which was unsuccessful and required the exercise of the put. In this example, the July silver chart has been modified to assume a decline much more severe than in the prior example. In the decline in Chart 12, the silver futures went down to 410.00, where it was trading on the January declaration date.

Except for the severity of the price decline, all of the other facts are the same as in Example O.

A long position is purchased at 470.00 (point A) and is protected by a six-month put struck at 470.00, costing $1,250. Silver rallies to 534.00 with one false point-and-figure sell signal given during the advance, and the long position is finally liquidated at the point-and-figure sell signal (point B) at 522.00. The ensuing decline, which triggered the liquidation sale, carries the price down to 476.00, where support seems to exist. Immediately after the upside reversal at 482.00 (point C), the price at which a long position is again purchased, silver begins a period of

CHART 12
SILVER—JULY (hypothetical chart)

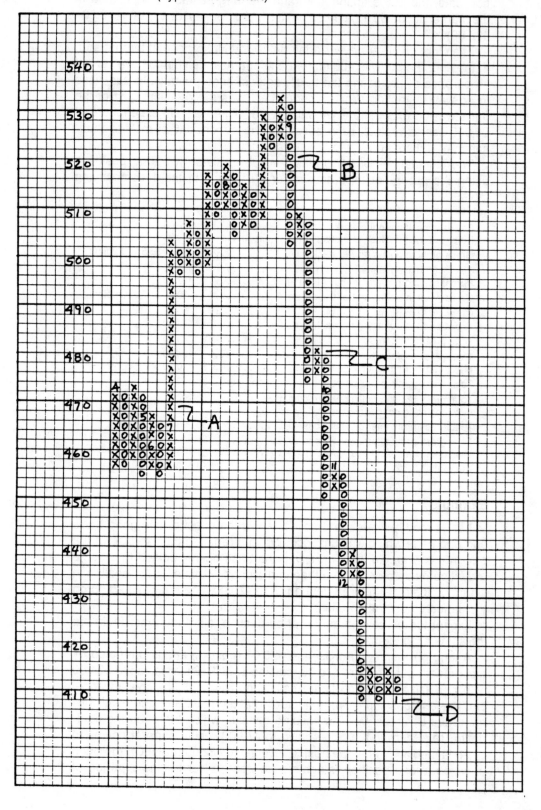

declining prices. When support is finally found at 410.00, silver goes through an extended period of base building and is still in this base building formation on the declaration date of the put (point D).

Since the market price of the future is below the strike price of the put, the put holder has no alternative but to declare the put at 470.00 and use the long position taken at 482.00 to offset the short. This loss of $600 on the long position certainly beats meeting margin calls during the price decline, being trapped in a limit move, or selling the position in the market at 410.00 for a $3,600 loss. Even adding the premium cost of $1,250, the commission of $100, and the $600 loss, the put provided invaluable protection in the second trade, in addition to the safety it potentially offered in the first trade.

To better understand this concept, the profit and loss figures are outlined in the accompanying table.

Sold long position in market at (B)	522.00
Purchased long position in market at (A)	470.00
Gross profit in points on transaction no. 1	52.00 = 5,200 points
Declared put going short at (A)	470.00
Purchased long position in market at (C)	482.00
Gross loss in points on transaction no. 2	12.00 = −1,200 points
Gross profit in points on transaction no. 1	5,200
Gross loss in points on transaction no. 2	−1,200
Total gross profit	4,000
Total gross profit	4,000
Multiplied by dollar point value	$ 0.50
Gross profit in dollars before commissions	$2,000
Gross profit in dollars before commissions	$2,000
Less dealer commissions (two × $100)	− 200
Gross profit after commissions	$1,800
Gross profit after commissions	$1,800
Less cost of put	1,250
Net profit	$ 550

4. Puts—trading against unprofitable options

Everyone guesses wrong sometimes. The guesses or hunches which fail to materialize in option purchases are no less common than in any other area of investments. The buyer of a put, expecting the commodity to collapse, as often as not believes the futures show unparalleled strength on the upside. It is always unfortunate to guess wrong and end up with an option on the wrong side of the market. But do not get discouraged and walk away from a put which proves unprofitable after the purchase. Purchasing an option is really just a purchase of time. A put struck below the currently trading price of the futures should be viewed positively, based on its remaining life, and this time should be employed and the put salvaged by trading against it.

Suppose Bill Clark, an option buyer, viewing Chart 13 at point A, becomes very bearish on the future price movement of the July silver

CHART 13
SILVER—JULY (hypothetical chart)

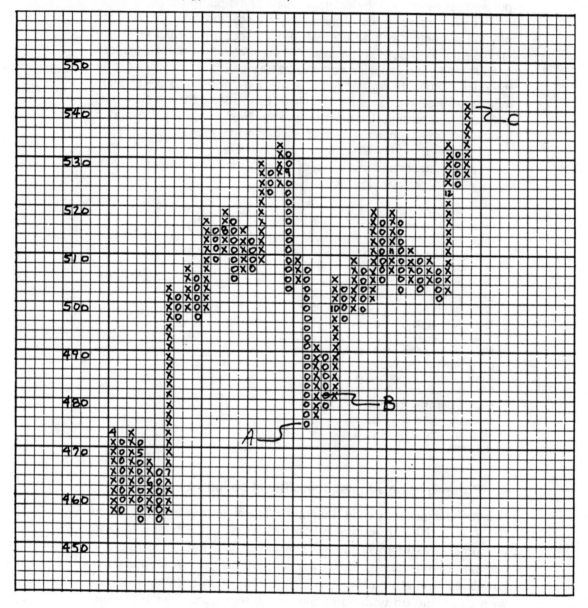

contract and believes the downside movement will continue until the 456.00 horizontal support level is reached. He then purchases a three-month put at 476.00 for a premium of 1,500 points, equivalent to $750. To his dismay, not only does silver fail to decline, but reverses to the upside and begins to develop all of the signs of having bottomed. Because our option trader has been a good little option buyer and, like all good little option buyers, he has thoroughly read and studied this book, he knows exactly what to do. He must simply go along on a futures contract of silver against the put. Even though his intention was never to trade against the put, he realizes if silver never goes below the strike price of the put, failure to go long futures against the put means he has thrown $750 away. Not wanting to be out the $750 and being absolutely convinced the next movement will be on the upside, he goes long at 482.00 (point B). His second hunch as to market action is as correct as his first was wrong, and silver rises, consolidates, and pushes forward again so that on the declaration date of the put in mid-December, July silver is trading at, and the long position is sold at 542.00 for a gross profit of 6,000 points, or $3,000. The gross profit less the $100 commission and the $750 premium cost of the put still leaves a net profit of $2,150, not bad for an investment which went sour from the inception and was nearly a $750 loss.

In this example, had silver immediately declined after the long position was purchased, the maximum loss would have been $1,150, calculated as the difference between the strike price of the put and the price at which the long was purchased (482.00 − 476:00 = $300) plus the $750 cost of the put and the $100 in commissions involved on the trade.

5. Puts—Hedges on profitable futures

One hopes there are a great many times in the life of a futures trader when a long position has worked perfectly and he is sitting with a substantial gain. The decision as to a logical course of action under these circumstances can be difficult. The profits must be protected against an abrupt market reversal, whipsaws should be avoided, and there should be no restriction placed upon the ability to profit from a continuation of the bullish trend. These parameters are enough to boggle the mind. A stop would not avoid whipsaws nor, if triggered, permit any additional profit action from a continuation of the upside movement. About the only technique that meets the needs of the speculator in this very pleasant, but trying, period would be the use of puts.

A put used as a hedge against a profitable futures position has the advantage of, first, protecting the profits by allowing the long position to be offset against the short created by the declaration of the put at the put striking price. Second, this protection offered by the put is not affected by whipsaws, the number of declines, or their severity. Third, the protection lasts through the entire life of the put, and thus only the ultimate move is important. And fourth, the put also permits the futures holder to profit from additional strength while having the peace of mind that, regardless of future market action, current profit is absolutely locked into a protected position.

Let us now look at an example. Assume a long futures position was established on March cocoa at 105.00 in late July (point A, Chart 14). Cocoa moves up smartly, exactly like it is supposed to, peaks at 138.00, and then declines with the same speed at which it rose. The decline does not concern Sue Stephens, the speculator, for although she is long-term bullish, when the future was trading at 138.00 (point B), she decided to purchase a put in order to hedge or protect her profit against such drops, while still looking over the intermediate term for substantial further upside movement. She has no real concern as to exactly how low the future price declines, for at any time she can dispose of the long, purchased at 105.00, at the 138.00 strike price of the put and thus effectively protect the 3,300 points, or $9,900 (3,300 points times $3 per point) gain. This protection costs only 1,000 points or the $3,000 premium of the four-month cocoa put with a striking price of 138.00.

She did not become nervous about the decline that carried the futures from 138.00 to 121.00, nor did she become concerned with the decline in November which carried the price down from the contract highs of 156.00 to 125.00, for the 105.00 long position was still protected at 138.00.

By the declaration date in mid-January, the March contract had once again recovered and was again making new contract highs. The put had to be discarded and the long liquidated in the market at 159.00 (point C). The net profit resulting from the transaction is $13,100, calculated by taking the gross transaction profit of 5,400 points, or $16,200, less both the commission of $100 and the $3,000 premium cost of the put.

Was the $3,000 premium cost of the put, which was ultimately abandoned, worth the cost? In light of the fact that it bought her peace of mind through two severe price declines while permitting her to ultimately liquidate the long 2,100 points higher than might otherwise have been possible, we would have to conclude it was definitely a good buy.

6. Puts—hedges on calls

The last major use of an option is to hedge, or lock in, profits on another profitable option. Now that the reader is thoroughly familiar with the trading concepts of both puts and calls, the two sides of this technique can easily be understood.

The first of the two sides of this technique is the use of puts to protect the profits in profitable calls. After July silver showed signs

CHART 14
COCOA—MARCH (hypothetical chart)

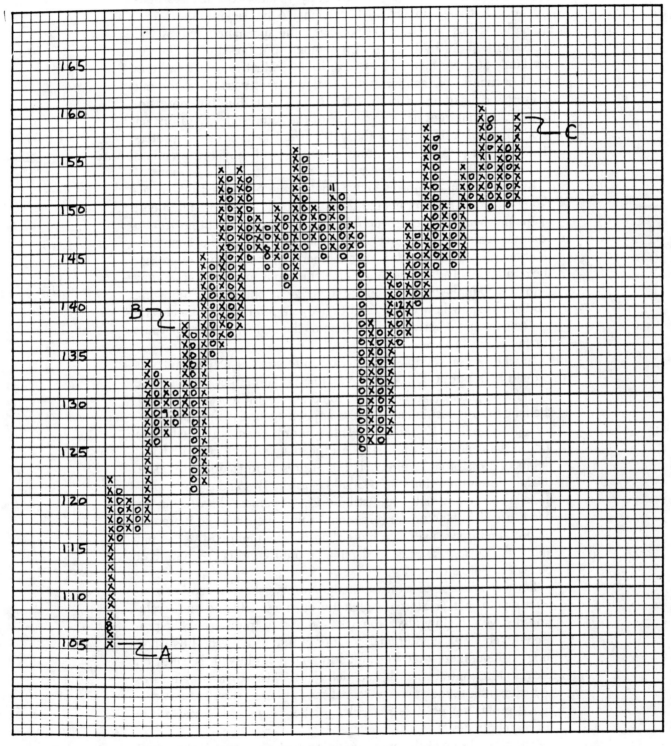

of bottoming in September, a six-month call is purchased at 486.00 (point A, Chart 15) for $1,500. By early January, the futures market price has risen to 552.00 but seems to be lacking short-term strength. At this 552.00 level (point B), the speculator hedges and locks in the profit by buying a three-month put for $1,000. The put need only be three months long in order to protect the call's two and one-half months of remaining life. If the market does drop, the put is exercised in order to protect the call's profit. But far more important, the put does not interfere with the futures ability to further profit from a continuation of the bull move. The cost of this protection, without jeopardizing future profits, is still only the premium cost of $1,000.

By comparison, a futures hedge could have been used which, although it would have protected the full amount of the premium cost of the put, would have prevented the trader from benefiting from a continuation of the bull move. A futures hedge is going short one contract month while remaining long another, under the assumption that the positions will move together. Some point-movement examples may help to explain the use of an option to hedge an option. The following paragraphs show how a put, used to hedge a profitable call, not only protects the profit existing at the time of the hedge, but also permits further profits to be realized.

In all of these examples, a call was purchased at 486.00 and was hedged by a put at 552.00. The variable is the market price on the declaration date. If, on the declaration date, the futures are at 450.00, the long futures position at 450.00 is applied against the put at 552.00 for a gross profit of 10,200 points. If the futures price were 486.00, the long at the same price would still be applied against the put with 6,600 points of gross profit resulting. If the futures were trading at 600.00, the long futures position would be sold in the market and the put abandoned. The gross profit would still be 11,400 points. Thus, for an expenditure of $1,000 for the three-month put, there was an increased potential return if silver rose more than the premium cost of the put above the puts strike price or declined more than this premium cost below the call's strike price.

For a comparison in a futures hedge, using a short in another contract month such as March, which moves in a one-to-one linear relationship with the July silver, the 6,600-point gross profit would be protected; yet, for each additional point of upside gain on the July silver long position, there would be an additional point loss in the short on the different contract month, and vice versa. Thus, when using futures to hedge futures, the premium cost of the option is saved, but no additional profits are possible regardless of how high or low the future ultimately trades.

The second side of the option-hedging option concept is the use of

CHART 15
SILVER—JULY

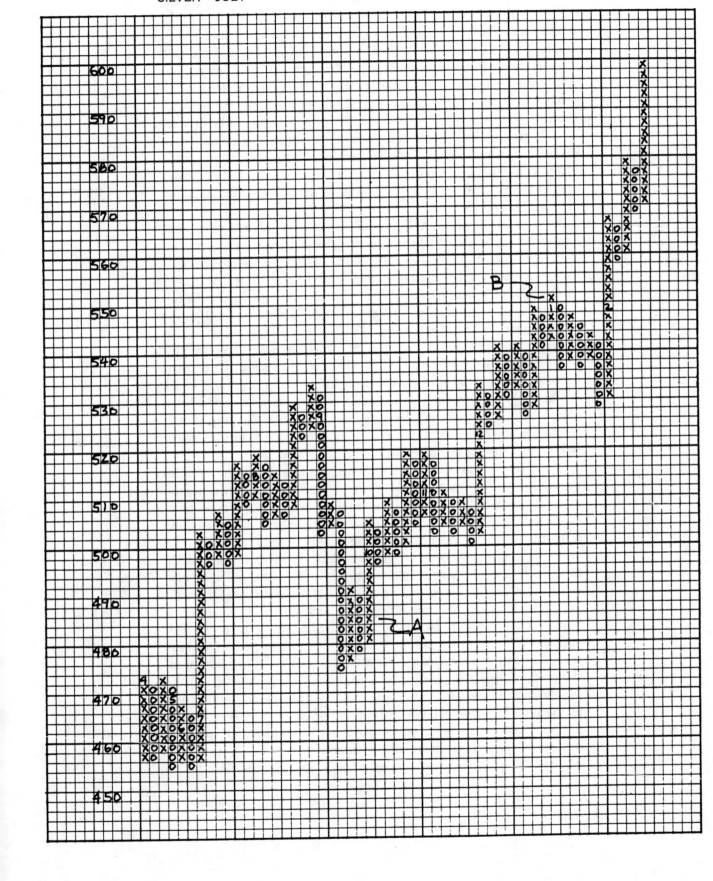

a call to hedge a profitable put position. Should the market rise, the call can be profitably exercised. But even more important, if the bearish move continues unabated, additional profits can be generated. The cost of this hedge is simply the premium cost of the call.

If the trading discussed to this point seems too complicated, you can always simply exercise the option when some predetermined profit has been achieved. There is absolutely nothing wrong with exercising early if you lack the confidence in being able to adequately pick trading points or lack the desire to squeeze a few more dollars out of an already profitable position through a complicated chain of transactions. You can never be criticized for keeping your system simple, and in many cases, the simplest techniques are the ones which work best.

Yet you owe it to yourself to read and reread these trading concepts until you understand them thoroughly so that you can compare them with the simple exercise. If, after obtaining a thorough, comprehensive knowledge of the various trading techniques, you conclude the exercise concept is still the best, stick with it. But in following the exercise idea, you might want to consider several points of refinement. First, since there is a 50–50 chance of being wrong on the direction of the market movement, in which case the entire premium is lost, there must be a profit objective of at least 100 percent on those options that do become profitable, just to cover the losses on the other 50 percent which ultimately must be abandoned for a complete loss. Therefore, before buying any option, be sure that if the future moves in the proper direction, the volatility of movement will at least double the invested capital.

The second refinement: One must never place a top on potential gains. The puts or calls which reach the 100-percent mark are the best investments and are the ones which probably should be held. If the calls are closed out into strength and the puts into weakness after a 100-percent return has been obtained, the profitability on the entire portfolio can never be greater than 100 percent, and those moves which could have generated the 200, 300, 400, or larger percentage returns are closed out at a mere 100-percent profit. It would be far better to have a price objective and, once the objective is reached, to use a stop, below the market price in the case of a call and above the market price in the case of a put to protect against reversals. At the same time, there would not be a ceiling on potential profits. These stops should also be moved in the direction of the profitable movement to protect gains made after the original setting of the stop. For example, when the price of silver futures is 550.00, a stop might be placed 1,000 points lower (at 540.00) in order to protect the profit of a silver call struck at 500.00 and costing $1,250. The stop should periodically be raised in a linear relationship to the market price as silver rises higher and higher. But it would always remain 1,000 points below the highest price reached by silver. Thus, when the market is 600.00, the stop would be 590.00, and when the market is 610.00, the stop would be raised to 600.00. If a profitable put were owned on silver at 500.00, with the market price currently at 450.00, a stop might be placed at 460.00, a distance of 1,000 points above the current market price. As the market declined, the stop would be lowered but would always remain 1,000 points above the lowest market price obtained. Methods other than this one-to-one linear method of moving stops can also be used.

The earlier sections have made the assumption that the trader was able to predict the major direction of futures price movements. But there are times in the commodities market when the best of speculators are completely confused as to the direction of the next major price move. There are also some people who have neither the ability nor the desire to attempt to predict the next move. The next section is for them.

THE SPECIAL DOUBLE

The special double option, sometimes referred to as a double option, is simply a combination of a put option and a call option which allows the purchaser to either buy or sell (but not both) a commodity at a fixed strike price for future delivery at any time prior to the declaration date. The premium cost of a double is usually close to, but slightly less than, the sum of the premium costs of both a put and a call purchased separately. Those familiar with stock option straddles should notice the one basic difference. Only one side of the double can be declared as opposed to both sides of the stock straddle.

While only one side of the double can be exercised, both sides can be traded against as many times as desired. Every trading trick discussed in the earlier chapters with regard to puts and calls, including the use of an option to hedge another option, options as hedges on futures, trading against unprofitable options, and the use of options in lieu of stop orders, will work equally well with either or both sides of the double. The only restriction is that only one side may ultimately be declared or exercised. This restriction should cause no problem because normally the buyer would only want to declare one side. If one has a substantial profit on the call side with several months of life remaining and expects a severe correction, one will trade (short) against the profitable call. Should the rally continue, the profit cannot increase, but the profit existing at the time a short was taken is protected. Likewise, should the price decline, the profit is protected, and when the short is covered, the call is left intact for a further upside move. A short has the effect of converting a call to a put, and should the price decline below the strike price of the double, there is double leverage. For each point below the strike, an additional point is made on the hedged call acting as a put, and a point is made on the true put side.

Since the premium cost of the double buys time because both sides can be traded against or hedged, and because there is the possibility of double leverage on a hedge should the price trade through the strike price, it seems silly to forego all of these advantages bought by the premium and related to the time life of the option by an early or premature exercise. If, instead of exercising early, the holder takes full advantage of all the time purchased with the premium, neither side will be declared until the last day. On the last day, if the market is above the strike price, the call is exercised, and if the market is below the strike price, the put is exercised, or if it is right at the strike price, the entire double is abandoned. Therefore, in taking full advantage of the option's life length, there is really no opportunity to exercise both sides and thus no advantage of having a straddle at a higher premium cost where both sides can be exercised.

The unique advantages of double options

The double option is one of the most exciting of investment vehicles to be developed in recent years. The double option offers all the advantages of puts and calls, including their minimum and calculable risk exposure, tremendous leverage, unlimited profit potential, and freedom from margin calls. But the double has one additional advantage which places it in a special category by itself. The purchaser of a put must attempt to predict the market. Except where the put is used in lieu of a stop to protect a new long position, or to hedge a profitable long position, the put buyer is anticipating a substantial drop in price. Likewise, the speculator who purchases a naked call, not bought with the expectation of immediately being used as a stop for a short futures position or as a hedge for a profitable short, is anticipating a major price move on the upside. The unique advantage of the double is that it frees the holder from dependence on market direction prediction. The double option, being the combination of both a put and a call, can be quite profitable regardless of whether the market advances or declines. This means the purchaser need never attempt to determine whether the next price movement will be up or down, probably the most difficult task in any investment program. All that is required to make money in doubles is a substantial price fluctuation which during the life of the double will carry the price of the futures either up or down more than the premium cost of the option.

It is far easier to determine the volatility than the direction the volatility will carry the price. And while every investor is saddled with the same need to predict volatility, not all investors must forecast the harder question as to which direction the volatility will move the price. No capital gains-oriented investor should purchase any stock, futures, or options unless he believes the price will move a reasonable amount. If investors risk $5,000 to purchase 100 shares of a $50 stock, expecting only a one-point upside movement, they are fools. Although different investors have different appreciation goals, they all realize there must be a potential appreciation rate in excess of the risk factor if they are to profit over the long run. Before putting dollars at risk, most investors must not only predict how much the price will move, but also in which direction. On the other hand, the purchaser of the double is only concerned with the easier of the two forecasts, that of predicting the amount of movement. Since there will be a profit from either a price advance or decline, the investor has no real interest in the actual price, only in the severity of the rise or fall in price. Puts and calls have potentially large risks in the absolute sense, meaning if the market goes the wrong way and no trades are made, the put or call is a complete or 100-percent loss. To compensate for the risk, options have fabulous return potential that can easily run to 200, 300, and 400 percent returns on invested capital.

In order to show the risk-reward relationship, assume a six-month put on silver costs $1,250, a call $1,500, and a double $2,200. A market decline of $4,000 below the strike price would represent a 220-percent return to the put holder as shown below.

$$
\begin{aligned}
\text{Gross profit} & \quad \ldots\ldots\ldots\ldots \quad \$4,000 \\
\text{Less put premium} & \quad \ldots\ldots\ldots \quad \underline{1,250} \\
\text{Net profit} & \quad \ldots\ldots\ldots\ldots \quad \$2,750
\end{aligned}
$$

$$
\text{Return on investment} = \frac{\text{Net profit}}{\text{Premium cost}} = \frac{\$2,750}{\$1,250} = 220 \text{ percent}
$$

The same decline would result in a 100-percent loss to the call buyer and an 82-percent profit to the purchaser of a double ($4,000 gross profit less $2,200 premium cost of double all divided by the $2,200 premium cost of the double).

If silver had risen in price by $4,000, the put investor would have a 100-percent loss, the call holder would have a 167-percent profit ($4,000 gross profit less call premium of $1,500 all divided by the call premium of $1,500), and the holder of a double would have made 82 percent.

In these examples, it is obvious the holders of puts and calls were taking the greatest risk if their judgment of the direction of the move was in error. Likewise, since their risk was the greatest, so were the rewards from being right. But since the double is a combination of a single put and call, the risk of error in judging the direction of movement is nonexistent. Since there is a cost to reduce the risk and since this cost is close to, but slightly less than, the sum of the premium costs of both the put and call, the ultimate return must be lower than having a single option on the correct side of the market.

Puts are generally cheaper than calls, and there is normally a premium savings by buying a double as opposed to purchasing a put and a call separately.

The next question which must be answered is just how volatile are the futures markets? This is an extremely important question, especially when considering the purchase of a double because of the relatively high investment outlay which must be covered by the future volatility. If a six-month double cost $2,200 on a commodity which traditionally has a total range between the high and low for any six-month period of only $2,100, the double is a horrible purchase. Yet, if the normal trading range for any six-month period is $8,000, the probability of earning a substantial return on the double is greatly increased. A later chaper will deal with the relationship of premium costs to market volatility and establish a simple, very effective method of determining whether an option has a reasonable profit potential. It will also explain a method of ranking various options in order to select the best of the offerings.

Chapter 5

Evaluation and profitability of options

FUTURES VOLATILITY AND ITS
RELATIONSHIP TO DOUBLES

The primary interest of this section is the double option. Since the double will benefit from either a price advance or decline, the first question which must be answered is whether the amount of the rise or fall of the futures price will be sufficient to cover the exercise commissions and the premium cost. Exact coverage is not enough. If the double buyer always gets back exactly what was invested, the game is pointless. Therefore, not only must the buyer of double options recover all costs, there must be a profit to be considered successful. The size of the return is the second question of vital concern. Answers to both questions will be covered in this section.

How volatile are commodity futures?—a chart view

Very few people trade the futures market. Why? Because they have been told how treacherous it can be. Being treacherous is the same as being extremely volatile. For proof, simply spend a moment reviewing the following charts of weekly price action of the five commodities having the greatest option volume in the London markets over the past five years. These five are sugar, cocoa, coffee, copper, and silver. Because a chart of weekly commodity price action is never as impressive a display of volatility as a chart of monthly price action, monthly charts have also been included on these commodities. Table 5–1 has also been provided to help understand the significance of the charts by showing such trading facts as the dollar value of a daily limit move, the dollar value of a daily range move, and the value of a point. Since it is uncertain at this writing as to what commodities will be optionable, the table contains information on all regularly traded commodities.

After having seen, in chart form, weekly and monthly trading ranges of these optionable commodities and having used the table to convert the movement into dollars, you must certainly be convinced that commodities are volatile (Charts 16–25). Of course, all are not always fast moving. Some commodities will trade in a narrow range for an extended period of time as did sugar in 1960, 1961, and the first half of 1962; others, like coffee, will not be regularly traded for years. But when a commodity like coffee does begin to move, it tends to move extremely fast and in broad ranges. Furthermore, once in this volatile phase, it will usually remain volatile for years, allowing ample time to make a number of extremely successful trades of double options.

But we still have not put a quantitative handle on the volatility in order to establish some guide lines as to just how profitable double options will be, and to set upper or maximum price limits that the

TABLE 5-1
TRADING FACTS

COMMODITY	EXCHANGE	TRADING HOURS N.Y. TIME	CONTRACT SIZE	PRICE QUOTATIONS	POINT VALUE	MINIMUM PRICE CHANGE	DAILY PRICE LIMIT	DAILY MAXIMUM RANGE
BARLEY**	WINNIPEG	10:30 a.m. 2:15 p.m.	100 Metric Tons	cents per ton	1¢ = $1.00 per contract	10¢	$5.00	$10.00
BROILERS	CHICAGO BOARD OF TRADE	10:15 a.m. 2:05 p.m.	30,000 lbs.	¢ and 1/100¢ per lb.	$3.00 per contract	2 1/2 points per lb.	200 points	400 points* NO LIMITS AFTER FIRST NOTICE DAY
CATTLE MIDWESTERN	CHICAGO MERCANTILE	10:05 a.m. 1:45 p.m.	40,000 lbs.	¢ and 1/100¢ per lb.	$4.00 per contract	2 1/2 points per lb.	150 points	300 points
CATTLE (FEEDER)	CHICAGO MERCANTILE	10:05 a.m. 1:45 p.m.	42,000 lbs.	¢ and 1/100¢ per lb.	$4.20 per contract	2 1/2 points per lb.	150 points	300 points
COCOA	NEW YORK COCOA	10:00 a.m. 3:00 p.m.	30,000 lbs.	¢ and 1/100¢ per lb.	$3.00 per contract	1 point per lb.	400 points	400 points NO LIMITS ON OR AFTER FIRST NOTICE DAY
COFFEE "C"	N.Y. COFFEE & SUGAR	10:30 a.m. 2:28 p.m.	37,500 lbs.	¢ and 1/100¢ per lb.	$3.75 per contract	1 point per lb.	200 points	400 points NO LIMITS ON OR AFTER FIRST NOTICE DAY
COPPER	COMMODITY EXCHANGE, INC.	9:50 a.m. 2:00 p.m.	25,000 lbs.	¢ and 1/100¢ per lb.	$2.50 per contract	10 points per lb.	300 points	600 points* NO LIMITS ON OR AFTER FIRST NOTICE DAY
CORN	CHICAGO BOARD OF TRADE	10:30 a.m. 2:15 p.m.	5,000 bushels	¢ and 1/4¢ per bu.	1/4¢ = $12.50 per contract	1/4¢ per bu.	10¢	20¢*
COTTON No. 2	N.Y. COTTON	10:30 a.m. 3:00 p.m.	50,000 lbs.	¢ and 1/100¢ per lb.	$5.00 per contract	1 point per lb.	200 points	400 points* NO LIMITS ON OR AFTER FIRST NOTICE DAY
CURRENCY	INTERNATIONAL MONETARY MARKET	9:45 a.m. 2:10 p.m.						
BRITISH POUND			25,000 BP	¢ and 1/100¢ per BP	$2.50	5 points	500 points	1,000 points*
MEXICAN PESO			1,000,000 MP	¢ and 1/1000¢ per MP	$10.00	1 point	75 points	150 points*
CANADIAN DOLLAR			100,000 CD	¢ and 1/100¢ per CD	$10.00	1 point	75 points	150 points*
DEUTSCHEMARK (Continued)			125,000 DM	¢ and 1/100¢ per DM	$12.50	1 point	60 points	120 points*

*Variable Limits

**Canadian Funds

March, 1977

TABLE 5–1 (continued)

COMMODITY	EXCHANGE	TRADING HOURS N.Y. TIME	CONTRACT SIZE	PRICE QUOTATIONS	POINT VALUE	MINIMUM PRICE CHANGE	DAILY PRICE LIMIT	DAILY MAXIMUM RANGE
CURRENCY (Contd)								
SWISS FRANC			125,000 SF	¢ and 1/100¢ per SF	$12.50	1 point	60 points	120 points*
FRENCH FRANC			250,000 FR	¢ and 1/1000¢ per FR	$ 2.50	5 points	500 points	1,000 points*
JAPANESE YEN			12,500,000 JY	¢ and 1/10,000¢ per JY	$12.50	1 point	60 points	120 points*
DUTCH GUILDER			125,000 DG	¢ and 1/100¢ per DG	$12.50	1 point	60 points	120 points*
						NO LIMITS ON LAST TRADING DAY		
EGGS (SHELL)	CHICAGO MERCANTILE	10:20 a.m. 2:00 p.m.	22,500 dozen	¢ and 1/100¢ per dozen	$2.25 per contract	5 points per dozen	200 points	400 points
FLAXSEED**	WINNIPEG	10:30 a.m. 2:15 p.m.	100 metric tons	cents per ton	1¢ = $1.00 per contract	10¢	$10.00	$20.00
GNMA MORTGAGE FUTURES	CHICAGO BOARD OF TRADE	9:50 a.m. 2:30 p.m.	$100,000 Face Amount	% and 1/32% of par	1/32% = $31.25	1/32%	3/4%	1 1/2%
						NO LIMITS ON OR AFTER FIRST NOTICE DAY		
GOLD	COMMODITY EXCHANGE, INC.	9:25 a.m. 2:30 p.m.	100 troy ounces	Dollars and cents per oz.	$1.00	10 points	1,000 points	2,000 points
						NO LIMITS ON OR AFTER DAY BEFORE FIRST NOTICE DAY		
GOLD	NEW YORK MERCANTILE	9:25 a.m. 2:30 p.m.	32.15 troy oz.	Dollars and cents per oz.	$.3215	20 points	1,000 points	2,000 points*
						NO LIMIT DURING DELIVERY MONTH		
GOLD	CHICAGO BOARD OF TRADE	9:25 a.m. 2:30 p.m.	96.45 troy oz.	Dollars and cents per oz.	$.9645	10 points	1,000 points	2,000 points*
						NO LIMIT ON OR AFTER FIRST NOTICE DAY		
GOLD	INTERNATIONAL MONETARY MARKET	9:25 a.m. 2:30 p.m.	100 troy ounces	Dollars and cents per oz.	$1.00	10 points	1,000 points	2,000 points*
						NO LIMITS ON LAST TRADING DAY		
GOLD	WINNIPEG	9:15 a.m. 2:30 p.m.	400 oz. (Standard) 100 oz. (Centum)	Dollars and cents per oz.	$4.00 $1.00	5 points 5 points	1,000 points 1,000 points	2,000 points 2,000 points
						NO LIMITS ON LAST TRADING DAY		
HOGS	CHICAGO MERCANTILE	10:15 a.m. 1:55 p.m.	30,000 lbs.	¢ and 1/100¢ per lb.	$3.00 per contract	2 1/2 points per lb.	150 points	300 points
LUMBER	CHICAGO MERCANTILE	10:00 a.m. 2:05 p.m.	100,000 board ft.	Dollars and cents per 1,000 board ft.	1¢ = $1.00	10¢ per 1,000 board ft.	$5.00 per 1,000 board ft.	$10.00 per 1,000 board ft.
OATS	CHICAGO BOARD OF TRADE	10:30 a.m. 2:15 p.m.	5,000 bushels	¢ and 1/4¢ per bu.	1/4¢ = $12.50 per contract	1/4¢ per bu.	6¢	12¢*
ORANGE FROZEN CONCENTRATE	CITRUS ASSOCIATES OF THE N.Y. COTTON	10:15 a.m. 2:45 p.m.	15,000 lbs.	¢ and 1/100¢ per lb.	$1.50 per contract	5 points per lb.	300 points	600 points
						NO LIMIT ON OR AFTER EIGHTH DAY OF DELIVERY MONTH		
PALLADIUM	NEW YORK MERCANTILE	10:20 a.m. 12:55 p.m.	100 troy ounces	Dollars and cents per oz.	$1.00 per contract	5 points per oz.	400 points	800 points
						NO LIMIT ON LAST TRADING DAY		

TABLE 5–1 (continued)

COMMODITY	EXCHANGE	TRADING HOURS N.Y. TIME	CONTRACT SIZE	PRICE QUOTATIONS	POINT VALUE	MINIMUM PRICE CHANGE	DAILY PRICE LIMIT	DAILY MAXIMUM RANGE
PLATINUM	NEW YORK MERCANTILE	9:45 a.m. 2:10 p.m.	50 troy ounces	Dollars and cents per oz.	50¢ per contract	10 points per oz.	1,000 points	2,000 points
						NO LIMIT ON LAST TRADING DAY		
PLYWOOD NEW	CHICAGO BOARD OF TRADE	10:00 a.m. 2:00 p.m.	76,032 sq. ft.	Dollars and cents per 1,000 sq. ft.	1¢ = 76¢	10¢ per 1,000 sq. ft.	700 points	1,400 points
						NO LIMIT ON OR AFTER FIRST NOTICE DAY		
PORK BELLIES	CHICAGO MERCANTILE	10:10 a.m. 2:00 p.m.	36,000 lbs.	¢ and 1/100¢ per lb.	$3.60 per contract	2 1/2 points per lb.	200 points	400 points
POTATOES (RUSSET)	CHICAGO MERCANTILE	10:00 a.m. 1:50 p.m.	80,000 lbs. (800 cwt.)	Dollars and cents per 100 lbs.	$8.00 per contract	1¢ per cwt.	50¢	100¢
POTATOES (MAINE)	NEW YORK MERCANTILE	10:00 a.m. 2:00 p.m.	50,000 lbs. (500 cwt.)	Dollars and cents per 100 lbs.	$5.00 per contract	1¢ per cwt.	50¢	100¢*
						NO LIMIT ON LAST TRADING DAY		
PROPANE	LPG ASSOCIATES OF THE N.Y. COTTON	9:45 a.m. 2:35 p.m.	100,000 gallons	¢ and 1/100¢ per gal.	$10.00 per contract	1 point per gal.	100 points	200 points
						NO LIMIT ON LAST TRADING DAY		
RAPESEED**	WINNIPEG	10:30 a.m. 2:15 p.m.	100 metric tons	cents per ton	1¢ = $1.00 per contract	10¢	$10.00	$20.00
RYE**	WINNIPEG	10:30 a.m. 2:15 p.m.	100 metric tons	cents per ton	1¢ = $1.00 per contract	10¢	$5.00	$10.00
SILVER	CHICAGO BOARD OF TRADE	9:40 a.m. 2:25 p.m.	5,000 troy oz.	¢ and 1/100¢ per troy oz.	50¢ per contract	10 points per oz.	2,000 points	4,000 pints
						NO LIMIT ON OR AFTER FIRST NOTICE DAY		
SILVER	COMMODITY EXCHANGE, INC.	9:40 a.m. 2:15 p.m.	5,000 troy oz.	¢ and 1/100¢ per troy oz.	50¢ per contract	10 points per oz.	2,000 points	4,000 points
						NO LIMIT ON OR AFTER DAY PRIOR TO FIRST NOTICE DAY		
SILVER COINS	NEW YORK MERCANTILE	9:35 a.m. 2:15 p.m.	$10,000 (10 bags)	Dollars per bag	$10.00 per contract	1 point per bag	150 points	300 points*
						NO LIMIT ON LAST TRADING DAY		
SILVER COINS (U.S.)	INTERNATIONAL MONETARY MARKET	9:50 a.m. 2:25 p.m.	$5,000 (5 bags)	Dollars per bag	$5.00 per contract	2 points	150 points	300 points*
						NO LIMIT ON LAST TRADING DAY		
SILVER COINS (Canadian)	INTERNATIONAL MONETARY MARKET	9:50 a.m. 2:25 p.m.	$5,000 (5 bags)	Dollars per bag	$5.00 per contract	2 points	150 points	300 points*
						NO LIMIT ON LAST TRADING DAY		
SOYBEANS	CHICAGO BOARD OF TRADE	10:30 a.m. 2:15 p.m.	5,000 bushels	¢ and 1/4¢ per bu.	1/4¢ = $12.50 per contract	1/4¢ per bu.	30¢	60¢*
SOYBEAN MEAL	CHICAGO BOARD OF TRADE	10:30 a.m. 2:15 p.m.	100 short tons	Dollars and cents per ton	$1.00 per contract	10 points per ton	1,000 points	2,000 points*
						NO LIMIT ON OR AFTER FIRST NOTICE DAY		
SOYBEAN OIL	CHICAGO BOARD OF TRADE	10:30 a.m. 2:15 p.m.	60,000 lbs.	¢ and 1/100¢ per lb.	$6.00 per contract	1 point per lb.	100 points	200 points*
						NO LIMIT ON OR AFTER FIRST NOTICE DAY		

TABLE 5–1 (concluded)

COMMODITY	EXCHANGE	TRADING HOURS N.Y. TIME	CONTRACT SIZE	PRICE QUOTATIONS	POINT VALUE	MINIMUM PRICE CHANGE	DAILY PRICE LIMIT	DAILY MAXIMUM RANGE
SUGAR (WORLD) No. 11	N.Y. COFFEE & SUGAR	10:00 a.m. 2:43 p.m. plus call	112,000 lbs.	¢ and 1/100¢ per lb.	$11.20 per contract	1 point per lb.	100 points	200 points*
						NO LIMIT ON AND AFTER FIRST BUSINESS DAY OF PRIOR MONTH		
SUGAR (DOMESTIC) No. 12	N.Y. COFFEE & SUGAR	10:00 a.m. 2:43 p.m. plus call	112,000 lbs.	¢ and 1/100¢ per lb.	$11.20 per contract	1 point per lb.	100 points	200 points*
						NO LIMIT ON LAST TRADING DAY		
T BILLS FUTURES	INTERNATIONAL MONETARY MARKET	9:35 a.m. 2:35 p.m.	$1,000,000 Face Amount	IMM Index	$25.00	1 point	50 points	50 points
						NO LIMIT ON LAST TRADING DAY		
WHEAT	CHICAGO BOARD OF TRADE	10:30 a.m. 2:15 p.m.	5,000 bushels	¢ and 1/4¢ per bu.	1/4¢ = $12.50 per bu.	1/4¢ per bu.	20¢	40¢*
WHEAT (KC)	K.C. BOARD OF TRADE	10:30 a.m. 2:15 p.m.	5,000 bushels	¢ and 1/4¢ per bu.	1/4¢ = $12.50 per bu.	1/4¢ per bu.	25¢	50¢
WHEAT (Minn.)	MINNEAPOLIS GRAIN	10:30 a.m. 2:15 p.m.	5,000 bushels	¢ and 1/8¢ per bu.	1/8¢ = $6.25 per bu.	1/8¢ per bu.	20¢	40¢*
WOOL (GREASE & CROSS BRED)	WOOL ASSOCIATES OF THE N.Y. COTTON	10:00 a.m. 2:30 p.m.	6,000 lbs.	¢ and 1/10¢ per lb.	$6.00 per contract	1 point per lb.	100 points	100 points
						NO LIMIT ON AND AFTER FIRST BUSINESS DAY OF PRIOR MONTH		

CHART 16

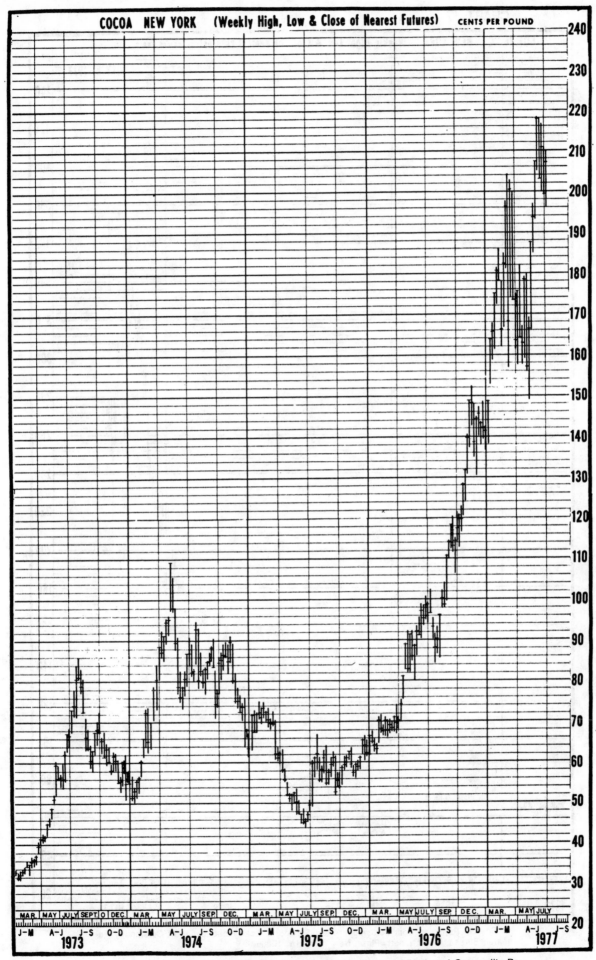

COCOA NEW YORK (Weekly High, Low & Close of Nearest Futures) CENTS PER POUND

1973 1974 1975 1976 1977

CHART 17

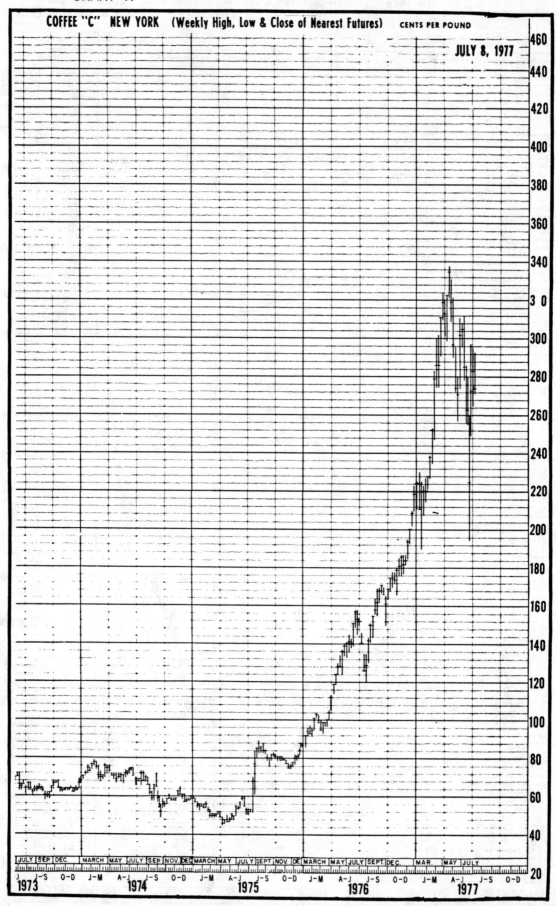

COFFEE "C" NEW YORK (Weekly High, Low & Close of Nearest Futures) CENTS PER POUND

JULY 8, 1977

Source: Reprinted from *Commodity Chart Service*, a weekly publication of Commodity Research Bureau, Inc., 1 Liberty Plaza, New York, N.Y. 10006.

CHART 18

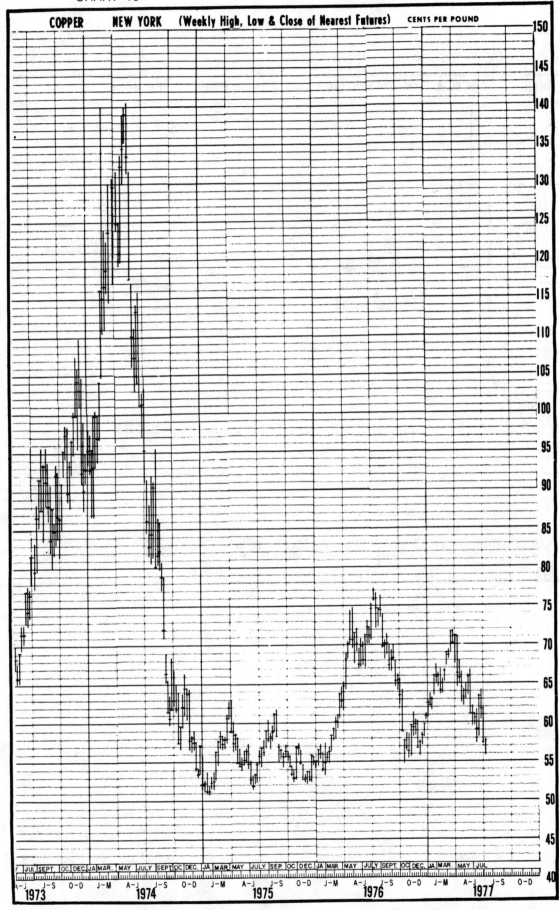

COPPER   NEW YORK   (Weekly High, Low & Close of Nearest Futures)   CENTS PER POUND

Source: Reprinted from *Commodity Chart Service*, a weekly publication of Commodity Research Bureau, Inc., 1 Liberty Plaza, New York, N.Y. 10006.

CHART 19

SILVER NEW YORK (Weekly High, Low & Close of Nearest Futures) CENTS PER OUNCE

Source: Reprinted from *Commodity Chart Service*, a weekly publication of Commodity Research Bureau, Inc., 1 Liberty Plaza, New York, N.Y. 10006.

CHART 20

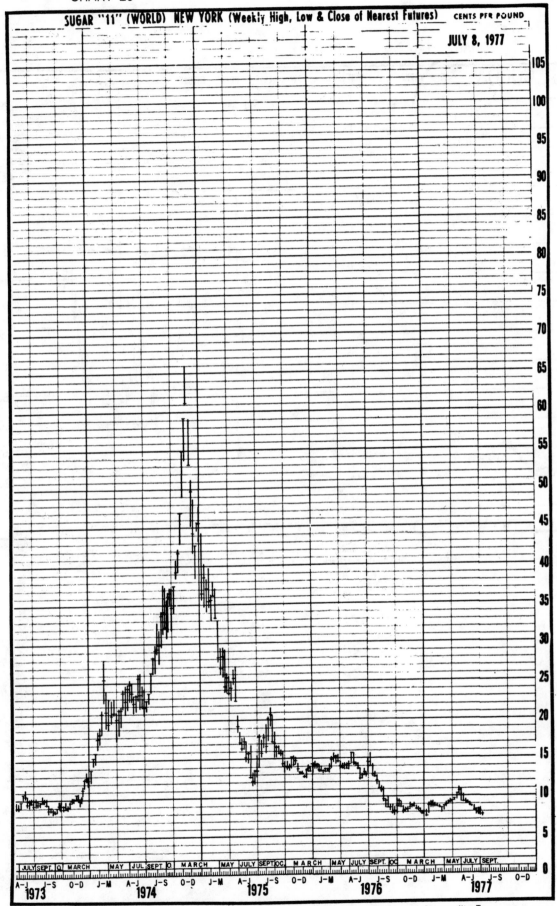

SUGAR "11" (WORLD) NEW YORK (Weekly High, Low & Close of Nearest Futures)   CENTS PER POUND

JULY 8, 1977

CHART 21

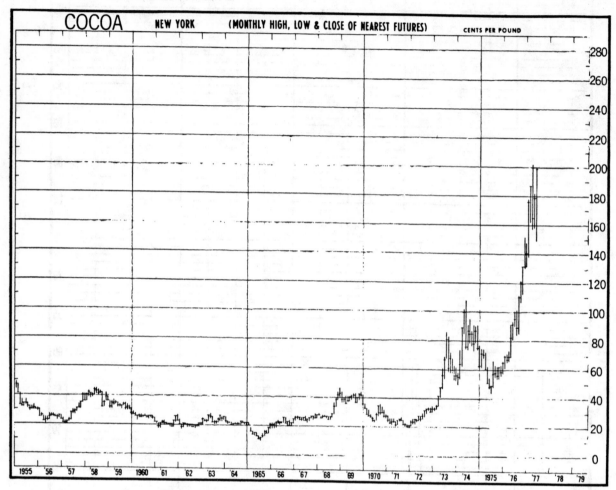

COCOA NEW YORK (MONTHLY HIGH, LOW & CLOSE OF NEAREST FUTURES) CENTS PER POUND

Source: Reprinted from *Commodity Chart Service*, a weekly publication of Commodity Research Bureau, Inc., 1 Liberty Plaza, New York, N.Y. 10006.

CHART 22

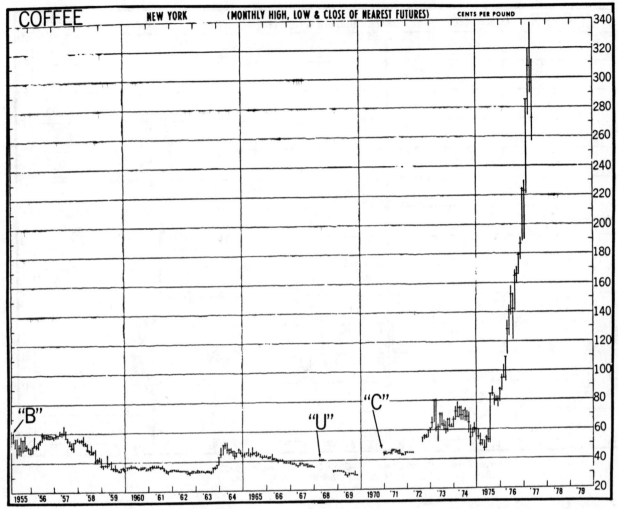

COFFEE　　　NEW YORK　　(MONTHLY HIGH, LOW & CLOSE OF NEAREST FUTURES)　　CENTS PER POUND

"B"　　　"U"　　"C"

Source: Reprinted from *Commodity Chart Service*, a weekly publication of Commodity Research Bureau, Inc., 1 Liberty Plaza, New York, N.Y. 10006.

CHART 23

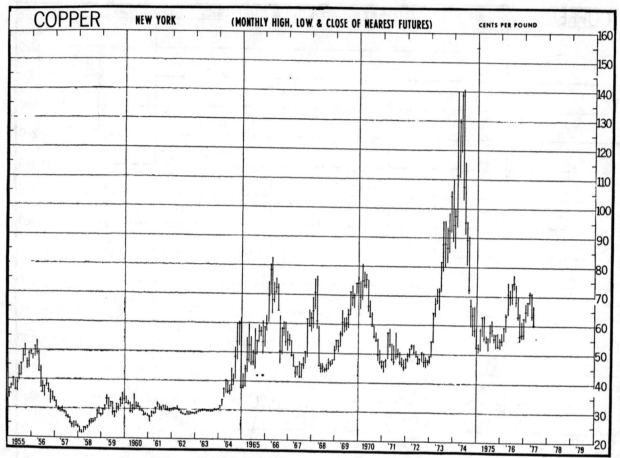

COPPER NEW YORK (MONTHLY HIGH, LOW & CLOSE OF NEAREST FUTURES) CENTS PER POUND

Source: Reprinted from *Commodity Chart Service*, a weekly publication of Commodity Research Bureau, Inc., 1 Liberty Plaza, New York, N.Y. 10006.

CHART 24

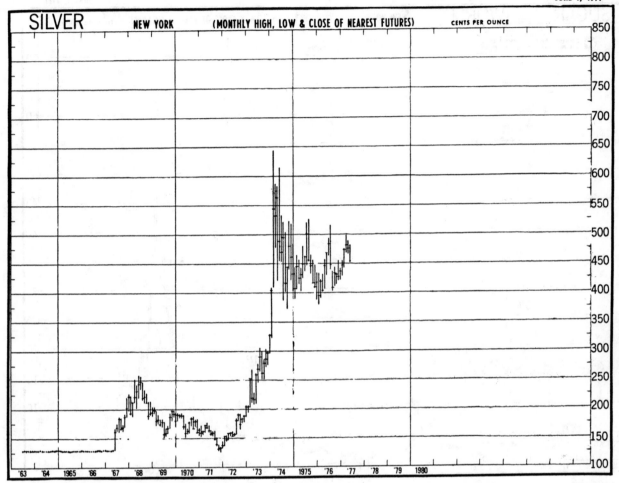

SILVER   NEW YORK   (MONTHLY HIGH, LOW & CLOSE OF NEAREST FUTURES)   CENTS PER OUNCE

Source: Reprinted from *Commodity Chart Service*, a weekly publication of Commodity Research Bureau, Inc., 1 Liberty Plaza, New York, N.Y. 10006.

95

CHART 25

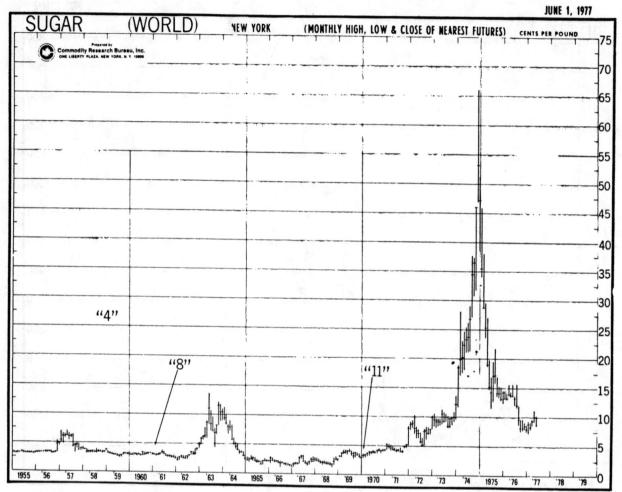

Source: Reprinted from *Commodity Chart Service,* a weekly publication of Commodity Research Bureau, Inc., 1 Liberty Plaza, New York, N.Y. 10006.

option buyer should be willing to pay without severely jeopardizing the profit potential. This will be the theme of the next section.

Volatility of commodities—a dollar average approach

There is nothing wrong with staring at charts in order to determine volatility. A more sophisticated approach, and one which is absolutely vital to successfully purchasing double options, is to do some very easy arithmetic calculations to determine average yearly trading ranges which establish the absolute top justifiable premium purchase price which can be paid and have a decent chance of earning a substantial investment return.

Please do not let a little arithmetic scare you away. All we are attempting to do is to find the average yearly trading range for each commodity and then break the yearly average into three-month, six-month, and nine-month ranges. These figures will then set the maximum price the buyer should be willing to pay for a double. The arithmetic for such calculations is simple and follows an orderly step-by-step procedure as outlined below for each commodity.

1. Obtain from your stock broker or commodity broker or your public library, or a commodity chart service charts of the weekly, monthly, or yearly high and low prices of the nearest futures month over a period of several years. The charts shown earlier, showing the weekly high, low, and close of futures contract, are an ideal type of chart to use for the calculations.

2. Calculate the year's trading range for each calendar year. This is done by locating the highest and lowest prices on the chart and then subtracting the lowest price for the year from the year's high. The resulting figure will be the price range for the year.

From the silver chart (Chart 24), it can be seen readily that the high price for silver in 1973 was 338 cents and the low was 208 cents. The range for the year is calculated by subtracting the low from the high. Thus, the range for 1973 is 338 cents — 208 cents, or 130 cents. Likewise, for 1974, the range is 641 cents — 329 cents, or 312 cents. This range should also be calculated for the current year if you are into July or a later month. If the year is less than six-months old, the year is omitted. Thus, if yearly calculations are made in May of 1978, the range to date for 1978 will be ignored, but if it is July, the 1978 range would be calculated and treated as if 1978 were an entire year.

3. List the yearly trading ranges in a column as was done in Table 5-3, and label the monthly period for any partial years.

4. Calculate the average yearly range. This is done by adding the ranges for the years studied and dividing the total by the number

of whom and partial years studied. Thus, in our example of New York silver, the sum of the yearly ranges from 1973 through 1976, with no partial years being used, was 717 cents. The sum of the yearly ranges is next divided by the number of years used in the summation, which in this case is four. Thus, the resulting average yearly range in points is 179.25 cents or 17,925 points (717 cents divided by 4).

5. Convert the average yearly range in points to an average yearly range in dollars. This is done by simply multiplying the average yearly range in points by the dollar value of a single point. Since one point in silver is equal to $0.50, the dollar value of the average yearly price range is $8,962.50 (17,925 points multiplied by $0.50).

6. Multiply the average yearly price range in dollars by 0.25, 0.50, and 0.75 to represent the average trading range for three months (25 percent of a year), six months (50 percent of a year), and nine months (75 percent of a year).

A student of the market with some mathematical abilities should realize this proportional dividing does not accurately represent the true average range for a period. Such a method sets up a conservative bias, but since we want conservative guidelines and because this proportional division is a simple method to calculate, it will be employed.

A conservative bias is interjected into this proportional method for the simple reason that the true range for one-quarter will generally overlap that of another quarter. If the first quarter range for silver was 450 to 500, the second quarter range 460 to 510, the third quarter range 470 to 520, and the fourth quarter range 480 to 530, the true average quarterly range would be 50 cents. Yet by proportion-

TABLE 5–2
YEARLY TRADING RANGES FOR NEW YORK SILVER

| Year | Price range from chart | | Yearly trading range, high minus low |
	High	Low	
1973	338¢	208¢	130¢
1974	641	329	312
1975	528	389	139
1976	516	380	136

A.	Sum of yearly trading ranges	717¢
B.	Average yearly range (A/4)	179.25¢
C.	Average yearly range in points (B × 100)	17,925
D.	Dollar value of one point	$ 0.50
E.	Average yearly range in dollars (C × D)	$8,962.50
F.	Average range for three months (E × 0.25)	$2,240.62
G.	Average range for six months (E × 0.50)	$4,481.25
H.	Average range for nine months (E × 0.75)	$6,721.88

ally allocating, the yearly range of 80 cents (530–450) would yield only a 20-cent quarterly range (80 cents × 25 percent). But as already stated, such conservative bias is great if it will raise the parameters and, by so doing, keep us out of potentially poor investments.

7. Repeat the steps above for each commodity. Table 5–3 shows the full calculation process and appropriate numbers for the optionable commodities for the period of 1973 through 1976. In order to test your comprehension of steps one through seven, it is suggested you make your own calculation of average yearly ranges in points and dollars from the charts provided earlier, and then check the results against the table.

8. Place the resulting 3-, 6-, 9-, and 12-month average range figures on a worksheet for further analysis.

The resulting average range or volatility figures for 3-, 6-, 9-, and 12-month periods are used as a method of preliminary screening the premiums charged by the dealers in order to determine if they are reasonable or totally out of line. Since the average annual range for copper is $11,550, if a premium for a 12-month double were $11,550, the price is too high; there would be little if any profit potential. Certainly, the contract year on which the option is based may have a much greater than normal volatility and experience a total range of $22,050 (as in 1974), or it may only have a $5,950 range (as in 1976). Even with the $22,050 range, if the double option were struck at the exact center of the range and the call was exercised at the exact top or the put at the exact bottom, there would still be a $525 loss.

On the other hand, if the 12-month premium cost for a copper double was only $3,000, and the volatility during the year following its purchase was anywhere near or above the average of $11,550 for the prior four years, handsome profits would result, regardless of where the option was struck. This concept is clarified and is structured as a basic guide for decision making as shown in the Comparison Rule.

The Comparison Rule—Always compare the premium for a double option with the average range over an equivalent period, (that is, three-month premium cost compared with three-month average range, six with six, and so forth), and reject those doubles costing as much as, or more than, the average range.

There is one exception to this rule. If the buyer does not believe the average past price range is representative of current volatility, the rule can be ignored. A case in point might be the coffee market. Because of the 1976 freeze in Brazil, there was every indication that the

TABLE 5-3
YEARLY TRADING RANGES FOR OPTIONABLE COMMODITIES

Year	N.Y. silver High	Low	Range	Sugar High	Low	Range	Cocoa High	Low	Range	Copper High	Low	Range	Coffee High	Low	Range
1973	338	208	130	10.10	5.00	5.10	86.00	31.80	54.20	109.80	49.00	60.80	81.00	52.00	29.00
1974	641	329	312	66.00	8.80	57.20	109.6	50.10	59.50	141.30	53.10	88.20	79.50	49.50	30.00
1975	528	389	139	47.80	11.70	36.10	75.20	44.00	31.20	62.90	50.90	12.00	89.00	45.50	43.50
1976	516	380	136	15.80	7.80	8.00	150.20	62.00	88.20	77.20	53.40	23.80	223.00	86.00	137.00

	N.Y. silver	Sugar	Cocoa	Copper	Coffee
Sum of ranges	717¢	106.40¢	23,310¢	184.80¢	239.50¢
Average yearly range	179.25¢	26.60¢	5,827¢	46.20¢	59.87¢
Average yearly range (pts.)	17,925	2,660	5,827	4,620	5,987
Dollar value of 1 point	$0.50	$11.20	$3.00	$2.50	$3.75
Dollar value of range	$8,962.50	$29,792.00	$17,481.00	$11,550.00	$22,451.25
Average range					
3 months	$2,240.62	$ 7,448.00	$ 4,370.25	$2,887.50	$ 5,612.81
6 months	$4,481.25	$14,896.00	$ 8,740.50	$5,775.00	$11,225.62
9 months	$6,721.88	$22,344.00	$13,110.75	$8,662.50	$16,838.44

Note: High and low prices are approximates from charts of weekly price action for the nearest futures contract. All prices are rounded conservatively.

volatility of 1976 through 1978 would be significantly greater than in the prior years of 1973 through 1975.

The Comparison Rule is meant to be a conservative guide to be used religiously if one believes the future is similar to the past. It can be totally ignored or modified to be more representative of recent trends, but to deviate creates risks which must be analyzed and borne.

The value premium ratio—a sensitive weighting guide to double option selection

Experience has shown that most double options satisfy the Comparison Rule of selection. For this reason, the requirement of using the Comparison Rule to eliminate from further study those double options which have premium costs greater than the average proportional trading range is not much good in helping to determine which options should be purchased. Furthermore, because the investment capital of most investors is far too limited to purchase all doubles meeting the Comparison Rule, and because investors are profit-oriented, a method must be developed to rank all available double offerings so those with the greatest potential profit return may be selected. The development and discussion of such a method is the crux of this section.

In order to effectively serve our requirements, a ranking method must have the following properties.

1. It must have a conservative bias.
2. It must be capable of ranking all offerings on the same basis.
3. It must work for both London and American option contracts equally well.
4. It must be able to rank a combination offering of doubles on different commodities.
5. It must be capable of ranking both single doubles and multiple doubles on the same contract.
6. It must be sensitive to recent volatility trends.
7. It must provide a risk-reward value function.

The method proposed to rank doubles as to their desirability is exceedingly easy to calculate and does a marvelous job in satisfying the requirements of an outstanding ranking method.

Very briefly, the ranking concept, which will be proposed, ranks doubles in order of their decreasing risk-reward ratios calculated as the function of the half-life price range divided by the full-life premium cost.

While the basic method is simple in nature and the calculations even easier, the verbal description sounds awesome. A very simple example will show that the concept is extremely easy to implement.

Ranking is a way to mathematically determine which double options offer the greatest potential return to the buyer. In this regard, a basic assumption is made that the near-term future volatility will be at least similar, if not identical, to recent volatility. In other words, it is assumed that if a commodity has been extremely volatile over the last three months, it will have similar volatility over the next three months. The term volatility as used here is nothing more than the spread or range between the high and low prices for a given period of time. It is not assumed that the highs and lows of the last three months will be equal to the highs and lows of the next three months, but only that the range or spread between the highs and lows of the last few months will be similar in value to the range between the highs and lows for the next few months. Stated differently, if coffee had wide price ranges over a recent period, it is more likely that these wide trading moves will continue than that they will stop. The price fluctuations might increase or decrease in intensity in the near future, but a radical departure from the recent intensity of price fluctuations is highly unlikely.

With the basic assumption that the volatility of price action in the next 3, 6, 9, or 12 months will be similar to the price fluctuations existing in the last 3, 6, 9, or 12 months, respectively, the next step, and really the first step, in calculating the ranking values is to compare the premium costs of doubles with their past volatility, or range. This comparison will provide a guide as to how potentially profitable the option might be in the future. But in order to enter an element of conservatism into the ranking, a half-life comparison is made with the premium for a full life. This means that while it is assumed a given period in the future will show the same price ranges as an equivalent length of time in the past, there is still the possibility that the future period may be considerably more volatile or much less volatile. Increased price fluctuations in the future only help to make the double more profitable, while decreased ranges are detrimental. If a double option were purchased for $2,000, based on a volatility range of $6,000 over the last six-months, and the volatility range turned out to be $10,000 during the six-month life of the double—great! But if the range declined to $2,000, the buyer would lose money unless the strike price was at the exact top or bottom of the range and the option was exercised at the opposite price extreme and commissions were ignored. In order to provide a cushion against those cases where the rate of price movement decreases, the double would be a justifiable investment for a given period in the future based upon the past volatility for a period equal to only half of the length of the option life. Stated differently, when analyzing a six-month double, look at the price action of the past three months. If the six-month double costs $2,000 and the range for the past three months is $5,000, even if it takes the next six months to achieve a $5,000 range, the double buyer is well protected. Thus, the half-life concept cushions against these cases where volatility is reduced.

Based upon the half-life concept of cushioning against future decreases in the rate of price change, the mathematical computation is the price range for the recent half life of the option divided by the double option premium cost for the whole life, or

$$\text{Rank} = \frac{\text{Price range for recent half-life period}}{\text{Double premium cost for whole life}}$$

For example, the premium cost of a six-month double on sugar would be divided into the price range for the past half-life of the future meaning half of the length of the life span of the double, or three months. Likewise, a premium on a 12-month double would be compared with volatility for six months. If the six-month sugar double costs $2,000 and the price range during the last three months for sugar futures is $4,000, the weight is $4,000 divided by $2,000, or 2.

The two factors in the division are easy to obtain. The option dealer will provide the premium cost of the double, while the price range for the half-life can be calculated by subtracting the lowest price during the half-life period of the nearest delivery month (not the month of delivery) from the highest price for the same period. A commodity chart of the nearest month, as opposed to the month of delivery for the option, is used because volatility almost always increases as the delivery month is approached. The lowest and highest prices are obtained from the nearest option month because the basis month of the option can be expected to act similar to the nearest delivery month as it approaches delivery. Thus, when analyzing a six-month double, find the lowest and highest prices on the futures chart, always using the chart of the nearest contract month, for the last three months (one half of the six-month life of the double), and then subtract the low from the high. The resulting answer when subtracting the low from the high is the price range for the option half-life, and into this price range will be divided the premium cost of the double option. The resulting figures from this division is the weight given to the double under analysis. From now on, this weight will be referred to as the Value Premium Ratio. The formula for its calculation is shown below:

$$\text{Value Premium Ratio} = \frac{\text{Futures price range for one half of double's life length}}{\text{Premium cost of the double option}}$$

The use of the Value Premium Ratio

The Value Premium Ratio has two basic functions. The first use is as a filter to eliminate from further analysis those double options with very little profit potential. The second is in ranking the doubles according to their profitability.

When used as a filter, the Value Premium Ratio mathematically eliminates those doubles from study which offer the least possibility of profit potentials. The buyer of a double will profit by such ownership only if the price of the futures contract moves substantially above or below the strike price. The greatest possible movement from the strike price is necessary. If the double is struck at or very near the high or low of a range, the returns will be much greater than if struck near the center of the price range because the movement will all be on the one side of the strike price. This means less total movement will be required in order to profit from an option struck at an extreme than in the case where the strike price is in the center of a range. For example, let us assume that a six-month double on silver costs $2,500, and the price range for the optioned period is 400.00 to 605.00. If the double were struck at 400.00, a move to 500.00 would double one's money, and exercising the call at 600.00 would generate a 300-percent return. But if the double were struck in the middle of the trading range at 500, the maximum possible return would be only 100 percent.

In order to be as conservative as possible, the filter must assume the worst possible strike price, meaning the option is struck in the center of the trading range. When purchasing a double, it is impossible to know whether the strike price will be in the center, at the upper or lower extreme of the range, or somewhere in between; therefore the worst strike price, that in the center, must be assumed. Under this conservative assumption, the total volatility must be twice the premium to insure that the premium cost is covered by price action on each side. If, in fact, the double were struck in the exact middle of a trading range and the trading range is twice the cost of the double option premium, the option would need to be exercised at the exact peak price or lowest price of the range in order to be even. But while few investors can pick true tops or bottoms, doubles are normally struck away from the center of a future price range, and the two tend to balance out. This all means, simply, that a double having a Value Premium Ratio under 2.00 must be disregarded. In other words, if the movement during the life of the double was exactly equal to the range of the historic half-life, and if the double option were struck in the midpoint of the range, the option would be a break-even situation at best if its Value Premium Ratio were 2.00 or less.

Value Premium Ratio rule—Disregard all options with a Value Premium Ratio under 2.00.

The second use of the Value Premium Ratio is in the ranking of options as to their desirability. The greater the volatility, in relationship to the premium cost, the better the option. Thus, the higher the Value Premium Ratio, the better the option.

To emphasize the point more strongly, let us consider several examples of Value Premium Ratio calculations.

If both six-month sugar doubles and six-month silver doubles were priced at $2,200, yet the volatility (range) over the past three months was $6,600 for sugar and $4,400 for silver, which is the better buy? Sugar is the better investment because its range is three times the premium cost as compared with only two times for silver.

All the ranking system is attempting to accomplish is to quantitatively express the relationship of premium costs to past price ranges, eliminate those totally undesirable options, and rank the remaining by desirability based on Value Premium Ratio (VPR) ranks.

Let us now look at some actual examples.

On June 15, 1976, a large option dealer offered London six-month double options for 49 pence on silver, for £50 on sugar, £148 on copper, £225 on cocoa, and £305 on coffee. The trading ranges in pence or pounds sterling for each of the futures for the prior three months, as taken from charts on the nearest contract month, are shown below:

Commodity	Three-month price range in pence or pounds sterling
Silver	73
Sugar	34
Copper	216
Cocoa	391
Coffee	697

Since it is no longer possible to eyeball the answer, as in the earlier silver and sugar comparison, the Value Premium Ratio must be calculated. The resulting calculations are shown below:

$$VPR = \frac{\text{Three-month price range in dollars for future}}{\text{Premium cost of six-month double}}$$

Commodity	Calculation	Value Premium Ratio
Silver	73/49	1.49
Sugar	34/50	0.68
Copper	216/148	1.46
Cocoa	391/225	1.74
Coffee	697/305	2.29

Because silver, sugar, copper, and cocoa have VPR values below 2.00, they fail to meet the Value Premium Ratio rule and automatically are rejected. Only coffee with its VPR of 2.29 qualifies as being suitable for purchase. But if you want to buy only the very best offerings, if more than one meet the criteria, those qualifying for purchase would be ranked in order of decreasing VPR figures. The doubles having the highest VPR values are the best purchases.

Table 5–4 shows the profits generated by all of the above options, if held to maturity and exercised on the last day (A) and if exercised at the best price existing during the contract life (B). It is interesting to note that while the highest VPR, coffee, did not earn the highest profit, cocoa did; its profit was a respectable 235 percent. Cocoa would not have qualified for purchase but had the second highest VPR. Those commodities with lower VPR figures did rather poorly. But, of course, they too would have been rejected. And while it is always possible for a commodity option having a lower VPR to yield a larger return as happened in this case with cocoa, the VPRs above 2.00 offer the most conservative and consistent method of trading for they have by definition the greatest probability of being profitable.

TABLE 5–4
PROFIT OR LOSS ON
SIX-MONTH DOUBLE OPTIONS
—PURCHASED JUNE 15, 1976

VPR assumption		Percentage return (loss)
Silver	1.49	
A		(79)
B		(14)
Sugar	0.68	
A		26
B		26
Copper	1.46	
A		(13)
B		4
Cocoa	1.74	
A		331
B		356
Coffee	2.29	
A		235
B		235

Note: A assumes exercised on last day of option life. B assumes exercised at best price.

Assuming several options have VPR figures greater than 2.00, why should a buyer consider any but the top VPR rated double for purchase? An option buyer should strive for some portfolio diversifica-

106

tion. If ample investment capital is available, our suggestion is to purchase the two top-rated doubles in order to spread the risk of decreased volatility in the top-rated future. If funds are limited, only the top-rated double would be purchased.

Ranking dealer options when they are combinations of commodities

Certain well-financed dealers from time to time are permitted to offer options against their inventory of commodities. These offerings could be single options, doubles on one commodity, or options on more than one commodity. A dealer in an attempt to sell options on inventory, or obtain client diversification, might offer combinations, and the knowledgeable buyer must be in a position to rank these special combinations right along with the single and double option offerings.

The ranking procedure is quite simple. If the offering is several doubles on the same commodity, simply calculate the cost per double by dividing the total premium by the number of doubles it purchases, and then divide the cost per double into the price range for the half-life historic period. Thus, to calculate the Value Premium Ratio on a special offering of five six-month doubles on silver for $10,000, the cost per double of $2,000 (total premium cost of $10,000 divided by the number of doubles purchased, 5) divided into the three-month price range in dollars of $4,000 for the half-life period as taken from a chart of the nearest month not in delivery gives a Value Premium Ratio of 2.00. This can then be compared with the VPR of other single offerings.

If, on the other hand, the offering is a combination of doubles on different commodities such as an offering containing one six-month double on silver, sugar, copper, cocoa, and coffee, the premium of the entire combination is divided into the sum of the price ranges for the half-life of the six. Assuming the offering cost of $10,000 and the sum of the three-month price ranges in dollars, as shown below, is $25,000, the VPR is $25,000 divided by $10,000, or 2.50, which can be compared with these offerings.

Commodity	Three-month price (volatility) range in dollars for the half-life
Silver	$ 4,000
Sugar	3,000
Copper	3,000
Cocoa	7,000
Coffee	8,000
Total volatility	$25,000

VPR calculations for different life lengths

The sophisticated buyer of doubles will naturally want to compare the purchase of 12-month double options with 6-month offerings as well as offerings of other lengths in order to purchase the very best available. When calculating the VPR for a 12-month double, divide the premium cost for the 12-month life into the price range for the past 6 months. The resulting VPR for all 12-month doubles can be directly ranked with those for 6-month options and, as always, purchases should be confined to only the top two VPR ranked doubles regardless of life lengths.

Six-month options are the most common, followed by 12-month double options. Yet, on occasion, option dealers offer doubles of an unusual length, such as five months. The simplest way to analyze life lengths other than those of 6-month and 12-month duration is to convert the unusual life length to a 6- or 12-month basis and then calculate the VPR as before.

When converting one life length into a 6-month or 12-month basis, convert to the closest standard life length. Thus, 3-, 4-, 5-, 7-, and 8-month doubles will be converted to 6 months, while 10- and 11-month doubles, and those longer than a year, will be converted into 12 months. Although a 9-month life is halfway between a 6 and 12, convert it to the most common 6-month basis. To convert, calculate the premium cost per month for the life of the double, and then multiply the monthly cost by 6, if converting to a 6-month length, or 12 for the 12-month life.

For example, a five-month sugar double, costing $1,500, would have a monthly premium cost of $300, calculated by dividing the five-month premium cost of $1,500 by the number of months of control the premium purchases, which is five. The $300 monthly premium cost is then multiplied by six. The resulting $1,800 cost is the standardized six-month cost. An eight-month copper double costing $2,400 would be converted to $1,800 for a standard six-month life ($2,400 premium cost for eight months divided by the eight-month life length equals $300, which is then multiplied by six).

The remaining VPR calculations and the ranking will be identical whether the option offered is a true 6- to 12-month double, or an unusual length which has been standardized to a 6- or 12-month length. Again purchase only the two top-rated doubles.

A review of the ranking method

It now seems appropriate to review the ranking method in a step-by-step manner from start to finish.

The following are the necessary steps which must be followed in order to provide a rational approach to the selection of double options. The strict adherence to the steps will result in the elimination of those offerings with little or no profit potential and many of those offerings which the dealer is high-pressure selling as "the best buys." It will also allow buyers to make their own investment selection with the confidence that they are buying the best doubles for their money. Lastly, this method eliminates the buyers' dependence on the evaluation made by others, including the dealers, which may be biased.

1. Calculate the average yearly price range in points for each commodity future for the past five years. The calculation is based on weekly range charts of nearest futures months and is computed as follows:
   a. Calculate the yearly range for each year by subtracting the year's low from the year's high.
   b. Calculate a total of yearly ranges by adding all of the yearly ranges together.
   c. Calculate the average yearly price range by dividing the sum of the total yearly ranges by the number of yearly ranges added together to arrive at the sum.
2. Convert the average yearly price range in points to a dollar range by multiplying the point average by the dollar value of one point.
3. Divide the average yearly price range in dollars into three-, six-, and nine-month periods. The calculations called for in steps 1, 2, and 3 need only be updated every six months.
4. Contact all commodity dealers with whom you deal, and believe to be reliable, in order to obtain their best double offerings since dealer markups *differ substantially*.
5. Disregard for future evaluation all but the cheapest offerings for each life length on each commodity, regardless of the dealer. Thus, if three dealers A, B, and C offered 6-month sugar doubles at $2,200, $2,150, and $2,300 and 12-month doubles for $3,400, $3,500, and $3,600, only dealer B's 6-month offering and dealer A's 12-month offering would be evaluated.
6. Convert all double offerings to either a 6-month or 12-month life length basis.
7. Break the total premium cost of all multiple offerings on a single commodity into the premium cost for a single double option.
8. Compare the premium cost with the proportional average price range in dollars for the same length, and reject from further consideration all offerings priced higher than the average historic range. In other words, a six-month double would be compared with a proportional price range in dollars for six months and be rejected if it costs more than the proportional price range.

9. Calculate the dollar price range for the last three and six months for each commodity. The formula for the calculation is high minus low equals point range, which when multiplied by the dollar value of one point gives the dollar price range.

10. Calculate the VPR (Value Premium Ratio) for each single offering. The VPR is calculated by dividing the premium cost of the double option into the dollar price range in a past period equal to one half the life length of the double. Thus, the premium for a 6-month double is divided into the dollar price range for the last three months, and the premium cost for a 12-month double would be divided into the dollar price range for the last 6-months.

11. Calculate the VPR for all compound offerings by dividing the premium cost of the compound offering into the sum of the dollar price ranges for the half lives of each commodity double contained in the compound offering.

12 Reject from further evaluation all offerings having a VPR figure of less than 2.00.

13. List in descending order of VPR figures all offerings.

14. Purchase those offerings having the highest VPR values.

All you need now to implement the VPR value system are the offering prices from one or more option dealers, long-term charts used to calculate the average yearly price ranges, and charts on near contract months in order to calculate the three- and six-month dollar price ranges, a pencil, and plenty of scratch paper.

OPTION PROFITABILITY

American off-exchange commodity options have been traded in the United States only since July of 1971, and it was mid-1972 before they gained wide acceptance. But because of widespread abuse, the business died within several years. This period was just too short to develop a statistically meaningful empirical study of option profitability. And at this writing the exchange options have not yet begun to trade so we cannot look to them for an answer to potential returns.

London options, while having been traded for years, are also not of much help in answering the profitability question because the data required for any meaningful research are virtually impossible to obtain. Four major brokerage houses were contacted for historic raw data on London options. The data requested included monthly volume, strike prices, and premium costs. All that was obtained from these requests were four very elementary two-, three-, and four-page fliers which were referred to as books, several interesting reprints from *Commodity Magazine* that failed to shed any light on the subject, and several Reuters sheets of daily prices and volume.

The process of obtaining the information required to calculate profitabilities of London options directly from London dealers proved just as laborious, thankless, and unrewarding. They, like their American counterparts, view their primary function as immediate selling. Helping an author is their last order of priority.

With no meaningful longevity of American trading and being unable to obtain the necessary data from London or from dealers in London options, the profitability question must be handled from a purely theoretical standpoint.

Any option seriously considered for purchase must have a Value Premium Ratio (VPR) of 2.00. Whether we are buying puts, calls, or doubles, the volatility or price range for the option's past half-life must be twice as great as the premium cost. This concept can also be referred to as times premium coverage, but regardless of the label, the basic idea is still the same. The price must fluctuate considerably more than the premium cost if the option is to ultimately be profitable.

It is logical that the greater the price range, the greater the profit potential. Thus a half-life range of $8,000 will offer far more profit potential than a range of $3,000 based on a $2,000 premium. This is another way of saying that the higher the times premium coverage or the Value Premium Ratio (VPR), the greater the profit potential.

The first basic assumption which must be made in order to arrive at a general profitability estimate is that no option will be purchased unless it has a VPR of 2.00 or greater. But one basic assumption is not enough on which to construct a meaningful theory of profitability. Several others are equally important.

The second basic assumption has to do with the relationship of half-life ranges to whole-life ranges for past periods. Tables 5–5, 5–6, and 5–7 show, for three different periods, the relationship between three-month and six-month price ranges. The three-month ranges would be used in all VPR calculations as the half-life figures for valuing six-month options. But the actual profit potential of a six-month option is related to market range for the next six months. The VPR uses a half-life range in order to interject a conservative element, but the future whole-life is the important determinant of profitability, and the future whole-life will be more similar to the past whole-life than the past half-life.

We still want to retain the conservative bias of the past half-life range for valuing options yet be able to easily estimate the past full-life range for profitability studies without having to again refer to the charts for the exact ranges.

What is the relationship between the half-life and full-life ranges? For one thing, the full-life range must be at least as large as the half-life because the half-life is contained in the full-life; therefore, the half-life period cannot contain higher peak prices or lower trough prices than the full-life of which it is a part. But conversely, the full-life can contain higher and/or lower prices than its half-life subset and thus can have a broader price range.

Tables 5–5 and 5–6 contain data on platinum and plywood because off-exchange American options were available on these commodities at the time the tables were developed, but omit coffee because it lacked option appeal and volume. Table 5–7 contains those commodities more often optioned in 1977.

To summarize this idea, the full-life range is equal to or larger than the range of its element, the half-life. But how much larger is the full-life range? Intuitively, if it is assumed that the range of any one three-month period is identical to that of any other three-month period, the six-month or full-life range would have to have one of three relationships to the three-month range. First, the six-month range could be the same size as the three-month range if both shared the same high and low price levels as seen in Chart 26. Second, the six-month range could be twice that of the three-month period if there were no price overlap between the two three-month periods. In other words, the low of the first three-month period represented the peak of the second period, or the high of the first is also the low of the second. Chart 27 shows both possibilities.

The third relationship, and the one which most often occurs, is when there is price overlap between the two three-month periods comprising the six-month whole-life; therefore, the six-month range will be less than double the three-month range. This concept is shown graphically in Chart 28.

In the real world, the assumption that ranges for all three-month periods are equal does not hold up. They tend to be similar in range size but rarely equal. But the third relationship of overlapping ranges still applies, and because the ranges are similar for similar periods, the six-month range generally tends to be larger than the three-month range—but less than twice its range.

Tables 5–5, 5–6, and 5–7 tend to substantiate the fact that the six-month range generally falls within the extremes of equal and double the range for a three-month half-life element of the six-month whole-life. In only one case were the three-month and six-month ranges equal (March 1973 copper), and in only two cases were the ranges for six-months more than double the three-month range (March 1972 plywood and July 1977 coffee). The other six-month ranges fell within the extremes of being 100 percent (equal) and 200 percent (double) the three-month range. The average six-month range was

TABLE 5-5
PERCENTAGE RELATIONSHIP OF THE SIX-MONTH PRICE RANGE OF SEPTEMBER 1971 THROUGH FEBRUARY 1972 TO THE THREE-MONTH PRICE RANGE OF DECEMBER 1971 THROUGH FEBRUARY 1972

Delivery month	Commodity	Six-month period			Three-month period			Six-month price range as a percentage of the three-month price range
		High	Low	Range	High	Low	Range	
March	Cocoa	26.30	20.20	6.10	25.40	20.20	5.20	117.3%
March	Copper	52.00	45.20	6.80	52.00	46.00	6.00	113.3
April	Platinum	117.00	96.00	21.00	112.00	96.00	16.00	131.2
March	Plywood	106.00	85.00	21.00	106.00	96.00	10.00	210.0
March	Silver—N.Y.	155.00	131.00	24.00	155.00	136.00	19.00	127.4
May	Sugar	9.65	4.45	5.20	9.65	5.20	4.45	116.9

TABLE 5-6
PERCENTAGE RELATIONSHIP OF THE SIX-MONTH PRICE RANGE OF AUGUST 1972 THROUGH JANUARY 1973 TO THE THREE-MONTH PRICE RANGE OF NOVEMBER 1972 THROUGH JANUARY 1973

Delivery month	Commodity	Six-month period			Three-month period			Six-month price range as a percentage of the three-month price range
		High	Low	Range	High	Low	Range	
March	Cocoa	34.60	28.90	5.70	34.60	30.80	3.80	150.0
March	Copper	55.00	47.20	7.80	55.00	47.20	7.80	100.0
April	Platinum	170.00	126.00	44.00	156.00	131.00	25.00	176.0
March	Plywood	163.00	103.00	60.00	163.00	125.00	38.00	157.9
March	Silver—N.Y.	207.00	169.00	38.00	207.00	181.00	26.00	146.2
March	Sugar	10.50	5.56	4.96	10.50	7.15	3.35	147.8

TABLE 5–7
PERCENTAGE RELATIONSHIP OF THE SIX-MONTH PRICE RANGE OF DECEMBER 1976 THROUGH MAY 1977 TO THE
THREE-MONTH PRICE RANGE OF MARCH 1977 THROUGH MAY 1977

Delivery month	Commodity	Six-month period			Three-month period			Six-month price range as a percentage of the three-month price range
		High	Low	Range	High	Low	Range	
July	Cocoa	199	124	75	199	151	48	156.2
July	Coffee	339	191	148	339	269	70	211.4
July	Copper	73.40	59.10	14.30	73.40	59.50	13.90	102.9
July	Silver—N.Y.	508	441	67	508	451	57	117.5
July	Sugar	11.23	8.22	3.01	11.23	8.48	2.75	109.5

CHART 26

THREE-MONTH AND SIX-MONTH RANGES IDENTICAL IN SIZE

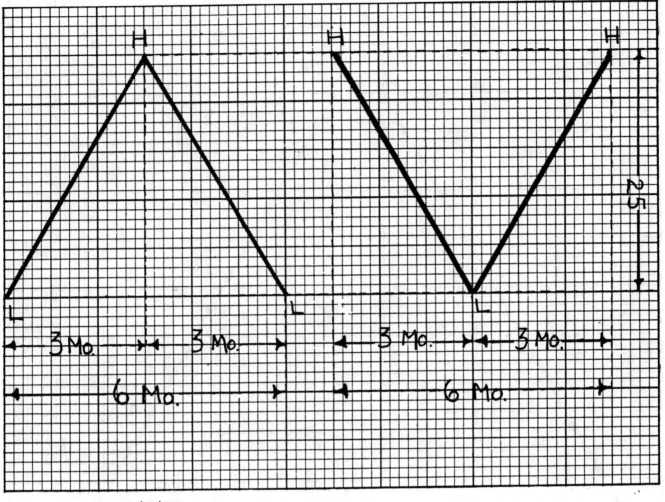

L = Low.
H = High.

140.7 percent of the three-month range for the commodities under study for the three time periods. For further analysis, 140 percent will be used for ease of calculations.

Granted, the sample size is too small to be statistically significant, but it is satisfactory for making the second assumption.

Assumption Number Two: The whole-life range is assumed to be 140 percent of the half-life range.

Based on Assumption Number One, that no option will be purchased unless the VPR is at least 2.00, and Assumption Two, that the whole-life is 140 percent of the half-life, and the general assumption

CHART 27
SIX-MONTH RANGE IS DOUBLE THE THREE-MONTH RANGE

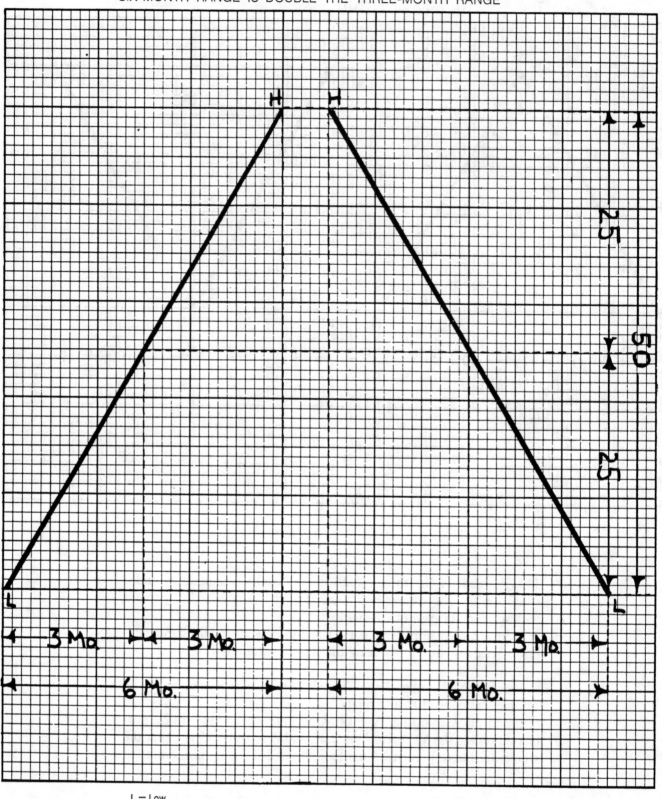

L = Low.
H = High.

CHART 28
SIX-MONTH RANGE IS GREATER THAN THE THREE-MONTH
RANGE BUT LESS THAN DOUBLE THE THREE-MONTH RANGE

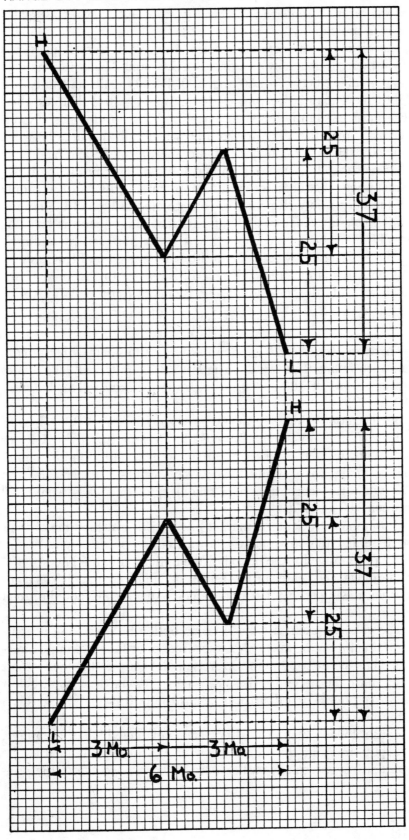

L = Low.
H = High.

that the future is similar to the past, it is possible to make estimates of option profitability.

The authors' experience in calculating VPRs for doubles has shown them to generally run between 1.00 and 3.50, with the vast majority falling between 1.50 and 3.00. Because calls and puts cost slightly more than 50 percent of the premium cost of doubles, their VPRs must be slightly less than twice the VPRs for doubles. Experience has shown the VPRs for both puts and calls to range between 1.90 and 6.00, with the majority falling between 2.85 and 5.50.

Mathematically, a Value Premium Ratio of 2.00 means there is a market price range of $2 for each $1 in premium cost. But this is only half the story. The VPR figures are constructed using half-life ranges, and if whole-life range has 40 percent more range than the half-life, the VPR figures can be converted to a whole-life basis by mulitplying the VPR figure by 1.40. By multiplying half-life VPR figures by 1.40, we arrive at a Ratio of Whole-Life Ranges to Premium Costs, which we will call the Whole Value Premium Ratio or WVPR.

Half-life value premium ratio $\times$ 1.40 = Whole-life value ratio VPR $\times$ 1.40 = WVPR

Therefore, the WVPR for doubles is 1.40 to 4.90, with the concentration falling 2.10 to 4.20. The WVPR for puts and calls ranges between a low of 2.66 and 8.40, with the majority falling between 3.99 and 7.70.

But because options are never purchased having VPR values of under 2.00, the WVPR cutoff would be 2.00 multiplied by 1.40, or 2.80. With the 2.80 value as a cutoff, the concentration of doubles eligible for purchase would have WVPR values between 2.80 and 4.20, while the concentration of eligible puts and calls would fall between 3.99 and 7.70.

Options are struck at the market price existing at the time of their purchase, but this strike price can turn out to be the highest point of the price range for the period of the option's life, the lowest point of the range, the center of the range, or (most commonly) a point between the upper and lower extremes but normally not the exact center.

The greatest profits are made on an option by exercising it at its farthest point on the range from the strike price in a profitable direction. Thus the most profitable exercise point for a call is the farthest point above the strike; for the put, it means the farthest point below the strike price. For a double, it means the farthest point regardless of the direction.

Thus it follows that a call struck at the extreme high of the range, or a put struck at the extreme low of the range, can neither be profitable nor return any cash toward a partial coverage of the principal. In other words, these options represent losses of 100 percent of the invested capital.

Conversely, a call struck at the low point of the range and a put struck at the peak of the range could be highly profitable. The maximum profitability, excluding commissions and assuming an exercise at the opposite price extreme of the range, will vary from 299 percent to 670 percent for puts and calls. These profit figures are calculated from the WVPR figures which defined the normal price fluctuations as being between $3.99 and $7.70 for each $1 of premium cost. When the extremes of the ranges and the premium costs are placed in the return on investment formula, the 299-percent to 670-percent figures are the result:

$$\text{Return on investment} = \frac{\text{Net dollar return}}{\text{Investment cost}}$$

Net dollar return = Gross return minus invested capital

Net dollar return at WVPR range of 4.28 = $3.99 − $1.00 = $2.99

$$\text{ROI} = \frac{\$2.99}{\$1.00} = 299 \text{ percent}$$

Net dollar return at WVPR range 7.70 = $7.70 − $1.00 = $6.70

$$\text{ROI} = \frac{\$6.70}{\$1.00} = 670 \text{ percent}$$

The profitability, or return on investment, for puts and calls therefore can be assumed to fall somewhere in the range between a 100-percent loss (where the call is struck at the high of the range or the put at the bottom) and a maximum profit return of 670 percent (where the put is struck at the extreme high and the call at the very bottom) with the option being exercised at the opposite extreme in price with the distance of the extreme points of the range being $7.70 for each $1.00 invested.

The double option will have a different potential profit range. Its range of potential profits will run from a loss of 100 percent of invested capital, in the case of absolutely no movement from the strike price, to a potential profit of 3.20 percent resulting from striking the double at the extreme high or low on the range and exercising it at the opposite extreme.

Net dollar return at WVPR range of 5.25 = $4.20 − $1.00 = $3.20

$$\text{ROI} = \frac{\$3.20}{\$1.00} = 320 \text{ percent}$$

But more realistically, the profitability range will not include a loss and will thus fall between a 0 and a 320 percent return on investment. Total losses on doubles will generally be nonexistent for two reasons. First, commodities do move. Second, the double is not purchased unless the VPR is 2.00, which defines the range as twice the premium; therefore, even if the double is struck at the exact center of a 2.00 range, the extreme is 1.00 from the strike price, a distance which will insure breaking even if the option is exercised at the price extreme.

To summarize, based on empirical VPR figures, and on the assumption that the investor will follow the VPR decision rules that the future price action will be similar to the past and that the price range for the whole life is 1.40 percent of the range for the half life, the option trader's return on the investment capital should fall between the extreme as shown below:

Puts .... (100 percent) to 670 percent
Calls .... (100 percent) to 670 percent
Doubles* .... 0 percent to 320 percent

* Showing most realistic maximum loss. (Trader could lose 100 percent if commodity fails to trade away from the strike price, a highly unlikely event.)

The actual returns can fall anywhere within the ranges shown above and could actually be even larger since the ranges were defined by the concentration of VPR figures and not by the range of VPR figures. But while actual profits can be larger than those shown, the losses can never be greater than 100 percent of invested capital.

It is absolutely impossible to determine where the returns for any individual option will fall within the range because the returns are dependent upon three variables. The first variable is the actual price range existing during the option's life. The second variable is the location of the strike price within the actual range. And the third variable is the price at which the option is ultimately exercised.

All of the return on investment figures shown above assumed no trading against the option. Trading can greatly increase the returns while not increasing the risks; therefore the returns shown above may be understated considerably for those option buyers with the ability, time, and desire to analyze the markets and successfully trade against the options. But even for those individuals whose only interest lies in successfully exercising their option contracts, the amount of return is far in excess of those obtainable in most other investment media.

If the option investor consistently averages only 10 percent of the maximum possible theoretical return, the return will still be 67 percent on puts or calls and 32 percent on doubles, and these are returns which will put a gleam in the eyes of any investor.

Chapter 6

The chart evaluation method of valuing double options

There always have been and probably always will be a group of investors who are not mathematically inclined or simply hate anything more complicated than simple addition and subtraction. This is not to say that the VPR is complicated, or requires a Ph.D. in theoretical mathematics, or requires even a single course in calculus. Nothing more than the simple tools of addition, subtraction, multiplication, and division learned in elementary school arithmetic are required to fully analyze any double offering in terms of the VPR method. But the VPR system takes time and involves a number of independent arithmetic calculations to arrive at the final answer and thus might scare some readers.

There are other readers with the time, desire, and ability to follow the easy step-by-step instructions but who, after arriving at the ranking of offerings by the use of VPR figures, still have doubts and would like to see still another way of achieving the same results. There are still other commodity traders who do not believe anything unless it is on a chart. This section is dedicated to all these groups of individuals.

The object of the Chart Evaluation Method is simply to draw various horizontal price objective lines on a futures chart, and then by viewing the ability of the price action in the past to trade through these lines, an assumption is made as to whether the price objective lines will be crossed during the option's life.

The lines which are drawn are totally related to one's profit expectations. If the object is a 50-percent return on the investment, one set of lines will be drawn. A goal of 100 percent will require another set; a profit objective of 200 percent still a different set of lines. In other words, each profit goal will be represented by a different set of horizontal lines.

In order to construct the horizontal lines, one must first know the premium cost of current offerings of double options. It should be pointed out that while the chart evaluation method will work with multiple offerings on the same commodity, it will not function with a compound offering of different commodities.

All horizontal lines are constructed from the premium cost. The first set of these lines are the break-even lines. Break-even lines are constructed from break-even points, calculated by adding together the premium cost of the double and the exercise cost, usually assumed to be $100, and converting the resulting figure, called the total double cost in dollars, into futures points.

The total double cost in points tells how many points the market must move above or below the strike price in order to be even on the investment, while the break-even points tell the upper and lower market prices at which the option is in a break-even situation. The two tell exactly the same thing but in different ways.

122

When the total double cost in futures points is subtracted from the striking, or current market, price, the resulting figure will be the downside break-even point. Should the futures price trade at or below this break-even point, the put could be exercised and the entire cost of the double returned. The total double cost in futures points is also added to the strike price, and the resulting figure will represent the upside break-even point. When the futures price trades at or above the upside break-even point, the call could be exercised and the entire cost of the double returned to the buyer.

The next step is to plot the upside and downside break-even points, rounded to the next more profitable round price. These break-even points are plotted as horizontal lines on the chart of the futures month on which the double would be purchased. The lines are extended forward and back in time equal to the length of the double's life. If the double were purchased for six months, the break-even lines would be extended back in time for six months and forward for six months.

Let us now run through an example. A six-month double can be purchased on September cocoa for $4,000. September cocoa is currently trading at 143.00, which would represent the strike price if the double were purchased. The total double cost, or the sum of the premium and the exercise commission, is $4,100 ($4,000 premium plus $100 commission). Once the future has risen or declined by $4,100, the purchaser could exercise and come out even. But how many points must cocoa move in order for the move to be equal to $4,100? The answer is found by dividing the total double cost by the value of one point, which is $3 for cocoa. Thus, when the September contract rises or declines by more than 1,367 points ($4,100 divided by $3) from the strike price of 143.00, the buyer is even. If the required point movement is to be expressed as a specific price level, the point movement must be both added to and subtracted from the strike price. Thus, the upside break-even point is 143.00 plus 13.67, or 156.67, and the downside break-even point is 143.00 minus 13.67, or 129.33. These two points are rounded to the next most profitable round points 157.00 and 129.00 and are drawn on the September cocoa chart as horizontal lines extending back six months, the length of the double, and forward the same amount, as shown in point-and-figure Chart 28 and line Chart 29.

After the horizontal lines are drawn, the potential buyer must study the relationship of the past price action to the upside and downside break-even lines and make a determination as to the likelihood of the current price crossing either of the two lines. If there is very little chance, disregard the option. If there is a strong possibility, go on to the next step in the analysis process.

The next step requires the setting of a profitability goal with the

CHART 29
COCOA—SEPTEMBER (hypothetical chart)

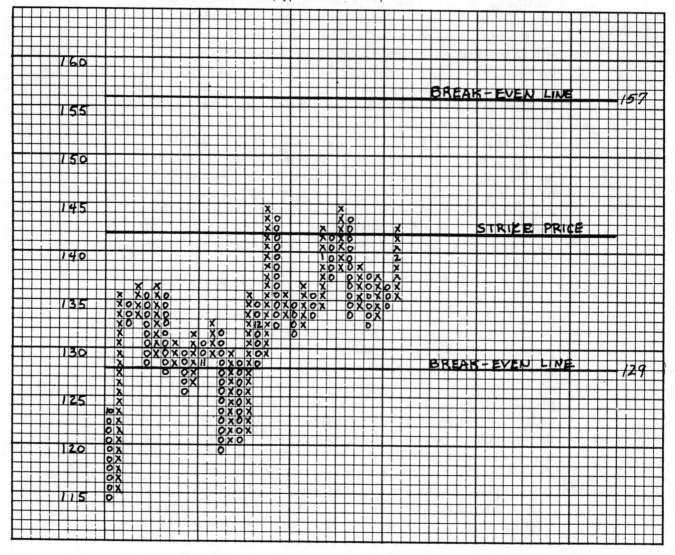

objective to earn a profitable return of 30, 50, 100, 200 percent, or more on the double option. Regardless of the profit objective the buyer may select, price objective lines above and below the strike price must be drawn to reflect these desired profit goals. The terms "price objective lines" and "profit objective lines" are synonymous, with the price objective lines showing the price levels at which desired profit objectives are reached.

In order to determine the profit objectives, add the premium cost, the desired profit in dollars calculated by multiplying the premium

124

cost by the desired percentage return on invested capital, and the $100 exercise commission. The resulting summation is then converted into futures points by being divided by the dollar value of one futures point. The answer from this calculation is the point distance above or below the striking price the future must trade in order to realize the profit goal. In order to draw the profit objective lines, the point distance must be added to and subtracted from the strike price.

Still working with the September cocoa example, if the buyer's profit objective is a 30-percent return on investment, cocoa must either advance or decline by $5,300, the dollar amount required to cover the premium cost of $4,000, the exercise commission of $100 which is not considered part of the investment for it is deducted from the proceeds on the exercise, and the amount of 30-percent profit on the $4,000 investment, or $1,200 ($4,000 × 0.30). But how many points of movement is $5,300? The answer is obtained by dividing the required dollar return by the $3 value of a one-point cocoa move. In order to meet the 30-percent profit goal, the cocoa contract must advance or decline from the 143.00 strike price by 1,762 points ($5,300 divided by $3). Or stated differently, it must rise to 160.62 (143.00 + 17.62) or decline to 125.38 (143.00 − 17.62) in order to yield a 30-percent return. These price objectives would be rounded to 161.00 and 125.00 for line plotting.

If the goal were a more optimistic 100 percent, the required dollar movement would be the sum of the $4,000 premium cost, the $100 exercise commission, and $4,000 profit ($4,000 investment multiplied by 1.00), or $100. This required dollar movement is equivalent to 2,700 points (8,100 divided by $3). Thus the price objective lines would be drawn at 170.00 (143.00 + 27.00) and at 116.00 (143.00 − 27.00), with no rounding necessary.

Both the 30-percent and 100-percent price objective lines have been drawn on the point-and-figure Chart 30, and similar lines could be drawn on a line chart if preferred. But, although both the 30-percent and 100-percent objective lines were drawn on the demonstration chart, the buyer of double options would only draw the one set of price objective lines which coincides with his or her specific profit desires.

Once the appropriate price objective lines have been drawn, the buyer must make his or her own determination, based on past price action, as to whether or not the futures price will reach either of the objective lines. If it appears there is a high probability the price will touch or exceed either the upper or lower price objective line during the life of the double, the double would be purchased. If there is little chance of the price advancing to the upper price objective

CHART 30
COCOA—SEPTEMBER (hypothetical chart)

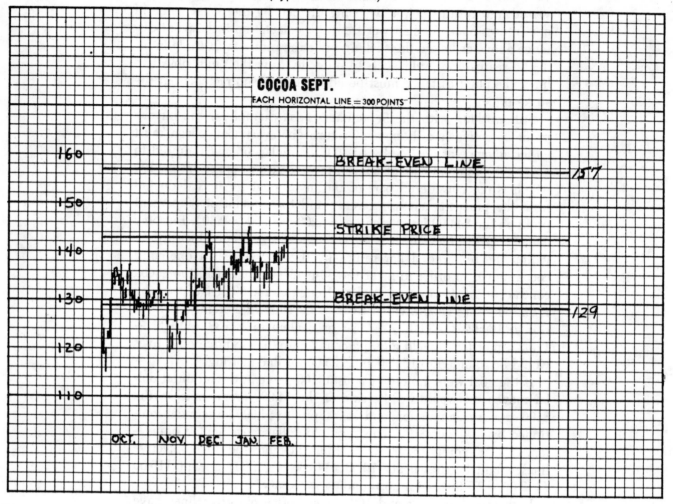

COCOA SEPT.
EACH HORIZONTAL LINE = 300 POINTS

BREAK-EVEN LINE 157

STRIKE PRICE

BREAK-EVEN LINE 129

line, or declining to the lower line, the double should be rejected.

Based on Chart 30, which covers only the prior five months, even though a six-month double is being purchased, plus the fact that volatility usually increases dramatically as the delivery month is approached, the six-month double looks like an outstanding purchase for those investors seeking a 30-percent return and a good investment for the more aggressive trader seeking to double his or her money. This decision is also based on the fact that, during the prior five months, the market crossed a 30-percent profit objective line three times, once in October, and twice in November. Whether the upper or lower price objective line is crossed is irrelevant. All that is significant is that an objective was touched, regardless of which one. Since the 100-percent line was also touched, but unfortunately only once, the investment is a reasonable selection for the portfolio of the more growth-oriented speculator.

If the trader had a profit objective of 200 percent, the September cocoa contract, having shown no past history on this chart of such dramatic price action, should be rejected.

How does one tell whether or not the price objective will be touched? The answer to this question is found in the combination of the very unscientific gut feeling and, partly, in how many times in the past either of the lines would have been hit. As already discussed in the September cocoa example, since both the 30-percent and the 100-percent price objective lines had been touched in the recent past, it is logical to expect that they will again be touched in the near future, and thus the double appears to be a reasonable buy for both a 30-percent and 100-percent profit move.

Let us now look at several additional examples in order to visualize the relationship between the premium costs and volatility. The ultimate profitability of a double is an inverse relationship with the premium cost, meaning that the higher the premium cost, the lower the profitability, assuming volatility is held constant. This concept also means that a six-month double costing $1,250 might be fabulously profitable as an investment; yet, if the same option cost $2,900, it might be a terrible investment. The following charts show this concept as well as provide additional practice in decision making under the Chart Valuation Method.

The price objective lines on Chart 31 are based on a premium cost of $1,250 for a six-month double on sugar based on a strike price of 13.00 and a profit objective of 100 percent. Is the double a good buy? Yes. But if the premium had been $2,900 instead of $1,250 (Charts 32 and 33), would the double have been a good buy? Based on the 100-percent profit objective line drawn, but not even approached, we would pass on its purchase.

The strength and weaknesses of the Chart Evaluation Method

There are several major weaknesses inherent in the Chart Evaluation Method.

First, not being quantitative, it can only help the potential buyer determine whether or not to purchase a specific double and cannot be used to rank alternatives in order that the best investment possibilities surface. The speculator using this method might analyze six offerings and get a buy recommendation on each but still not know which double represented the best purchase.

CHART 31
COCOA—SEPTEMBER (hypothetical chart)

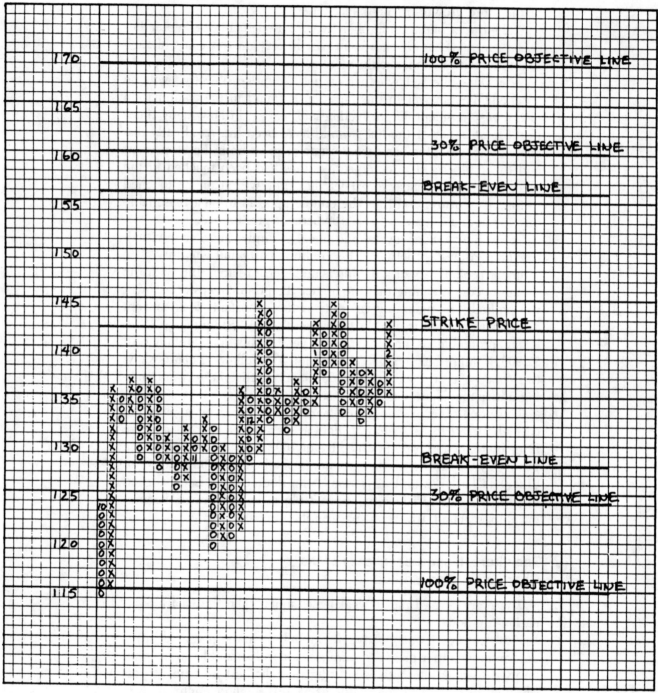

Note: Price objective lines = profit objective lines.

128

CHART 32
SUGAR—SEPTEMBER (hypothetical chart)

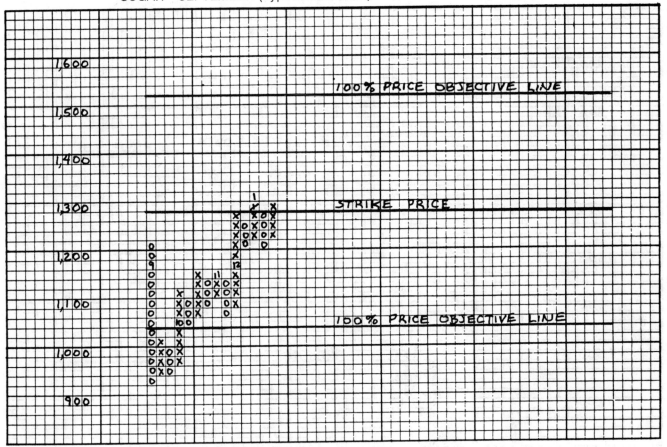

Chart shows 100 percent price objective lines based on a premium cost of $1,250 for six-month double options.

The second weakness is that a compound offering, meaning those containing doubles on two or more different commodities, cannot be analyzed in this manner.

The third weakness is that it is extremely unscientific, and by necessity, the decision rules rely on guesses.

But even in light of these weaknesses, the Chart Evaluation Method is useful in that it forces the buyer to set concrete profit goals, something few investors normally do. The method also is helpful in analysis because it is a graphic representation of the relationship of the key ingredients in trading doubles, the volatility versus the costs. The costs include the premium, commissions, and profit objective.

Should a speculator use this method? The answer is a qualified yes. The Chart Evaluation Method complements the VPR method.

CHART 33
SUGAR—SEPTEMBER (hypothetical chart)

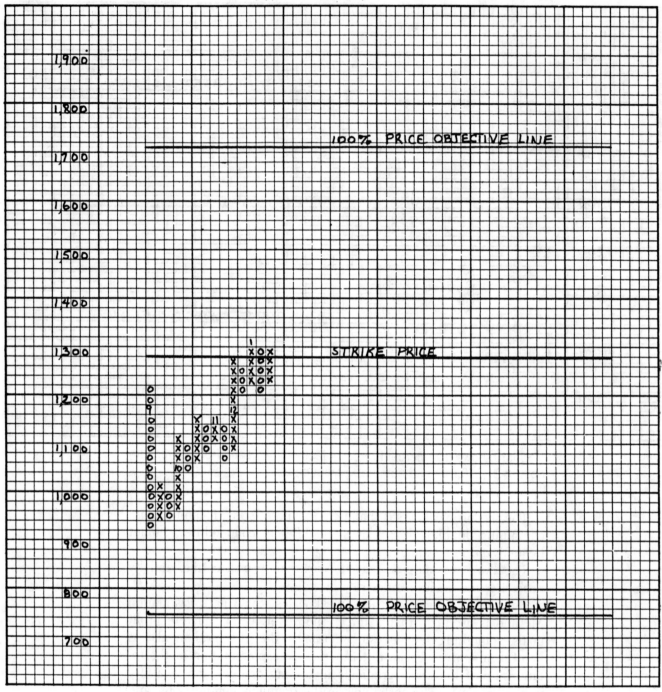

Chart shows 100 percent price objective lines based on a premium
cost of $2,900 for six-month double options.

130

The VPR can quantitatively rank all types of doubles, thus overcoming all of the weaknesses of the Chart Evaluation Method, while the latter supplements the VPR by forcing goal setting and by being graphic.

There is also one additional and very strong advantage of the Chart Evaluation Method. This method can greatly assist in setting stop-loss levels in order to protect realized returns. The way this is done is to simply ignore the double after its purchase until the market price of the contract penetrates either the upper or lower price objective line, at which time a stop order is placed to hedge the profitable side should a reversal occur.

Never place a limit order to liquidate above the call's strike price or below the put's strike price and right at the price objective. In other words, if the upper price objective is 200.00 and the future is trading at 190, do not limit the profit by entering an order to sell at the profit objective line at 200.00. This will set a limit on the maximum profit which can be earned. The proper way to close out the profitable side is by the use of a stop to sell a future against the call, with the stop placed below the upper price objective once the futures price has reached the price objective, or a stop to purchase a futures contract against the put placed above the lower price objective once the futures price has penetrated the lower price objective.

Once the stop against the call has been placed, it should be raised as the futures price rises in order to allow the holder to profit from the additional upside movement. Yet it should remain close enough to the current market price to protect against a reversal. Likewise, the stop against the put should be lowered as the futures price declines below the price objective.

Just where should the stops be placed and how rapidly should they be raised? The proper use of stops has been the subject of a great many books, articles, and late-night bull sessions, and there have been as many solutions to the subject as participants. It is not the purpose of this book to add any additional and revolutionary thoughts to the volumes already published or even to discuss the merits of one stop-setting method over another. But it is our purpose to show one method which can be used very successfully to protect existing profits, yet allow the holder of the double to profit from further moves.

In order to accomplish the objective of protecting profits on the profitable side, yet not jeopardizing additional profits, a stop is immediately established when either the upper or lower objective is touched. The stop is placed at a three-box point-and-figure reversal from the price objective. This means that if an upper price objective is hit on cocoa at 220.00, and if each point-and-figure box in cocoa is equal to 100 points, the stop to sell against the call could be placed three boxes lower, or 217.00. This stop would never be lowered but would be raised by one box, or 100 points, each time the futures price rises 100 points. Thus, when the futures price of cocoa hits 221.00, the stop would be raised to 218.00. This process would continue until cocoa traded at 223.00 and the stop reached the price objective line at 220.00.

Once the stop is at the price objective line, and thus the desired return on investment is protected, the stop should then allow for wider price fluctuations. This will permit taking advantage of the major trend without having the position stopped out on a minor reversal. The best way to do this is to hold the stop at the price objective level until the point-and-figure sell signal has reached the price objective, and from then on the stop would be set at the point-and-figure sell point.

Chart 34 shows more specifically how the stops would be raised with the stop levels being designated by numbered circles. When the price objective of 220.00 was hit, the stop was placed at 217.00 (Circle Number 1). When the future hit 221.00, the stop was raised to 218.00 (Circle Number 2). Likewise, when the future hit 222.00, the stop was raised to 219.00 (Circle Number 3). The stop was finally raised to the price objective of 220.00 (Circle Number 4) when the future hit 223.00. The stop remained at this level until the

CHART 34
STOP-LOSS ORDER ENTRY POINTS

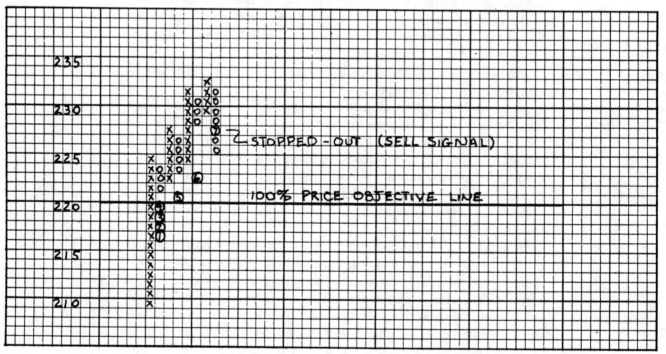

132

sell point established the stop point. Ultimately, the stop was raised to 228.00, the seventh level at which it was set and the level at which it was triggered.

Had a limit order to sell been placed at the price objective even before the future had reached that level, the call would have been hedged at 220.00 instead of 228.00, and that is a lot of foregone point-and-figure sell point caught up, and then the point-and-figure profit.

Chapter 7

London commodity futures and options markets

Although most American traders focus their attention on the U.S. markets, there has been a growing trend toward American participation in foreign markets. The age of satellite communications and computer sophistication has brought about a change of attitude in Americans trading on foreign markets. Rapid telecommunications via satellite between the United States and London have made London commodities markets readily accessible to American traders.

Even though there may be some hesitation about trading on the London futures markets, the active ones are as viable as the active U.S. futures markets. London markets are in some ways similar to American futures markets. London commodities exchanges provide international market places for buying and selling futures and options contracts on metals and foodstuffs. London markets are particularly appealing to international commercial dealers and large speculators. Commodity option transactions constitute a relatively small part of trading volume on these exchanges. Commercial dealers in London commodities grant (sell) put and call options primarily as a hedge against price fluctuation on commodity inventories.

Before proceeding further, some concepts and definitions germane to the London markets should be introduced:

Actuals　The physical commodities—also referred to as "physicals."

Basis price　The price agreed between seller and buyer of an option to become the price at which the option can be exercised. The basis price is usually the current market price of the commodity, for the delivery month, at the time the option is sold. (Also "striking price.")

Call option　A call option gives to the purchaser the right to buy a futures contract from the seller on the terminal market at an agreed price (the basis price) at any time from time of purchase to the expiration of the option. A call option is bought, therefore, in the expectation of a rise in price.

Clearing house　The separate agency associated with a futures exchange through which futures contracts are offset or fulfilled and through which financial settlement is made.

Declaration (of options)　To exercise his or her rights under his or her option the purchaser must make a declaration (through his or her broker to the broker of the party granting the option) before the prompt date. Failure to do so is construed as abandoning the option.

Double option　A double option provides the purchaser the right to *buy from or sell to* the seller on the futures market a futures contract at an agreed price (the basis price) at any time during the life of the option.

136

Essentially, therefore, it is a combined put and call, except that only the put side or the call side of the option may be exercised, not both. When the purchaser buys more than one option, he or she may exercise each one independently of the others. A double costs approximately twice as much as a put or call and is used when the purchaser expects the price to move radically but not sure which way.

Hedge   The establishment of an opposite position in the futures market from that held in the physicals.

Kerb   Literally means trading conducted outside the exchange on the kerb (curb) of the street—nowadays also means on the telephone or any other dealings after ring trading ends.

Lot   The minimum unit of trading for a particular commodity. The lot sizes are cited in Appendix B.

Option   An option provides the investor the right to buy from or sell to the grantor of the option at any time before its expiration a specified quantity of the commodity concerned at an agreed price (the basis price). The cost to the purchaser of the option is called the "premium" and, depending on the volatility of price movements and duration of option, is usually about 10 percent of the cost of the commodities contract.

Put option   A put option provides the purchaser the right to *sell* to the grantor of the option on the futures market a futures contract at an agreed price (the basis price) at any time during the life of the option.

A put option therefore is bought in the expectation of a fall in price.

Ring   The formal trading periods on the London Metal Exchange.

Tender   Delivery against a futures contract.

Taker   The taker is the party who purchases an option.

Grantor   The grantor is the writer of an option who sells it to the taker for a consideration (premium).

Premium   The cost to secure the right to a put or call one contract unit of a given commodity. The premium is governed by the length of time the option has to run and the degree of volatility in the market. In general, premiums will fluctuate between 5 percent and 15 percent (for a six-month period) of the market value of the contract at the time of the grant. Premiums are quoted in pounds sterling per ton (tonne), or in pence per troy oz. The total premium cost is determined by multiplying the premium by the number of tons (tonnes) in the contract. For example, the cost of a cocoa option quoted at £16 would be £80 (£16 × 5 tons = £80); for a sugar option at £5, it would be

£250 (£5 × 50 tons = £250). Premium is payable at the time the option is purchased.

London futures markets provide commercial dealers with a hedging vehicle to obtain price insurance against adverse price volatility in the spot markets. London markets also provide statistical information to the public on the factors that affect supply and demand of commodities essential to the economy of the United Kingdom. London markets serve as potential delivery markets whereby commodity dealers can receive assurances of fulfillment of their futures contracts. The active London commodities markets have attracted broad commercial and speculative participation, which is essential to the viability of a contract market.

The primary commodities traded on the London futures markets are sugar, coffee, cocoa, copper, lead, rubber, silver, soybean oil, tin, wooltops, and zinc. Commodity options trading is permitted only for sugar, cocoa, coffee, lead, copper, silver, rubber, tin, and zinc. These are the contract markets that the Commodity Futures Trading Commission (CFTC) may approve for options trading on U.S. commodity exchanges in Spring 1978.

Before trading London futures or option contracts, one should be aware of the basic differences between U.S. and London commodities markets. Conceptually, the futures markets are similar but differ significantly in the mechanics of trading and regulation. London option contracts differ significantly from domestic options in that they lack the trading flexibility and governmental regulatory controls prevalent in the U.S. options markets.

The Commodity Futures Trading Commission has broad powers to monitor the activities of U.S. commodity markets and intervene, if necessary, to insure orderly markets, prevent fraud, and halt price manipulation. The CFTC also advises executives and members of U.S. commodity exchanges on trading policies, compliance procedures, registration requirements, and other legal matters germane to the protection of the public's interest.

The CFTC sets position limits for speculative accounts on domestic commodities markets such as wheat, corn, soybeans, cattle, and hogs. The purpose of setting trading limits on speculative positions in domestic commodities markets is to prevent the possibility of price manipulation on commodities essential to the American economy.

No government regulatory agency closely monitors trading or insures compliance of exchange rules and regulations on the London commodity markets. London options on agricultural commodities are guaranteed by the International Commodities Clearing House

(ICCH), and options on metals are guaranteed by a member of the London Metal Exchange (LME).

The International Commodities Clearing House, Ltd. (ICCH) fulfills the functions of (a) checking, settling, and reporting the day's business on the commodities exchange; (b) guaranteeing fulfillment against default of each contract made on the exchange; and (c) assigning tenders and retenders. The ICCH performs these functions for commodities exchanges other than the London Metal Exchange (LME).

Trading on the LME is on a principal-to-principal basis between members. Unlike most U.S. markets, there is no clearing house, and each member is liable for its own commitments. Thus, if customers buy silver contracts from ABC member firm, in order to liquidate they would have to sell back to ABC company. If the customers chose to accept delivery, ABC company would be required to deliver the silver at the date specified in the contract. In addition, customers who purchased a three-month forward contract liquidate via offset by selling the date it was to mature, not another three-month futures contract.

The major differences between London and U.S. commodities markets are (1) brokerage commissions, (2) margin requirements, (3) daily price limits, (4) price quotations, (5) trading hours, and (6) contract sizes and deliverable grades of a commodity.

Commissions for trading on U.S. commodity exchanges are generally offered at a fixed rate with possible negotiation on large orders. This is true for London futures contracts with the exception of the metals. The nonmember round turn commission on the LME is based on a percentage of the initial value of the transaction, usually ranging from 0.5 to 1.0 percent. For example, the nonmember round turn commission for a LME silver contract would be calculated as follows, assuming the three-month futures price is 450.00 U.S. cents.

10,000 troy oz. $\times$ 450.00 cents $\times$ 0.5 percent = 225.00 U.S. dollars

U.S. commodity exchanges have minimum, fixed margin requirements for speculative and commercial (hedge) account customers. The brokerage firm's subjective policy is the primary determinant of how much margin it requires from its customers.

Most U.S. brokerage firms require at least some margin for London trades, usually the amount equivalent to the margin required for transactions on U.S. markets. For example, a London silver futures contract is 10,000 troy oz., whereas a New York COMEX silver contract is 5,000 troy oz. A U.S. brokerage firm may require $2,000 for a COMEX contract but would require $4,000 for LME silver contract because it is twice as large as the COMEX contract.

U.S. commodities exchanges have continual trading from the opening bell to the closing bell. U.S. commodity exchanges open and close at times specified by the contract market. Trading outside the established time periods is not permitted on U.S. commodity exchanges.

London markets operate under a split session arrangement in which there are trading sessions in the morning and in the afternoon with a break between (see Table 7–1 for LME contracts). For certain commodity markets, trading is allowed outside official hours. Trading on these markets after the formal sessions close is referred to as the "Kerb market." The five- to six-hour time difference between London and U.S. markets provides the rationale for the existence of the Kerb markets because it allows traders in London to adjust to prevailing price conditions on U. S. markets. Of the most active London markets, metals and sugar have Kerb markets, while coffee and cocoa do not.

U.S. commodity exchanges have imposed set daily price limits within which a commodity's daily price fluctuations are confined.

TABLE 7–1
TRADING TIMES

Morning session	
First ring	
Copper (wirebars and cathodes)	12:00–12:05
Silver	12:05–12:10
Tin	12:10–12:15
Lead	12:15–12:20
Zinc	12:20–12:25
Interval	12:25–12:35
Second ring	
Copper (wirebars)	12:35–12:40
Copper (cathodes)	12:40–12:45
Tin	12:45–12:50
Lead	12:50–12:55
Zinc	12:55– 1:00
Silver	1:00– 1:05
Afternoon session	
First ring	
Lead	3:30–3:35
Zinc	3:35–3:40
Copper (wirebars and cathodes)	3:40–3:45
Tin	3:45–3:55
Silver	3:55–4:00
Interval	4:00–4:05
Second ring	
Lead	4:05–4:10
Zinc	4:10–4:15
Copper (wirebars)	4:15–4:20
Copper (cathodes)	4:20–4:25
Tin	4:25–4:30
Silver	4:30–4:35

Note: Inter-office trading occurs throughout the day. For Eastern Standard Time, subtract five hours from the above table, Central Standard, six hours, and so forth.

London futures have almost no restrictions on a commodity's daily price fluctuations. There are no daily limits on the LME, whereas New York COMEX copper has a daily permissible range of 6.00 cents. New York COMEX silver maximum permissible range is 40.00 cents. Daily price limits for expiring contract months are lifted or modified on some U.S. exchanges to allow the futures and cash prices to converge during the delivery month.

London commodities price quotations may cause some problems for American traders because of differences in contract sizes and currency conversions. London commodities are usually quoted in pound sterling (£) per long, short, or metric tonne or in pence per troy oz.

In recent years, the pound sterling has fluctuated widely since going on a floating exchange rate with other currencies. U.S. traders on London markets can incur currency conversion risks due to the fluctuation of the pound. That is why it is important for traders to keep abreast of the current pound versus dollar exchange rates if they are going to know the correct price of London commodities compared to their U.S. equivalents. Table 7–2 compares the different prices of London cocoa with various exchanges rate for the pound.

TABLE 7–2

Pound sterling exchange rate in U.S. dollars	U.S. equivalent price quotation	Price quotation on London market
$2.00	90.00¢/lb.	1,008£/ton
1.90	90.00¢/lb.	1,061£/ton
1.80	90.00¢/lb.	1,120£/ton

CURRENCY CONVERSION

General rule: Conversion from a price quoted in pounds sterling per long ton can be made by dividing the London price by a factor, CF, where:[1]

$$CF = \frac{2{,}240}{\text{Exchange rate in U.S. cents}} = \frac{2{,}240}{200} = 11.20; \text{ or } \frac{2{,}240}{190} = 11.78$$

1. Divide a £/ton quote by factor obtained.
2. Multiply a cents/lb. price by factor obtained.

London silver is quoted in pence per troy oz. One pence = 1/100 pound sterling.

$$\frac{\text{Exchange rate}}{100} \times \text{Quote in pence} = \text{Quote in cents per oz.}$$

$$\frac{1.90}{100} \times 3 = 5.7 \text{ cents per oz.}$$

$$5.7 \times 10{,}000 \text{ troy oz.} = \$570 \text{ per contract—profit (or loss)}$$

---

[1] Long ton = 2,240 lb.; metric ton = 2,204.63 lb.; short ton = 2,000 lb.

CONTRACT SIZES

For both London and U.S. commodity options, the contract size of the options and the contract size of the futures contract on which they are based are the same. This is so because one option is the right to one specific future contract. For example, one London call option on cocoa is the right to acquire one London cocoa future. Likewise, one U.S. call option on cocoa is the privilege to buy one cocoa future on the New York cocoa exchange. This does not mean that an option on cocoa in London is the same size as an option on cocoa in New York, but only that a London option on cocoa is exactly equal to a London futures contract, and a U.S. cocoa option is exactly equal in size to the New York cocoa futures. The London cocoa future is 10 metric tons, or 22,046 pounds, while the New York cocoa futures is 30,000 pounds. Stated another way, a London option is exercizable only against London futures which is always identical in size. A U.S. option controls only a contract traded on a specified U.S. commodity exchange. The size specifications of futures contracts change on occasion. A detailed comparison of futures and options contracts are presented in Table 7–3. Appendixes A and B contain more detailed information with regard to contract specifications for London and U.S. commodities markets.[2]

TABLE 7–3
LONDON FUTURES MARKETS

Commodity	London futures and option size specification*	U.S. futures and option size specification*
Cocoa	10 long tons (22,400 lb.)	30,000 lb.
Coffee, Robusta Contract	5 metric tonnes (11,023 lb.)	37,500 lb.†
Copper	25 metric tonnes (55,116 lb.)	25,000 lb.
Silver	10,000 troy oz.	5,000 troy oz.
Sugar	50 long tons (112,000 lb.)	50 long tons
Lead	25 metric tonnes (55,116 lb.)	
Rubber	15 metric tonnes (33,069 lb.)	33,000 lb.
Tin	5 metric tonnes (11,023 lb.)	
Zinc	25 metric tonnes (55,116 lb.)	

* Contract size specifications as of September 1977.
† Coffee "C" contract of the New York coffee and sugar exchange.

---

[2] TABLE 7–4 also provides a detailed comparison between London and U.S. options markets.

ARBITRAGE OPPORTUNITIES

Arbitrage is the simultaneous buying and selling of equal quantities of similar commodities between different markets. For example, a cocoa processor located in New York notices that cocoa prices on the London terminal are higher than prices on the New York cocoa exchange. He would therefore sell London cocoa futures and buy New York cocoa futures in order to profit from an unusual price spread between London and New York markets. Similar examples can be given for New York copper versus London copper, New York silver versus London silver.

An astute trader who studies the price differentials between the U.S. and London markets will take advantage of occasional situations where the price spread between London and U.S. markets have diverged too far offering high return/low risk trading opportunities for arbitrage.

Arbitragers run a risk of unpredictable changes in currency exchange rates. A devaluation in the pound sterling could cause a rise in commodity prices traded on London markets. A re-valuation of the pound sterling would result in a decline in London commodity prices compared to their U.S. equivalents. If commodity prices become artificially high or low due to uncertain currency exchange rates, international commodity dealers and speculators can arbitrage, thereby bringing commodity prices of that market back into line with other world markets. These temporary price distortions between international markets can afford traders ample opportunities to arbitrage London and U.S. markets using a combination of futures and options contracts.

Arbitrage opportunities may result from unstable economic and political developments that affect the currency exchanges rates with other countries. Sometimes these events are short-lived, but other times they may be enduring. For example, the economic and political events that caused the first major devaluation of the British pound in 1972 lasted until the pound sterling declined from a high of $2.44 in 1974 to a low of $1.55 in 1976. In this situation, owners of British pounds could arbitrage as a means of preserving more favorable exchange rates by buying London futures and selling simultaneously New York futures contracts, since devaluation of the pound sterling would cause commodity prices in London to rise faster than New York commodity prices.

CURRENT STATUS OF LONDON COMMODITY OPTIONS IN THE UNITED STATES

On December 9, 1976, the Commodity Futures Trading Commission (CFTC) established the first set of regulations for U.S. trading

TABLE 7-4
COMPARISON OF LONDON OPTIONS AND U.S. EXCHANGE OPTIONS

Trading mechanics		U.S. exchange options	London options
Trading time and place and market features	Location and method	Open outcry in central market place.	Some on exchanges; some office-to-office.
	Trading hours	Specified and limited, approx. 10 a.m.–2:30 p.m.	Normal U.K. business hours (7 a.m.–12 noon, New York time).
	Continuous price dissemination	Customer's broker can receive continuous prices on a ticker or screen or by direct-line telephone from exchange floor.	Customer's broker obtains quotes from U.S. wholesaling broker, London broker, or London dealer by telephone. No continuous quotes available.
	Trade price dissemination	Trade-by-trade price runs *without* trade time available.	Estimated but not necessarily traded "settlement" prices published. No price runs available.
	Volume and open interest dissemination	Volume and open interest published daily.	Volume and open interest available on ICCH.
Contract terms	Quotations	Two-way buy/sell market. Customer-broker-floor broker interaction by telex or telephone. Competing floor brokers.	Selling quotes only: Option close-out only by exercise. Communications by telephone and telex to customer-broker-dealer.
	Contract and trading terms	Well-defined, easily understood contracts with fixed striking price and fixed maturity date.	Contract terms vary: All have variable striking prices; some have fixed maturity dates, some do not.
	Assignability	None.	None.
	Nature of option buyer's right	Right to convert contract to a futures contract (which one must then margin or sell).	Right to convert contract to a futures contract (which one must then margin or sell).
	Can be liquidated by offset	Yes.	No.
	Customer's costs	Premium plus single, defined, moderate brokerage.	Premium plus U.K. broker's commission plus U.S. broker's (not always moderate) commission or markup.
	Premium payments	Paid in full.	Paid in full.

		United States	United Kingdom
Costs; disposition and protection of customer funds	Customer's premium funds	Held in dollars in U.S. bank.	Currently paid to grantor who deposits sterling or (more frequently) asks a U.K. bank to issue a sterling-denominated guarantee to ICCH.
	Customer's profits	Can be calculated in and are paid in dollars.	Can only be calculated by reference to commodity price (in sterling) and sterling/dollar exchange rate for relevant forward date and are paid in sterling which U.S. customer must then convert to dollars.
	Striking price currency	Dollars.	Sterling.
	Protection of customer's premiums	Margin deposits with clearinghouse segregated in U.S. bank.	Customer's funds held either by grantor or (Part B) foreign commodity exchange in U.K.
	Protection of customer's profits	Customer's profit is segregated for own benefit either with clearinghouse or in own account with broker.	
Legal framework and constraints	Applicable law	United States.	United Kingdom.
	CFTC jurisdiction	Yes, along entire chain.	Only at FCM level; no influence over rules.
	Protection of customer from fraud	Customer's broker must be registered FCM.	Customer's broker must be registered FCM if customer is in U.S.
	CFTC recourse to unwarranted changes in contract or trading terms	Can nullify.	Cannot nullify; can only withdraw "recognition" after an undesired act.
	Ability to time-stamp orders within one minute	Probably not.	No.
	Books and records available to CFTC	Yes.	No.

of commodity options which heretofore were being bought and sold in a totally unregulated environment. These first federal regulations were designed to assure that options buyers would receive full details of each transaction, options sales would be conducted only through persons and firms registered with the CFTC, and each firm engaged in commodity options transactions would maintain a minimum adjusted working capital figure as established by the CFTC.

The net effect of these regulations was to drive undercapitalized firms and those using high pressure sales techniques not backed by written disclosure out of business which gave stronger moral tone to the industry. Of course, the regulations did nothing to improve one's ability to make money from the purchase of an option, for only market movement can do this; but it did mean that the public was better informed when they purchased options, and the likelihood of losing money through dealer bankruptcies and embezzlements was greatly lessened.

Although these first regulations went a long way toward improving the quality, integrity, and viability of the industry, they were only interim in nature designed to fill the void until even stronger regulations governing both London and domestic or American commodity options could be published. A second set of regulations were published in draft form in late 1977. Their primary objectives were to establish rules and guidelines for the trading of American commodity options on U.S. exchanges and to refine the original interim regulations to curb certain abuses and correct problem areas not adequately addressed in the earlier regulations. Under the watchdog eye of the CFTC with its arsenal of regulations, enforcement procedures, and sanctions, we now have a fully regulated American market for commodity options traded on both the London and U.S. exchanges.

Chapter 8

Tools of analysis
for trading
commodity options

Now that readers are familiar with basic concepts and terminology of commodity trading, we will discuss the problems of developing a trading plan that is both dependable and profitable. This chapter will describe the tools of analysis available for making profitable trading decisions. In a general way, the commodity trader is faced with the following problems:

1. Formulating a long-term price forecast of a commodity market; that is, is the price of the commodity expected to rise, or decline, over the next three- to six-month period? Why should the price of the commodity rise, or decline, during that period?
2. Determining the price trend of the commodity. Is the current price trend up, down, or a series of random movements without an identifiable trend?
3. Should I buy, sell, or stay out of the market at the present time?
4. What is the fair value for the particular commodity option I am considering buying, or writing? Is the particular call option (or put option) on the commodity underpriced, overpriced, or fairly priced with respect to its present market price?
5. How much should I diversify my positions in the market? Should I trade only one or two commodities, or should I trade a portfolio of commodities?
6. What are some of the analytical tools available to assist me in making profitable trading decisions?

The remainder of the chapters in this book address themselves to these salient questions. We want to stress that there is no one best way to make trading decisions. Our objective here is to present a variety of techniques and methods available for making these decisions. Individual needs and preferences for specific trading methods will ultimately determine the development of a personal trading plan. However, we will begin with methods for forecasting commodity prices.

METHODS OF FORECASTING PRICES

Methods of forecasting commodity prices range from astrological predictions to sophisticated computer forecasting models. Because of the great diversity of techniques available, we will restrict our discussion to fundamental and technical analysis of commodity prices. The tools of fundamental and technical analysis can be used to complement each other in formulating accurate near-term and long-term price forecasts. The large number of interacting variables that influence commodity prices causes the apparent instability and randomness of price behavior. At any point in time, commodity prices are either (a) going up, (b) staying unchanged, (c) going

148

down, (d) following an identifiable trend, or (e) moving randomly without an apparent trend—random walk.

Crop failures, severe weather conditions, stockpile surpluses, changes in governmental policies, and fluctuating interest rates are only a few of many significant factors that generate volatile prices so often seen in commodity markets. How can traders profit from these price gyrations under conditions of so much uncertainty? The partial answer to this question is the formulation of a long-term price forecast based upon a fundamental analysis of the market. Fundamental analysis attempts to answer the questions: Is the price of this commodity expected to rise or decline over the next three to six months? How much is it expected to rise or decline during that period?

Technical analysis, on the other hand, attempts to answer the following questions: What is the *current price trend* of the market—up, down, or sideways? At what point should I buy, sell, or close out my positions? Thus, fundamental analysis tells the trader what the long-term perspectives and expectations of the market are. Technical analysis tells the trader when to initiate or close out positions in the market. Stated another way, fundamental analysis provides a *rationale* for either buying or selling a particular commodity, and technical analysis tells the trader *when to do it*.

Before proceeding further, several points of clarification might help the reader. Price forecasting models make the implicit assumption that knowledge of past events can be utilized with sufficient reliability in making inferences about future events. This is a reasonable assumption and the best one considering the degrees of uncertainty of the market place. We would like to emphasize that future price changes in the market are not necessarily related to past price patterns. Price forecasting models can not predict the future but can only make inferences and probability statements about future price expectations within certain limits of reliability. Drastic changes in international economics, governmental policies regulating commodities, formation of cartels, or unusual worldwide weather conditions can bring about fundamental deviations in commodity prices from their historical patterns. The extraordinary events that occurred in the commodity markets in the 1970s bear witness to this statement. For example, from 1955 to 1973, world sugar prices ranged from a low price of 2.5 cents per pound to a high of 15.0 cents per pound. In 1974 the price of world sugar skyrocketed to 65 cents per pound. No forecasting model could have predicted that the price of sugar would have reached 65 cents per pound based upon past price history. Similar situations were also observed in the world coffee, cocoa, copper, gold, and silver markets, to name only a few!

Past price history of a commodity can bear significant influence on future price direction and degree of change because of psychological expectations shaped by previous history. As an example, when sugar prices attained 65 cents per pound in 1974, and the market began to show technical weaknesses in maintaining its previous strong momentum, experienced traders liquidated their long positions and sold short for a long downhill trend. The psychological impact of sugar prices never having been 65 cents per pound before in history, heavy consumer resistance to buying sugar at those prices, and technical weaknesses of the market added oil to the skids when sugar prices began to fall sharply in 1975. The financial rewards for being correct in selling sugar at 65 cents per pound and buying back contracts at 12 cents per pound would have been $59,000 with only a $12,000 investment in Sugar No. 11 futures contracts, or a rate of return equal to 492 percent.

Forecasting commodity prices is an essential but oftentimes frustrating aspect of commodity trading. The rationale for most price forecasting methods is that future price behavior can be inferred with sufficient accuracy from past price events. The word "sufficient" is the teaser here. Commodity price forecasting, like weather forecasting, carries both penalties and payoffs for being "right" or "wrong." If the weather forecaster says there is a 20-percent chance of rain tomorrow, and your family is planning an all-day picnic, what are the payoffs and penalties associated with the probable occurrence of rain? Your family may be very angry if the picnic is called off and tomorrow turns out to be a beautiful day. They may be angrier if the forecast is not heeded, and the picnic is ruined by thunderstorms. Based upon past weather forecasts, a 20-percent chance of showers may be too small to discourage the family from going on their picnic. On the other hand, a forecast of 80-percent chance of rain may be high enough to make your family consider cancelling the picnic in favor of another day.

Formulating an accurate price forecasting model for trading commodities is only a part of the problem, albeit a very important part. Formulation of a decision-making model that takes into account the probable payoffs and penalties associated with each trading decision enhances significantly the capabilities of both speculator and hedger to make intelligent decisions.

Price forecasting may involve the applications of probability and statistics in formulating forecasting models. Probability and statistics are those areas of mathematics that deal with states of uncertainty. The analysis of price variability, price trends, and correlations of commodity prices with significant variables are some of the objectives of price forecasting methods. Price forecasting models range from elementary statistical models involving only two or three

150

variables to complex multivariate models that include ten or more variables in their analysis.

Computer time sharing has made the utilization of these sophisticated forecasting models more accessible to speculators and hedgers because computer programs can be written and tailored to the needs of both speculators and commercial hedgers. However, since most commodity traders do not have access to computer facilities, we will discuss other methods and techniques in later chapters for making trading decisions that are valid and reliable—but do not need a great deal of mathematical sophistication. We will now turn our attention to the role of fundamental analysis in a personal trading plan.

FUNDAMENTAL ANALYSIS

Fundamental analysis as it applies to commodity price forecasting involves the study of supply/demand and consumption/production variables that are known to affect significantly the price of a particular commodity. For example, the world cocoa grindings report issued by Gill & Duffus can provide traders with an indication of the current demand for cocoa beans compared to previous years. Gill & Duffus statistics on world cocoa crop production are important indicators of the relative supply of cocoa beans for grinding. If world crop statistics suggest an abundant crop of cocoa beans for next year and the cocoa grindings report indicate a decrease in cocoa beans being processed for chocolate, cocoa prices will most probably decline since expected supply is presumed to be greater than expected demand. If the production of cocoa beans is expected to be nearly equal to the demand for beans, prices will most likely remain stable. If severe weather conditions (frosts, floods, droughts) should alter the growth and maturity of next year's cocoa crop, and the demand for cocoa is expected to increase, cocoa prices could take a sharp rise, which they did in 1976 after severe frosts hurt the Brazilian (Bahia) cocoa crop.

Commodity markets always have two sides to the equation for determining price—consumption and production. When consumption and production are in equilibrium, prices will remain relatively stable. If one side of the equation is altered, price disequilibrium results in either rising or falling market prices. Commodities differ greatly with respect to their *elasticity of demand*. Some commodities are said to have a greater elasticity of demand than others. Elasticity of demand is an important concept for understanding the three-way relationship between supply, demand, and price. A commodity characterized by elasticity of demand decreases much less in price when available supplies of the commodity become greater, whereas a commodity characterized by inelastic demand will exhibit a steep decline in price as available supplies become greater. Figure 8–1 shows the graphic relationship of changes in price versus changes in supplies for commodities with elastic and inelastic demand curves. For this reason, a speculator or hedger must have clearly in mind the elasticity of demand for the particular commodity(ies) in studying the fundamentals of a commodity market. For example, what would be the anticipated change in cocoa prices if the available supplies were increased by 15 percent next year? Or what would be the change in cocoa prices if cocoa grindings declined by 10 percent next year? The main point here is that a trader must know the degree of relationship between price and available supplies of a commodity to determine its elasticity of demand. Correlational analysis is a useful tool for determining this relationship.

Correlational analysis

Correlational analysis is a mathematical procedure for determining the degree of relationship between price and supply/demand variables. The question that correlational analysis asks is: What is the relationship between the price of commodity ABC and some

FIGURE 8–1
ELASTICITY OF DEMAND CURVES

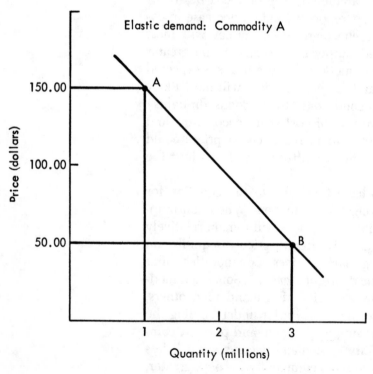

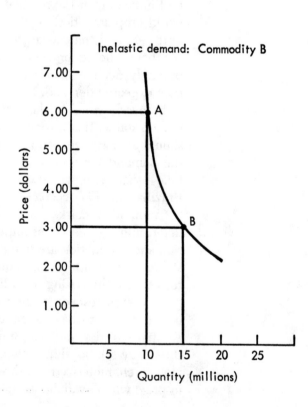

variable X? Is the relationship between the price and variable X strongly positive, strongly negative, or nonexistent? A strongly positive relationship means that as prices increase, variable X also increases in value; that is, a positive correlation exists between price and variable X. A strongly negative relationship means that as the price increases, values of variable X decrease; that is, a negative correlation exists between price and variable X. A nonexistent relationship means that changes in price are independent of changes in values of variable X; that is, no correlation exists between price and variable X. Naturally, we are only interested in those variables that exhibit either a strongly positive or strongly negative relationship (correlation) to the price of a particular commodity. (Refer to Figure 8–2 for graphic illustrations of commodity prices correlated with different variables.)

Correlational analysis is not a complete tool by itself, but is actually related to a more powerful statistical forecasting technique known as *regression analysis*. Correlational analysis allows us to determine which supply/demand variables are significantly related to the price of a particular commodity. Regression analysis tells us a great deal more about the degree and type of relationship that exists.

Regression analysis

Regression analysis is an extremely powerful method for forecasting commodity prices. It involves plotting different price levels of a commodity against one or more significantly correlated supply/

FIGURE 8–2
GRAPHIC ILLUSTRATIONS OF CORRELATIONS OF VARIABLES
X, Y, AND Z WITH PRICE OF COMMODITY ABC

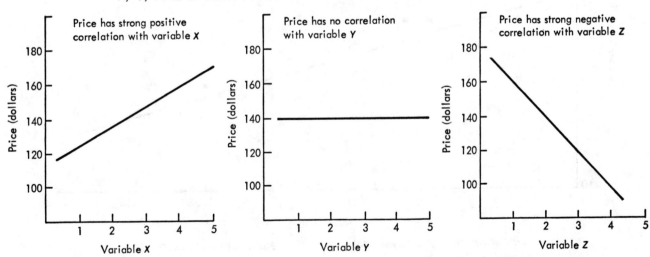

153

demand variables. If prices are plotted against varying values of only one variable, this is called *linear regression analysis.* If two or more variables are used, then *multiple regression analysis* is used to determine the relationships among price and the other variables. Either a straight line or a continuous curved line is drawn to show the graphic relationship of price to other variables. (Refer to Figure 8–3 for an example of linear regression.)

Price is considered to be a dependent variable because all other variables are considered to operate independently of it, or stated another way, price is considered to be a function of the other variables. Of course, this is an oversimplification of reality since changes in price can effect changes in the other variables being studied through complex interaction. For example, chocolate processors may curtail their purchases of cocoa beans during times of sharply rising prices. Likewise cocoa producers may hold their beans off the market during times of rapidly falling prices. Thus price is a "regulating" variable that significantly influences the relative supply and demand for commodities. Nevertheless, the diverse and changing expectations about the market place by producers and consumers are all reflected in the price of a commodity.

The primary task of fundamental analysis in price forecasting is

FIGURE 8–3
HYPOTHETICAL GRAPH SHOWING RELATIONSHIP BETWEEN
PRICE VERSUS AVAILABILITY OF A COMMODITY

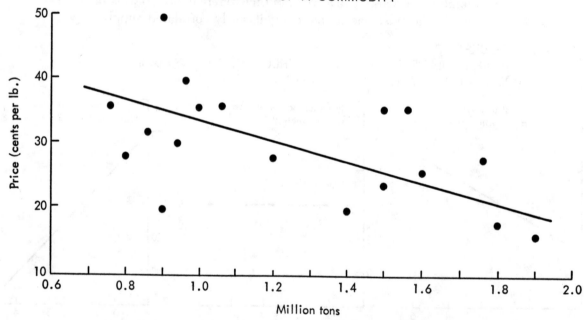

Linear regression analysis is used to plot relationship between price and availability.

154

to determine the salient variables that account for price variability. This task becomes very difficult when we realize that the effects on price caused by these variables can change significantly over time. Fundamental factors that may have had an important impact on price variability one year may be much less important next year. If a trader had devised a statistical regression model that included variables X, Y, Z to account for the primary variances in the price of a commodity, his model might give incorrect forecasts because variable D (which was previously excluded from the model) intervened to alter the valadity of the original assumptions on which the model was based. For example, the exchange rate of the British pound sterling was not a significant variable in affecting London and U.S. commodity prices until 1972 when the pound sterling was devalued. A statistical forecast model that did not include the probable effects of currency devaluation yielded inaccurate price forecasts since a currency devaluation will arbitrarily cause commodity prices to rise in the country with the devalued currency. This example illustrates the necessity of revising forecasting models in light of fundamental changes in the market.

Fundamental analysis by itself is not a complete tool for making trading decisions because "extraneous" factors can interfere with the supply/demand equation to alter both direction and magnitude of price movements during a brief period. An unexpected political announcement, a severe weather warning, or a technological breakthrough can cause a brief flurry of trading activity with little long-term consequence to a commodity market.

The objective of fundamental analysis is to provide a rationale for buying or selling an option or futures contract. Since the buying or writing of an option is a long-term proposition compared to a futures position, a thorough fundamental study of the market increases the likelihood of making a correct trading decision. Option traders must take a long-term perspective of a market because they are buying *time value* when they purchase an option—and selling *time value* when they write an option. Commodity traders can enhance the dependability and profitability of their trading program considerably if they have a good grasp of the fundamentals and technical conditions of the market. Technical analysis of market conditions assists traders in timing their buy/sell decisions to optimize their return on investment. We will now discuss some of the more commonly used methods of technical analysis.

TECHNICAL ANALYSIS

Technical analysis involves the study of price behavior irrespective of any fundamental (production/consumption) factors. An implicit assumption of technical analysis is that all relevant factors of the market are reflected in price variability, open interest, and volume of trading. Technical traders look for "signs" to give them indications when a major price move—up or down—is about to begin, or when a key reversal has occurred in a previous price trend. Technical signs may take many forms depending upon the orientation of the trader.

The more frequently used methods of technical analysis are (1) bar-graph charting, (2) point-and-figure charting, and (3) moving averages. Point-and-figure charting techniques are presented in greater detail in Chapter 9. Bar graphs and point-and-figure charts provide an extremely useful pictorial view of past and present price behavior. One can obtain at a glance the "price zones" on a graph of potential supply and demand for a commodity. When commodity prices fall too low, buyers enter the market to purchase commodities. Prices are said to be supported in this area—support zone. When prices rise too high, sellers will enter the market to drive prices lower. Prices are said to meet resistance in this area—resistance zone. Support zones are areas of potential demand for a commodity, and resistance zones are areas of potential supply of a commodity.

Bar-graph charts are created by plotting the daily (weekly or monthly) high, low, and closing prices on standard graph paper. (See Chart 35.) A bar graph reveals the spread between the high and low price of the period, the location of the closing price in relation to previous closing prices, and previous high and low prices. If the trend of the closing prices is successively lower, then the market is said to be in a downtrend. If the trend is successively higher, then the market is said to be in an uptrend. Bar graphs become extremely useful tools when the volume of trading and open interest of a commodity are plotted on the same graph. If the open interest and volume of trading increase significantly coupled with either a sharp rise (or decline) in price, the market is referred to as being technically strong, and some type of market action (buy, sell, or liquidation) may be indicated. Whereas if the open interest and volume of trading do not confirm each other, the market is called technically weak, and usually no market action is indicated. Bar-graph charts provide a wealth of visual information for primary and secondary zones of price support and resistance.

Bar-graph and point-and-figure chartists look for the primary and secondary price support and resistance zones to give them cues about when a market may be overbought or oversold. They also look for specific graph configurations such as head-and-shoulder formations, flags, pennants, channels, and saucer-shape patterns to generate buy or sell signals. These configurations are used because they

CHART 35
BAR GRAPH CHART SHOWING THE DAILY HIGH, LOW, AND
CLOSING PRICES FOR N.Y. COFFEE "C" FUTURES CONTRACT
(daily figures for volume of trading and open interest are also shown on
chart)

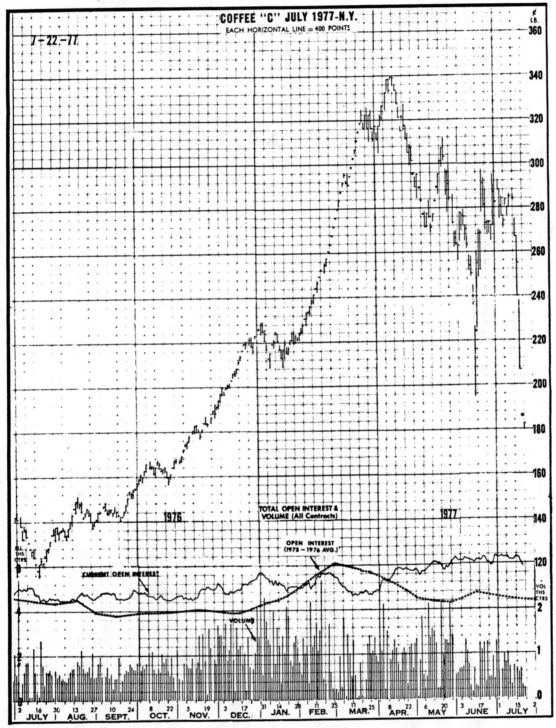

Source: Reprinted from *Commodity Chart Service*, a weekly publication of Commodity Research Bureau, Inc., 1 Liberty Plaza, New York, N.Y. 10006.

157

have demonstrated varying degrees of reliability and validity—depending upon the individual skills of the trader—in forecasting market trends.

Moving averages

Technical traders who use moving averages are not really attempting to forecast prices, but rather to identify an established price trend. Various types of moving averages can be used to make trading decisions—simple moving averages, weighted moving averages, and exponential movings averages.

Moving averages may be calculated on a 5-, 10-, or 20-day basis to provide a mechanical system for generating buy and sell signals. A simple (unweighted) ten-day moving average, for example, is calculated by summing up the previous ten days of closing prices and dividing by ten. On the 11th day, the closing price for the earliest day is dropped and replaced by the latest closing price to maintain a current moving average. A moving average system is updated each day in this manner. Table 8–1 shows calculations for both 5-day and 10-day moving averages using gold prices over a 20-day period.

Buy and sell signals are generated when either the five-day moving average rises above, or falls below, the ten-day moving average

TABLE 8–1

COMPUTATION OF FIVE- AND TEN-DAY MOVING AVERAGES OF GOLD PRICES

Day	Closing price	Five-day total	Ten-day total	Five-day moving average	Ten-day moving average
20	$141.00				
19	141.50				
18	141.25				
17	142.00				
16	142.50	$708.25		$141.65	
15	142.00	709.25		141.85	
14	142.75	710.50		142.10	
13	143.00	712.25		142.45	
12	142.50	712.75		142.55	
11	143.25	713.50	$1,421.80	142.70	$142.18
10	144.00	715.50	1,424.75	143.10	142.48
9	145.00	717.75	1,428.25	143.55	142.83
8	144.50	719.25	1,431.50	143.85	143.15
7	145.00	721.75	1,434.50	144.35	143.45
6	145.50	724.00	1,437.50	144.80	143.75
5	145.25	725.25	1,440.75	145.05	144.08
4	146.00	726.25	1,444.00	145.25	144.40
3	146.50	728.25	1,447.50	145.65	144.75
2	146.75	730.00	1,451.75	146.00	145.18
1	147.00	731.50	1,455.50	146.30	145.55

158

value. A buy signal is generated when the five-day value rises above the ten-day value. Likewise a sell signal is generated when the five-day value falls below the ten-day value. See Table 8–2. Simple (unweighted) five-day and ten-day moving averages are used here as examples. Any combination of moving averages may be used—4-, 9-, 18-day, or 10-, 20-, 40-day moving averages—depending upon the objectives of the trading system.

TABLE 8–2

Ten-day values	Five-day values	Buy/sell signal
$135.00	$135.00	No signal
135.00	136.00	Buy signal
135.00	135.00	No signal
135.00	134.00	Sell signal

A primary disadvantage of using simple moving averages is that the closing prices of all the days carry equal weight in computing the average. Many traders argue that the closing prices of the nearest days should carry more weight than the more distant days in computing the average. The closing prices of a moving average can be weighted by various factors to give more significance to the nearest days and less to the more distant days. For example, using the figures in Table 8–3, we can calculate a five-day weighted moving average as follows:

TABLE 8–3

Day	Closing prices		Factor		Total
First	$136.00	×	3	=	$ 408.00
Second	134.00	×	2	=	268.00
Third	135.00	×	1	=	135.00
Fourth	133.00	×	1	=	133.00
Fifth	132.00	×	1	=	132.00
Total	$670.00		8		$1,076.00

$$\text{Simple moving average} = \frac{670}{5} = 134.00$$

$$\text{Weighted moving average} = \frac{1,076}{8} = 134.50$$

The primary advantage in using a weighted moving average versus a simple moving average is that a weighted average is more sensitive to changes in price trends and, therefore, more responsive to generating buy/sell signals when a price trend begins or ends.

A weighted moving average should signal a trend change more quickly than a simple moving average because the nearest days are given additional weighting in computing the average. Stated another way, a simple, unweighted moving average has a greater lag time built in to its computation in signaling changes in price trends.

Let us wrap up our discussion of moving averages as a valuable tool by describing the primary advantages and disadvantages of using them in an options trading program:

A. Advantages
  1. Purely mechanical trading approach for generating buy/sell signals.
  2. Moving averages smooth out erratic price gyrations to identify current trends in the market.
  3. Moving averages are easy to calculate and update as needed with an electronic hand calculator.
  4. No charting is really necessary but may be helpful to give a graphic view of price trends.
  5. Moving average systems are flexible in that almost any combination of averages and weightings on closing prices can be used to develop a reliable trading system.
B. Disadvantages
  1. Moving average systems may generate too many false buy/sell signals in whipsaw markets.
  2. Moving average systems do not attempt to forecast the direction and magnitude of price trends as other technical methods do; moving averages tell only what the current trend is and signal its beginning and its end according to the parameters of the moving average system used.

This concludes the chapter on tools of analysis for trading options. Many brokerage firms with commodity research departments have a staff of fundamental and technical analysts to provide trading recommendations, research reports, and other services to their customers. The financial resources and technical capabilities for conducting commodity research and making it available to the firm's customers are extensive and by all means should be used by both speculators and commercial traders in making trading decisions.

160

Chapter 9

Do-it-yourself point-and-figure charting: The basics

Point-and-figure charting has long been associated with images of serious-minded men hunched over notebooks in the dark corners of brokerage offices and trading floors making cryptic marks on box-ruled paper. Part-time speculators usually think of it as a valuable tool that is beyond their grasp, either because it is too expensive in terms of time to be invested, is too complicated, or because it requires access to time and sales data that aren't always available. This chapter will correct these misconceptions while showing how it rates as a good trading system.

The attributes of a good trading system are ease of maintenance, simplicity, the ability to understand its functioning, the involvement of the trader in the discussion-making process, and, of course, its profitability. On all these criteria point-and-figure ranks high. It is simple to understand, and costs virtually nothing to maintain, but it does demand daily personal involvement. It can serve as a scapegoat for bad trades, and yields credit to the user for winning trades —and it is profitable!

Anyone can keep point-and-figure charts just as easily as the more common bar graphs. All that are needed are pencils and erasers, graph paper, daily high-low prices for each contract to be plotted, and an understanding of a few simple rules. The results will be a trading tool that is more accurate than the standard bar chart, presents clearer pictures of what prices are doing, more positive indications of where to get in and out of a market, and more reliable predictions of how far price moves are likely to go.

The success of point-and-figure charting will be analyzed in depth later in this chapter, but it might be interesting as an introduction to examine a handful of trading signals generated by the system during 1977. During this period, September frozen concentrated orange juice gave a buy signal at 85.60 and a sell later at 99.20. A short position was signaled in July 1977 sugar at 12.40 and held open for ten months for a $5,000 move. July soybean meal gave a sell signal at $285 and proceeded to decline to $190. Frozen pork bellies signaled a short at 56.80-cents basis February 1978 and subsequently declined to 47.00 before being covered on a buy signal at 48.60. October cattle declined from 43.80 to 40.60 between the short and cover signals; July silver dropped from 498.00 to 464.00 following the sell; and August soybeans rose by $13,500 between the long and the close out point.

And best of all, every one of these signals was generated by the simplest of point-and-figure charting techniques without the aid of a computer, without hours of fundamental analysis, without the services of a high-priced advisor, and without the slightest understanding of exponential moving averages, slope tests, curve fitting, oscillators, regression analysis, or any of the other techniques currently in vogue.

This is thus an introduction to simple point-and-figure charting. It is the beginning set of do-it-yourself instructions, so let's get started.

THE TOOLS

As already mentioned, the only things necessary for successful point-and-figure charting of commodity future contracts are a pencil, an eraser, graph paper, daily high and low prices for each commodity contract being monitored, and the understanding of a few very simple rules.

The pencil should be a soft lead type which can be easily erased. The eraser should leave the paper smudge-free, and the paper should have ten squares to the inch with heavy rulings every five boxes. Other square sizes and rulings can be used, yet the ten squares and heavy fifth rulings provide squares sufficiently large for notations yet small enough to permit a large number or rows and columns per page. Graph paper of the appropriate type is readily available at most office supply stores.

THE RULES

Point-and-figure charts are unique in three ways. First, only large significant moves are noted and minor fluctuations are ignored as having no relevance to the overall trend. Second, point-and-figure charts ignore the passage of time. Dates may be indicated on the chart, but this is done solely as a matter of convenience and has no relevance to decision making or to signal descriptions. Third, point-and-figure charts denote movements by the letters "X" and "O" and not by lines, as in the more commonly seen line/bar charts. Examples of a line/bar and point-and-figure chart can be seen in Charts 36 and 37.

The basic premise of point-and-figure charting and trading is that the law of supply and demand, and nothing else, governs the price of a commodity. When demand is stronger than supply, the price rises; when supply exceeds demand, the price declines; when supply and demand are contesting for supremacy, the price moves sideways.

Every point-and-figure chart contains the following elements: long columns of Xs signifying greater demand than supply and, therefore, a rising price; long columns of Os used to depict a falling price resulting from supply exceeding demand, and short alternat-

CHART 36
LINE/BAR CHART

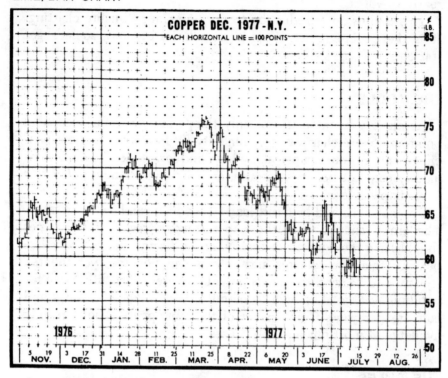

COPPER DEC. 1977 - N.Y.
EACH HORIZONTAL LINE = 100 POINTS

Source: Reprinted from Commodity Chart Service, A Weekly Publication of Commodity Research Bureau, Inc., 1 Liberty Plaza, New York, N.Y. 10006.

ing columns of Xs and Os where supply and demand are contesting for supremacy from a relatively equal position. The point-and-figure chart is, therefore, a pictorial record of the contest between the forces of supply and demand.

Now for the specifics of drawing point-and-figure charts. The first task is to scale the chart. This means assigning a uniform value to the boxes. Table 9–1 provides the box sizes currently being used in the traditional, or non-optimized, method. Although these box sizes remain constant over long time spans, during periods of extremely high or very low volatility the box sizes will be increased or decreased in unit value in order to provide the most representative and useful picture of the price action.

Once the chart is scaled as shown in Chart 38 for March New York silver, the next step is the entry of price movements. This is accomplished by observing the daily high and low prices for the contract in *The Wall Street Journal* or any other newspaper providing daily highs and lows. Since there are no entries on the chart, the spread between the high and low is important. If the spread spans

CHART 37
POINT-AND-FIGURE CHART

COPPER   December 1977

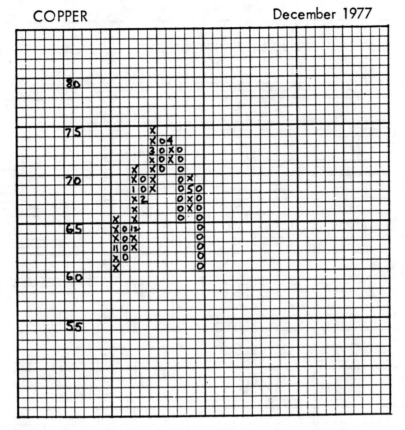

TABLE 9–1
BOX SIZES FOR THE TRADITIONAL (NONOPTIMIZED) THREE-POINT REVERSAL METHOD OF POINT-AND-FIGURE CHARTING (June 3, 1977)

Commodity	Value of one box	Commodity	Value of one box
Broilers	20 pts.	Orange juice	100 pts.
Cattle	20 pts.	Platinum	200 pts.
Cocoa	100 pts.	Plywood	100 pts.
Coffee	100 pts.	Pork bellies	20 pts.
Copper	100 pts.	Potatoes (Maine and Idaho)	10 pts.
Corn	2 cents	Silver (N.Y. and Chicago)	200 pts.
Cotton	100 pts.	Silver coins	20 pts.
Eggs	20 pts.	Soybeans	10 cents
Grain	20 pts.	Soybean meal	500 pts.
Gold	100 pts.	Soybean oil	20 pts.
Hogs	20 pts.	Sugar	20 pts.
Lumber	100 pts.	Wheat	2 cents
Oats	1 cent		

CHART 38
A SCALED CHART FOR MARCH NEW YORK SILVER

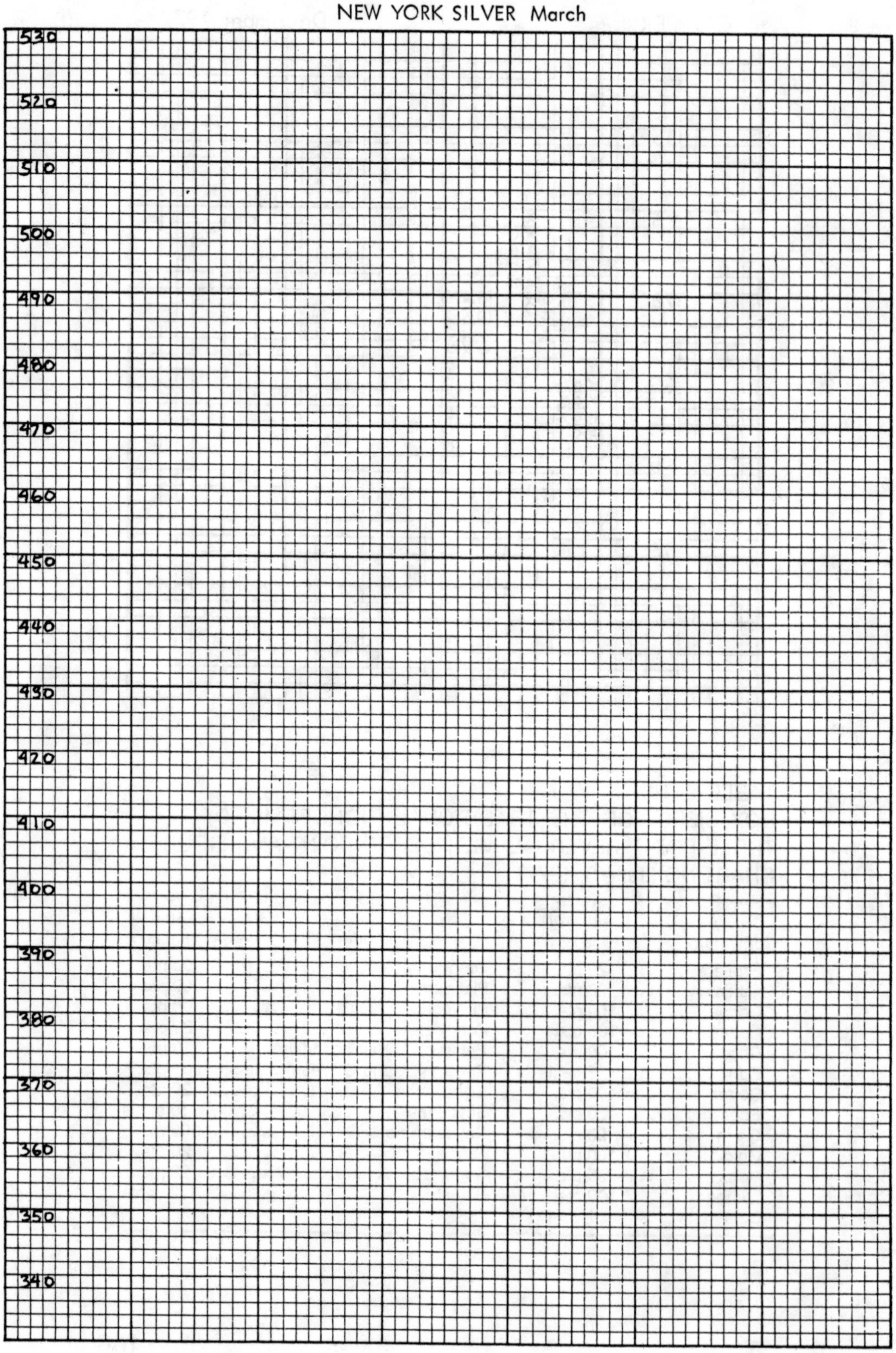

NEW YORK SILVER March

530	
520	
510	
500	
490	
480	
470	
460	
450	
440	
430	
420	
410	
400	
390	
380	
370	
360	
350	
340	

the value of three or more boxes and the price closes above the center of the range, draw the appropriate number of Xs. For example, if March silver had a high of $5.56 and a low of $5.51 and closed at $5.54, Xs would be drawn in the 552, 554, and 556 boxes. If the contract closed below the center of the range, Os would be drawn. Thus, had the close been $5.52, Os would be entered in the 556, 554, and 552 boxes.

If the range between the high and low failed to span three boxes, dots are placed in the boxes that were spanned, for later evidence will be required to dictate the direction. For example, had the silver's high been $5.56 and the low $5.54, dots would be placed in the 554 and 556 boxes. The dots serve as reminders of which boxes have been crossed. If on the following day the contract had a range of $5.58 to $5.55, a third, and higher, box has been reached, so the two dots are replaced by Xs and an X is drawn at 558. Had the second day's range been $5.55 to $5.52 instead, a lower box was crossed, and the dots are replaced with Os and an O is drawn at 552.

RISING PRICES

Now that the first column has been drawn, the continuation becomes considerably easier. The technique is as follows: If the current or most recent column is composed of Xs, the daily high is reviewed. If the high is at least one box higher than the highest X in the current column, the appropriate number of additional Xs are drawn. If the current column is an X column with Xs at 552, 554, 556, and 558 and the daily high is $5.61, a new X would be drawn at 560. A daily high of $5.65 would have required the drawing of Xs at 560, 562, and 564.

If the daily high is high enough to require the drawing of one or more additional Xs in the current column, the daily low is totally ignored. This same pattern of looking first at the highs and drawing more Xs continues as long as each succeeding daily high is one or more boxes higher than the last X drawn in the current column.

But finally there will come a time when the daily high will not permit the drawing of new Xs. Only when this occurs will the daily low be of interest. Therefore, if the daily high was not at least one box higher than the highest X, the daily low is reviewed to determine whether the price advance has reversed. If the low is lower than the highest X by the value of three boxes, the price advance is considered broken and a column of Os is drawn with the first O being placed one column to the right of the X column and one box below the highest X.

Assume, for example, that the highest X is at 666, the daily high is $6.67, and the low is $6.60. Since the 667 is not high enough to permit the entry of a new X, attention is focused upon the daily low: 660. Because the 660 spans three boxes of 664, 662, and 660, the trend has reversed and Os are drawn down beginning one column to the right of the X column and with the highest O one box below the highest X. Chart 39 shows this price reversal. Had the low been $6.58, four Os would have been entered. Had the low been $6.56, five Os would be drawn. But if the low were $6.61, only two boxes would have been penetrated. And, since the "three-point reversal method of point-and-figure" does not consider that a trend has reversed until three boxes are spanned, no entries are made and the price is still believed to be advancing.

CHART 39: PRICE REVERSAL
FROM AN X COLUMN
TO AN O COLUMN

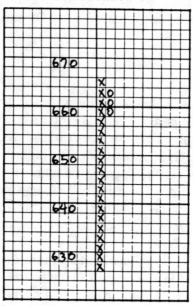

If neither one new X nor three new Os can be drawn, no entry is made and the procedure begins anew the following day.

On the following and each succeeding day and as long as the trend is still up (meaning the current column is an X column) the high is reviewed first for new entries, and only if no new Xs can be drawn, is the low analyzed for a three-box reversal. And regardless of how low the low may be, if the high permits the drawing of at least one new X, the trend is still up and the low must be disregarded. If the trend has truly reversed, even though a new X was drawn, the directional change will be revealed the following day

168

when a higher high is lacking and the low is three or more boxes below the highest X.

FALLING PRICES

If the current column is a declining column or a column of Os, the daily procedures are reversed. In this case the daily low is analyzed first. If the low is one or more boxes below the lowest O in the current column, the appropriate number of additional Os are drawn and the daily high is ignored. If the current column runs from 560 down to 552 and the day's low is $5.48, new Os are entered at 550 and 548, and the high price for the day is of no concern. Yet, if the low fails to permit the entry of one or more additional Os, as in the low of $5.51, the high would be analyzed to determine if a three-box reversal had occurred. If the high were $5.58 or higher, a reversal has occurred and a new column of Xs is drawn immediately to the right of the Os with the lowest X being entered one row higher than the lowest O in the most current of O columns. A reversal from an O to an X column is shown in Chart 40.

CHART 40: REVERSAL FROM
AN O COLUMN TO AN
X COLUMN

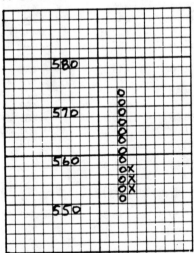

If no new Os can be added and a reversal failed to occur, no entries are made for the day and the procedure begins again the following day.

In order to clear up any confusion that may exist, a good idea would be to practice charting the March 1975 New York silver contract from the data provided in Table 9–2, which shows the daily

TABLE 9–2

HISTORIC DAILY HIGH AND LOW PRICES AND CHART ENTRIES
FOR MARCH 1975 NEW YORK SILVER

Date		High	Low	Chart entries
January	2	$351.70	$346.80	
	3	353.00	347.10	O — 352, 350, 348
	4	346.00	340.80	O — 346, 344, 342
	7	352.80	335.00	O — 340, 338, 336
	8	361.00	353.00	X — 338, 340, 342, 344, 346, 348, 350, 352, 354, 356, 358, 360
	9	357.50	350.50	O — 358, 356, 354, 352
	10	359.80	349.70	O — 350
	11	365.00	360.00	X — 352, 354, 356, 358, 360, 362, 364
	14	373.50	367.30	X — 366, 368, 370, 372
	15	374.50	370.00	X — 374
	16	382.20	366.10	X — 376, 378, 380, 382
	17	390.50	384.30	X — 384, 386, 388, 390
	18	400.10	385.70	X — 392, 394, 396, 398, 400
	21	410.10	410.10	X — 402, 404, 406, 408, 410
	22	420.00	403.00	X — 412, 414, 416, 418, 420
	23	399.50	393.50	O — 418, 416, 414, 412, 410, 408, 406, 404, 402, 400, 398, 396, 394
	24	408.60	404.40	X — 396, 398, 400, 402, 404, 406, 408
	25	418.60	418.60	X — 410, 412, 414, 416, 418
	28	428.60	418.00	X — 420, 422, 424, 426, 428
	29	428.00	418.60	O — 426, 424, 422, 420
	30	416.00	409.50	O — 418, 416, 414, 412, 410
	31	423.20	410.00	X — 412, 414, 416, 418, 420, 422
February	1	432.10	426.20	X — 424, 426, 428, 430, 432
	4	442.10	442.10	X — 434, 436, 438, 440, 442
	5	457.10	457.10	X — 444, 446, 448, 450, 452, 454, 456
	6	472.10	448.00	X — 458, 460, 462, 464, 466, 468, 470, 472
	7	486.50	477.00	X — 474, 476, 478, 480, 482, 484, 486
	8	496.90	496.90	X — 488, 490, 492, 494, 496
	11	511.90	511.90	X — 498, 500, 502, 504, 506, 508, 510
Holiday	12			
	13	526.90	526.90	X — 512, 514, 516, 518, 520, 522, 524, 526
	14	541.90	532.00	X — 528, 530, 532, 534, 536, 538, 540
	15	556.90	556.90	X — 542, 544, 546, 548, 550, 552, 554, 556
Holiday	18			
	19	571.90	541.90	X — 558, 560, 562, 564, 566, 568, 570
	20	575.20	570.00	X — 572, 574
	21	590.20	590.20	X — 576, 578, 580, 582, 584, 586, 588, 590
	22	605.20	605.20	X — 592, 594, 596, 598, 600, 602, 604
	25	620.20	620.20	X — 606, 608, 610, 612, 614, 616, 618, 620
	26	635.20	635.20	X — 622, 624, 626, 628, 630, 632, 634

170

TABLE 9–2 (continued)

Date		High	Low	Chart entries
	27	655.20	617.00	X — 636, 638, 640, 642, 644, 646, 648, 650, 652, 654
	28	604.80	604.80	O — 652, 650, 648, 646, 644, 642, 640, 638, 636, 634, 632, 630, 628, 626, 624, 622, 620, 618, 616, 614, 612, 610, 608, 606
March	1	593.00	584.80	O — 604, 602, 600, 598, 596, 594, 592, 590, 588, 586
	4	586.00	564.80	O — 584, 582, 580, 578, 576, 574, 572, 570, 568, 566
	5	546.50	546.50	O — 564, 562, 560, 558, 556, 554, 552, 550, 548
	6	546.50	526.50	O — 546, 544, 542, 540, 538, 536, 534, 532, 530, 528
	7	549.60	545.20	X — 530, 532, 534, 536, 538, 540, 542, 544, 546, 548

high and low figures for March 1975 New York silver from January 1, 1974, through March 7, 1974. This contract was selected because many people believe silver is one of the easier commodities to chart because of familiarity and this period was one of the most volatile ever for silver. The column entitled "Chart entries" shows the entries that should be made from these figures. It is suggested that this column be covered and only used to check postings. The resulting chart is shown by Chart 41.

THE BASIC CHART PATTERNS: THE SIMPLE BUY AND SIMPLE SELL

Point-and-figure chart patterns are neither shrouded in mystery nor are they merely random configurations. They are neither one nor the other because they repeat themselves 99 percent of the time. The actions of buyers and sellers, whether they are hedgers or speculators, must necessarily be reflected in price changes. Every purchase and sale of a contract is made at a certain price, affects the price, and ultimately changes the price. The method used to record these price changes is what causes the appearance of recurring patterns of Xs and Os. The ability to recognize and interpret these patterns provides the chartist with the knowledge of the correct position to take at any particular time. These patterns are referred to as formations and range from very simple to very complex patterns.

The most basic of all formations—and necessary elements in more complex formations—are the simple buy and simple sell formations, sometimes called the double top and double bottom formations.

The simple buy formation, as shown in Chart 42, occurs when

171

CHART 41: POINT-AND-FIGURE CHART
NEW YORK SILVER (January 1, 1974
through March 7, 1974)

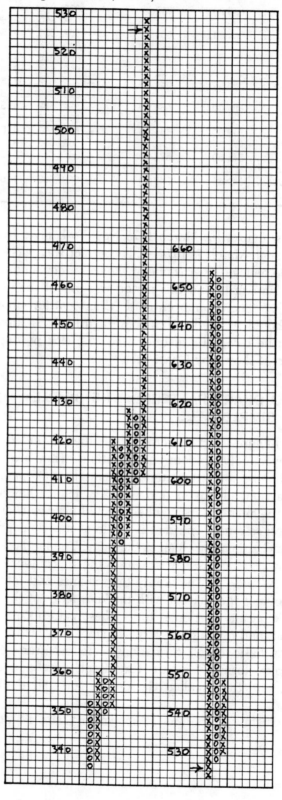

CHART 42
SIMPLE BUY FORMATION

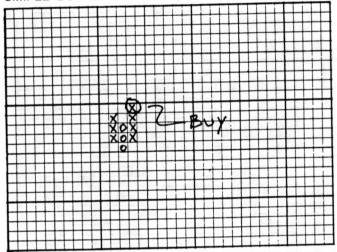

the current X column rises one box higher than the top X in the prior column of Xs. Notice that a simple buy formation occurred in March silver at 362 (Chart 41). A simple buy signal can also be seen at 67 on December 1977 copper (Chart 37). These charts contain more than just one simple buy signal, and yet it only took one to reap a substantial profit in both contracts.

The simple buy formation is more than an entry point for a long position. It also represents the price at which any short position in the contract should be covered. Thus, the simple buy formation is both an entry signal for longs and a stop-loss point for shorts.

The other basic formation is the simple sell or double bottom formation. It is composed of two columns of Os and one intervening column of Xs and occurs when the current column of Os falls one box below the lowest O of the prior column. An example of this type of formation can be found in Chart 43. Another example of this formation can be seen at 70 in December 1977 copper (Chart 37).

The simple sell formation signals two market strategies—to liquidate long positions, providing guidance for the placing of stop-loss orders, and to short the contract.

Additional signals can be found in soybean, corn, oats, cattle, hogs, pork bellies, and broilers in Chart 44. An easy to follow graphic display of charting techniques is provided in Chart 45.

CHARTING FUTURES OR OPTIONS?

Our discussion has centered on charting futures with no mention of charting options, but is this the correct way to proceed?

173

CHART 43
SIMPLE SELL FORMATION

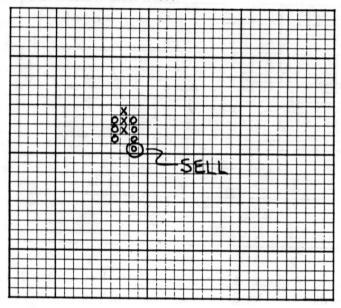

There are differences of opinion as to whether it is best to chart the futures contracts or the options on the futures. One school holds steadfast to the idea that options mirror futures, and therefore by charting futures one knows when to buy, sell, or exercise an option, or when to use futures to hedge against an option or to reverse the process and use an option to protect a futures position.

The other school believes that option prices or premiums over extended periods of time can and do move independently of futures because they are influenced by supply and demand for options rather than the immediate price action of the underlying futures contract.

We are not proposing any solution to these differences of opinions other than to point out that such differences do exist and either futures or options or both can be effectively charted. We must admit that we are at a disadvantage in discussing the charting of options because at this writing, they are not yet traded on American exchanges. A period of trading history will be required before appropriate scales can be established for maximum profitability. We also have no profitability data on the success of point-and-figure charting as it applies to options and must also patiently wait for a data base to build before studies can be performed.

But even though we are unable to provide concrete statistics as to the profitability of trading options from point-and-figure charts of options, the following section shows the results of years of re-

174

CHART 44
ADDITIONAL SIGNALS

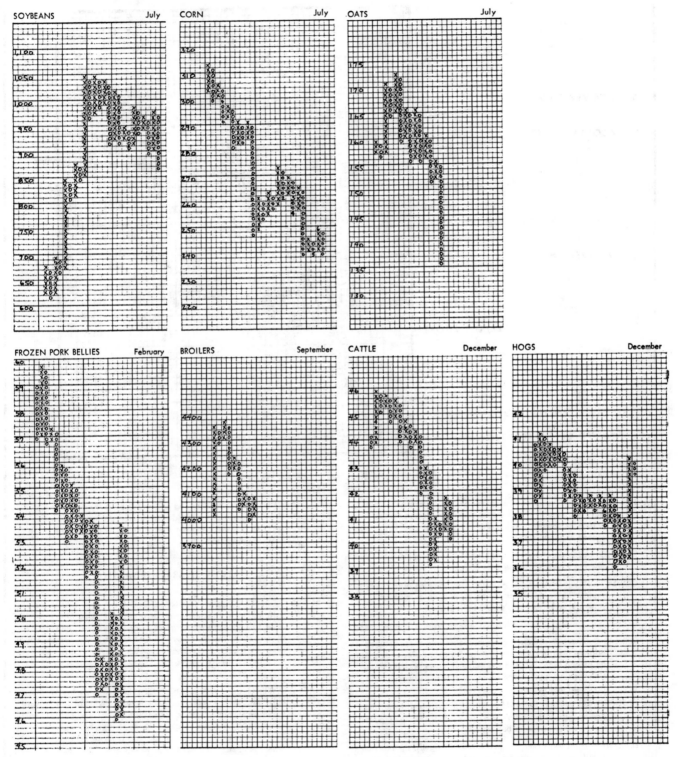

CHART 45
CHARTING TECHNIQUES

EXPLANATION of CHARTS

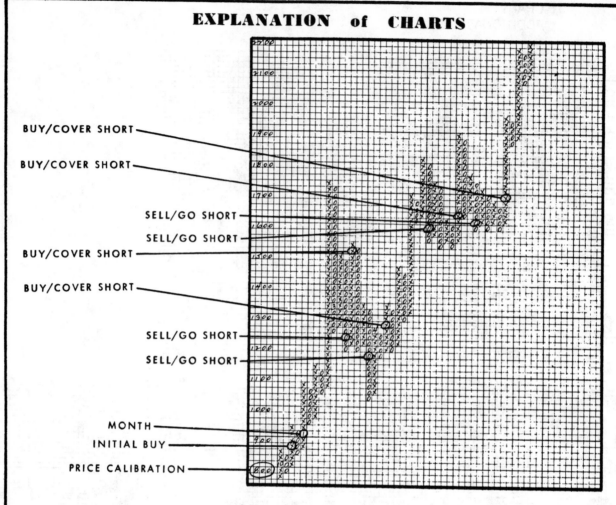

BUY/COVER SHORT

BUY/COVER SHORT

SELL/GO SHORT

SELL/GO SHORT

BUY/COVER SHORT

BUY/COVER SHORT

SELL/GO SHORT

SELL/GO SHORT

MONTH

INITIAL BUY

PRICE CALIBRATION

POINT & FIGURE TECHNIQUES

BUY SIGNAL – Occurs when a column of Xs rises one box higher than the highest X of the prior X column. Since this point can be anticipated, a stop order to enter the position can be placed at the buy point.

SELL SIGNAL – Occurs when a column of Os declines one box below the lowest O on the prior O column.

COVER POINT FOR A SHORT – Exactly the same point as the buy signal. Since this point can be determined in advance, a stop-loss order to cover should be in the market.

CLOSEOUT OF A LONG – Exactly the same point as the sell signal.

ORDERS – Since all entry and stop-loss points can be determined prior to their occurrence, entry and closeout stop orders can be placed beforehand in the market. But remember these signal points change and all orders should be periodically reviewed and adjusted.

TRADITIONAL ENTRY SIGNALS – The first buy signal following one or more sell-short signals and the first sell-short signal following one or more buy signals.

BULLISH – If the most recent signal was a buy signal, the position is bullish and remains bullish until a sell-short signal occurs.

BEARISH – If the most recent signal was a sell-short signal, the position is bearish and remains bearish until a buy signal occurs.

PULLBACKS – Rather than taking an immediate entry on a signal, if a reversal is anticipated after a signal, a strategy involving less risk is to take the position after the signal but at a price closer to the stop.

DAILY CHART UPDATING

IF THE CURRENT COLUMN IS AN X COLUMN – Look first at the daily high. If the daily high permits the drawing of one or more X's, draw them and ignore the daily low. If, and only if, no new Xs can be drawn, look at the daily low and determine whether a reversal has occurred. If a reversal has not occurred, make no entries at all.

IF THE CURRENT COLUMN IS AN O COLUMN – Look first at the daily low. If the daily low permits the drawing of one or more Os, draw them and ignore the daily high. If, and only if, no new Os can be drawn look at the daily high to determine whether a reversal has occurred. If a reversal has occurred draw the appropriate number of Xs. If a reversal has not occurred make no entries at all.

There can never be Xs and Os drawn on the same day. On a daily basis there is either a continuation of the current column, a reversal, or no new entries are made.

search into the profitability of this trading tool as applied to both stocks and commodity futures.

HOW PROFITABLE?

How well has point-and-figure charting performed over an extended period of time, and how well has it performed recently? These seem like questions whose answers would be easily obtainable since point-and-figure is the second-most popular charting technique in use today, topped only by bar charts. But just try to find the answer to these questions. We tried because we make a living studying the performance of major trading systems, but the answers were nowhere to be found. Point-and-figure chartists have generally accepted the system on faith and—having once accepted it—tend to follow it blindly without the need for reliance upon constantly updated performance records. Therefore, it seems that few empirical studies were ever conducted.

The only historic profitability studies on point-and-figure charting we discovered were the research results of Robert E. Davis and Charles C. Thiel, Jr., published by Dunn and Hargitt in limited printings.

In 1965, Davis wrote *Profit and Probability,* which provided the results of an extensive test of traditional point-and-figure techniques as applied to common stocks. This study covered two stocks for the period of 1914 through 1964, and 1,100 stocks representing all industrial groups for the period 1954–64. It revealed that the simple buy signal (which occurs when the current column of Xs exceeds the prior X column by one box) was profitable 80.3 percent of the time when closed on a simple sell signal, and when profitable it showed a net return of 38.7 percent realized in 11.5 months. In the 19.7 percent of the cases where losses occurred, the average loss was 13.1 percent and the loss occurred in 4.6 months. The simple short-sell signal (which occurs whenever the current O column falls one box below the lowest O of the prior column of Os) was found to be profitable 82.1 percent of the time, and profits were realized in 4.7 months and averaged 22.7 percent. Losses occurred on 17.9 percent of the signals, cost 9.7 percent of the investment, and were realized in 5.5 months.

All percentage profit-and-loss figures were based on a nonmargined investment and were after commissions.

Davis' research then switched to commodity futures, and his next book, coauthored with Thiel, entitled *Point and Figure Commodity Trading: A Computer Evaluation,* was published in 1970. It was a brilliant research model designed to provide trading results for a variety of point-and-figure box sizes and reversal distances, in an attempt to determine the optimal box size and reversal distance for each commodity. Although the optimal box and reversal values seldom coincided with the values generally used by chartists today, the results are invaluable because they reveal that for the period of 1960–69, with two delivery months six months apart, the maximum results which would have been attained regardless of the box size or reversal distance. The returns with conventional box sizes and the standard three-box reversal value would naturally be lower, simply because this is not always the best set of rules by which to play.

Table 9–3 summarized the Davis-Thiel results, assuming the optimal strategy for each commodity. The results are spectacular: 53 percent of all 799 signals were profitable, and the average net profit on all trades (including both profitable and unprofitable ones) was $311.

TABLE 9–3
RESULTS OF OPTIMAL BOX SIZE AND REVERSAL VALUES FOR POINT-AND-FIGURE TRADING

Commodity	Contracts covered	Delivery years covered	Profit/total trade ratio for both delivery months	Percentage of trades profitable	Average net profit per trade
Wheat	May	1960–69			
	December	1960–69	25/49	51%	$ 154
Corn	July	1960–69			
	December	1960–69	25/46	54	104
Oats	May	1961–69			
	December	1960–69	8/17	47	42
Soybeans	January	1961–70			
	July	1960–69	60/111	54	245
Soybean meal	January	1961–70			
	July	1960–69	16/28	57	188
Soybean oil	January	1961–70			
	July	1960–69	26/39	67	284
Live cattle	July	1965–69			
	December	1965–69	19/27	70	331
Pork bellies	February	1961–70			
	August	1963–69	28/47	60	438
Eggs	September	1960–69			
	November	1960–69	46/114	40	− 25
Potatoes	May	1961–69			
	November	1960–69	48/86	56	61
Copper	March	1962–69			
	December	1961–69	34/67	51	1,455
Sugar	March	1962–70			
	September	1962–69	21/43	49	297
Cocoa	March	1961–70			
	September	1960–69	45/87	52	244
Orange juice	March	1968–70			
	September	1968–69	15/31	48	368
Silver	May	1968–69			
	December	1967–69	6/7	86	2,447

Note: Total profit/total trade ratio, 422/799; percentage of all trades profitable, 53 percent; and average net profit per trade for all trades, $311.

To our dismay, however, we ascertained that the Davis-Thiel research represented the complete universe of published data on the profitability of point-and-figure charting. Furthermore, as good as this research was, it ended in 1969; and we as traders are interested in the here and now, in markets almost unrelated to those of the 1960s in terms of volume, volatility, and values. It was therefore imperative that we examine modern markets.

TODAY

The current studies of the profitability and reliability of point-and-figure charting focused on two key questions. Whether the traditionally accepted box sizes and reversal distances existing in 1974 as displayed in Table 9–4 (values are slightly different in some cases in 1977 with the 1977 figures displayed in Table 9–1) were the best set of parameters by which to play the game, and whether a comparison could be drawn between theoretical results working backwards in time and the more realistic results of forward analysis. All of this research work was done by Kermit C. Zieg, Jr., and Perry J. Kaufman and was published in 1975 in a book entitled *Point and Figure Commodity Trading Techniques.*

TABLE 9–4
PARAMETERS FOR THE THREE-BOX-REVERSAL METHOD OF POINT-AND-FIGURE CHARTING (traditional method)

Commodity	Box size	Reversal size
Broilers	100 pts.	3 boxes
Cattle	20 pts.	3
Cocoa	100 pts.	3
Coffee	100 pts.	3
Copper	100 pts.	3
Corn	2 cents	3
Cotton	100 pts.	3
Eggs	100 pts.	3
Hogs	20 pts.	3
Lumber	100 pts.	3
Oats	1 cent	3
Orange juice	20 pts.	3
Platinum	200 pts.	3
Plywood	100 pts.	3
Pork bellies	20 pts.	3
Potatoes	5 pts.	3
Silver	200 pts.	3
Silver coins	20 pts.	3
Soybeans	10 cents	3
Soybean meal	500 pts.	3
Soybean oil	20 pts.	3
Sugar no. 11	10 pts.	3
Wheat	2 cents	3

To answer the first question seemed simple enough empirically. How could a set of box size and reversal parameters selected in the early 1960s and chosen without any significant research for use in the traditional method continue to be the best set today? And along the same line—isn't it ridiculous to believe that the same box sizes which might work well for cotton would work equally well for broilers, cocoa, coffee, copper, eggs, and lumber? The answers seemed obvious but we tested anyway. The testing program involved an examination of the profitability and reliability (percentage of profitable trades to total trades) of hundreds of combinations of box sizes and reversal distances for each commodity in order to select the optimal combination, meaning that combination of variables with the highest profit and reliability, with a weighting bias toward reliability.

Once the optimal combination was selected, the profitability and reliability of these optimal variables were compared with the variables used in the traditional approach. Table 9–5 shows the results.

TABLE 9–5
PROFITABILITY OF THE OPTIMIZED METHOD OF POINT-AND-FIGURE CHARTING FOR 135 TRADING DAYS ENDING JUNE 28, 1974

Commodity	Delivery month	Total cumulative net profit (after commissions)	Total percentage return for period	Percent reliability
Broilers	November 1974	$ −700.90	−100%	0%
Copper	September 1974	9,244.70	154	100
Cattle	October 1974	1,246.02	138	56
Cocoa	September 1974	15,948.00	399	100
Coffee "C"	September 1974	3,928.25	131	100
Corn	September 1974	6,440.00	515	80
Cotton	December 1974	5,974.99	92	80
Eggs	November 1974	1,206.99	134	63
Hogs	October 1974	−1,744.26	−145	38
Lumber	September 1974	3,440.00	382	50
Oats	September 1974	2,375.00	317	70
Orange juice	October 1974	510.75	57	100
Platinum	October 1974	4,026.00	201	75
Plywood	September 1974	864.12	96	50
Pork bellies	August 1974	11,491.49	1,149	83
Potatoes (Maine)	May 1975	940.50	118	100
Silver (N.Y.)	September 1974	27,164.75	320	63
Silver coins	October 1974	−10,670.76	−534	33
Soybeans	August 1974	1,334.00	59	33
Soybean meal	October 1974	4,162.04	416	100
Soybean oil	October 1974	1,330.05	74	100
Sugar (world)	October 1974	8,318.25	416	56
Wheat	September 1974	5,877.49	261	60
Totals		$102,707.19	199%	
Average				66%

For the 135 trading days ending June 28, 1974, the traditional approach usually called the "three-box-reversal method of point-and-figure charting" generated a profit of $51,490.82, representing a 100 percent return on margin; 41 percent of all trades were profitable, and 13 of the 23 commodities were profitable. Using the optimal box size and reversal value for each commodity, we found that the 23 commodities generated a profit of $102,707.19, representing a 199 percent return; 66 percent of the total trades were profitable, and 20 of the 23 commodities showed cumulative profits.

Based upon the results of the studies cited here plus the dozens of others covering different periods of 1974 (all of which showed a similar superiority of the optimized approach over the traditional approach) Zieg and Kaufman were able to conclude that no one set of variables in a trading system will or can be the optimal values for every commodity. An optimized system requires that optimal values be selected for each commodity and these values must be periodically reevaluated. The system of value selection requires the testing of hundreds and sometimes thousands of different values for each delivery month of each commodity, until the best set of variables is found, with the optimal set being the one which combines the greatest profitability and reliability.

It is a time-consuming and expensive process, but the results justify the means. Through the process of optimizing the standard point-and-figure method, the dollar returns for 135 trading days were increased from $51,490.82 to $102,707.19 and the percentage return from 100 percent to 199 percent. The number of profitable trading commodities increased from 13 to 20, and the reliability was increased from 41 percent to 66 percent of profitable trades to total trades.

And as exciting as these results are, one problem still existed. In selecting the optimal values Zieg and Kaufman examined every reasonable combination of box sizes and reversal values for 135 trading days, found the best and then said, "Look how much better the optimized variables performed as compared with the traditional ones." And this was a perfectly reasonable way to approach the problem for it was the intention of this research to determine whether a different set of variables might have performed better.

As already discussed, there are more effective combinations of variables than the traditional ones, and thus it became necessary for Zieg and Kaufman to construct a testing routine more similar to the results traders might actually receive. In the first study the traditional method results accurately portrayed the after commission profits accruing to traders using it because they knew the rules of play in advance or at the start of the 135-day test period. The only deviation from the study results and the real-world returns would be the losses due to skids. A skid is defined as the difference between where you want to execute a trade and the price actually received. Thus if a buy signal would be given at 55.20 on July copper as the market traded at 54.50 and the order was in to buy July copper at 55.20 stop, but the execution was at 55.40, the skid is 20 points—the difference between the signal price and the actual execution. And there are skids because in trading on stops you buy on strength and sell into weakness. Locked limit moves preventing reasonable executions also fall into the category of skids.

Thus, except for not accounting for unpredictable skid costs, the traditional returns were realistic but the optimized were not. The latter could not have been realized by a trader because the variables or rules of the optimized game were known only after the 135-day test period. To overcome this problem the next study involved choosing the rules for the future markets in advance by analyzing prior data. Thus at the end of each quarter new variables were chosen based upon the examination of the trading characteristics of the past 12 months of price history. Once selected, these variables were announced in "Commodities Point-and-Figure Charts," a weekly publication of Economic Research, Inc., and thus locked into the system for the following quarter. Table 9–6 displays the results of this study of the optimized system applied to real-time markets for an entire year. In this study, three of the four quarters were profitable overall. The net return of trading on the delivery month of 24 commodities (gold was added) and the contract months traded where the high volume months were closest to, but not in delivery, was $43,065—this represented a 163 percent return on investment based upon July 1, 1975 margins. Fully 18 of the 24 commodities proved profitable, and 170 or 43.8 percent of the 388 total trades were profitable. The average net profit per trade was $108.42.

These results can be compared with those found in Table 9–7, a display of the results of optimizing the variables over a 12-month period and then calculating the results over the same period as tested using only one delivery month. Notice that the results are improved substantially, with 22 of the 24 commodities being profitable, 52 percent of all trades being profitable, the average return being $393.28, and the total return being $118,771.20 or 462.1 percent on margin.

WHAT DOES IT MEAN?

The substantial difference between the optimized results tested over the same time period as used to optimize the system and the much lower but still substantial returns generated when trading on

TABLE 9–6

POINT-AND-FIGURE SYSTEM PERFORMANCE—SELECTING BOX SIZES AND REVERSAL VALUES AND TESTING RESULTS THE FOLLOWING QUARTER (assumed roll-forward always trading main near month contract not in delivery 12 months ending September 30, 1975)

	4th qtr. 1974		1st qtr. 1975		2d qtr. 1975		3d qtr. 1975		Total		
	Profit	Trades*	Profit	Trades*	Profit	Trades*	Profit	Trades*	Profit	Trades*	Reliability
Broilers	$ −562	1/4	$ 603	1/1	$ −1,299	1/2	$ −1,201	3/11	$ −2,459	6/18	33%
Cattle	−562	1/3	1,976	2/2	532	2/3	−143	4/6	1,803	9/14	64
Cocoa	2,925	1/2	−1,858	2/3	2,793	2/2	−647	2/4	3,213	7/11	63
Coffee	—	—	−1,848	3/8	1,443	2/5	6,580	2/7	6,175	7/20	35
Copper	1,489	1/1	−1,671	0/1	1,654	1/1	−585	2/4	887	4/7	57
Corn	−128	2/3	2,234	1/2	−1,504	0/2	691	1/3	1,293	4/10	40
Cotton	3,595	3/4	−587	3/7	1,877	3/3	−1,397	3/7	3,488	12/20	60
Eggs	722	2/5	2,948	1/1	−595	0/1	−2,682	0/6	393	3/13	23
Gold					495	1/6	900	3/8	1,395	4/14	28
Hogs	−1,629	1/6	−3,108	0/3	3,116	1/1	3,688	3/5	5,067	5/14	35
Lumber	−600	3/6	−264	2/6	1,944	3/4	1,200	2/5	2,280	10/21	47
Oats	950	1/1	1,101	2/2	−308	2/6	1,847	3/5	3,590	8/14	57
Orange juice	60	1/1	470	1/2	88	1/2	130	2/4	748	5/9	55
Platinum	−1,390	3/8	770	1/1	−485	3/7	55	3/7	−1,050	10/23	43
Plywood	−123	0/1	1,255	1/1	−554	0/1	259	2/3	837	3/6	50
Pork bellies	5,076	3/4	−4,120	1/6	1,621	3/5	9,480	3/3	12,059	10/18	55
Potatoes			364	1/1			−636	1/7	−272	2/8	25
Silver CBT	7,340	4/6	−1,400	5/13	−2,061	5/12	−1,528	3/13	2,351	17/44	38
Silver coins	−3,860	1/2	−460	4/9	−2,210	2/9	1,860	6/11	−4,670	13/31	41
Soybeans	−275	2/5	6,262	1/2	−5,572	2/5	826	4/7	1,241	9/19	47
Soy meal	695	2/3	2,637	1/2	−1,013	0/2	−3,307	0/4	−988	3/11	27
Soy oil	−5,954	0/4	−1,080	2/5	−1,814	2/5	1,658	5/11	−7,190	9/21	42
Sugar 11	24,902	3/3	−14,074	2/6	7,794	1/1	−9,176	1/5	9,446	7/14	50
Wheat	−1,950	0/2	2,581	1/1	−706	1/2	2,503	1/3	2,428	3/8	37
	30,751		−8,260		5,236		10,375		42,065	170/388	43.8

Note: Average profit per trade = $108.48; total profit based on July 1 margins ($25,700) is 163 percent.
* Profitable trades/total trades.

a time unit not used for optimizations indicates that as we get further away from the time period used to optimize the variables, the effectiveness of the values diminish—a totally understandable occurrence, but one not fully understood or discussed by most researchers or system promoters. Any system will achieve remarkable results when tested over the same period used to select the variables, but the true test of a system is its ability to cope with the real world, or data entirely different from that used in the system design. And although the results are reduced substantially in a forward-looking test, a return of 163 percent over a 12-month period coupled with the simplicity of the system makes point-and-figure charting a truly remarkable technical approach to market analysis and trading.

And while it must be remembered that the effectiveness of a system's variables diminishes with time, the variables used to generate Table 9–7 are displayed in Table 9–8.

TABLE 9–7
PROFITABILITY OF THE OPTIMIZED METHOD OF POINT-AND-FIGURE CHARTING FOR 12 MONTHS ENDING OCTOBER 9, 1975 COVERING SAME PERIOD AS OPTIMIZED

Commodity	Delivery month	Profitable trades per total trades	Reli- ability	Cumulative dollar profit net of commissions	Return on minimum exchange margin
Broilers	November 1975	5/11	45%	$ 470.09	62.7%
Cattle	December 1975	13/22	59	4,103.99	342.0
Cocoa	December 1975	5/7	71	1,473.00	98.2
Coffee "C"	December 1975	10/19	53	14,934.97	995.7
Copper	December 1975	12/26	46	4,140.97	552.1
Corn	December 1975	3/4	75	6,166.49	616.6
Cotton	December 1975	3/5	60	1,277.52	127.8
Eggs	December 1975	2/5	40	−4.00	−0.4
Gold—N.Y.	December 1975	4/11	36	4,159.99	277.3
Hogs	December 1975	5/6	55	6,947.98	772.0
Lumber	November 1975	2/9	22	−1,616.00	−230.9
Oats	December 1975	8/19	42	943.00	125.7
Orange juice	January 1976	5/12	42	667.51	148.3
Platinum	January 1976	3/5	60	1,845.00	184.5
Plywood	November 1975	5/7	71	1,029.78	147.1
Pork bellies	February 1976	5/11	45	7,906.40	790.6
Potatoes—					
Maine	November 1975	5/8	62	1,147.00	191.2
Silver—CBT	December 1975	16/33	48	7,698.47	641.5
Silver coins	January 1976	10/19	63	6,150.00	410.0
Soybeans	November 1975	5/7	71	9,913.48	566.5
Soybean meal	December 1975	5/9	56	669.50	67.0
Soybean oil	December 1975	6/9	67	841.49	84.1
Sugar	March 1976	11/22	50	25,977.59	1,298.9
Wheat	December 1975	9/16	56	11,926.98	954.2
		157/302	52%	$118,771.20	462.1%

Note: The average trade was $393.28.

184

TABLE 9–8
PARAMETERS FOR THE OPTIMIZED
METHOD OF POINT-AND-FIGURE
CHARTING OPTIMIZED OCTOBER 1975

Commodity	Box size	Reversal size
Broilers	17 pts.	2 boxes
Cattle	10 pts.	1
Cocoa	45 pts.	8
Coffee	3 pts.	5
Copper	20 pts.	1
Corn	2½ cents	6
Cotton	16 pts.	11
Eggs	24 pts.	7
Gold—N.Y.	60 pts.	3
Hogs	21 pts.	8
Lumber	60 pts.	8
Oats	90 pts.	3
Orange juice	10 pts.	9
Platinum	105 pts.	9
Plywood	45 pts.	10
Pork bellies	14 pts.	14
Potatoes	5 pts.	4
Silver	350 pts.	1
Silver coins	9 pts.	7
Soybeans	4 cents	8
Soybean meal	200 pts.	2
Soybean oil	15 pts.	8
Sugar no. 11	24 pts.	2
Wheat	5 cents	1

SUMMARY

The Davis, Davis-Thiel, and Zieg-Kaufman studies all show that point-and-figure charting is profitable and reliable. Its returns and accuracy of market predictions can be improved by adjusting the variables to fit the changing characteristics of the markets, but regardless of whether the optimized or traditional approach is taken, the system works. And this profitability coupled with its simplicity, ease of maintenance, and the satisfaction of personal involvement make it an outstanding approach to market analysis.

Or we could summarize the system differently by saying that it is a valuable trading tool. It yields specific prices at which to go long or short, and it displays the location of stop-loss points. It provides order, meaning, rationality, and consistency. It forces discipline in the trading world where this most important ingredient is so often lacking. But best of all, it works.

True, there are whipsaws and false signals. The system is not perfect. But, as a rule, it cuts losses short, lets profits run, and is right a high percentage of the time. It is also always "in" on the major moves. These are the components of a good trading system, and point-and-figure charting does it in an easy-to-understand format.

The system can be coupled with fundamentals to comprise a valuable trading team. The fundamental data will indicate the commodity futures or option contracts to trade and the long-term trends. The chart will provide the timing of the trades. Or the point-and-figure system can be used alone if one subscribes to the philosophy that all fundamentally caused movements will ultimately be reflected on the chart so why bother with fundamentals. But regardless of which method is used, numerous research studies have shown that the system will work.

Chapter 10

Decision theory and theoretical valuation of option premiums

This chapter introduces several mathematical concepts that can assist speculative and commercial traders in estimating market risks and profitability associated with trading decisions. Later in the chapter, a theoretical model is presented and explained that computes expected values for option premiums. The trader can then compare the expected value of an option to the current market price to determine if an option premium is under-, over-, or fairly valued. We will begin with a discussion of how decision theory can be utilized in evaluating market risks associated with *what* and *when* to buy or sell.

DECISION THEORY AND RISK

Variability and volatility are words that are often used interchangeably when a trader refers to fluctuations in commodity prices. They are simply a measure of the degree to which commodity prices have advanced or declined over specific time intervals in the past. A highly volatile commodity is one that has taken sharp advances or declines in previous time periods. Commodities that have a particular variability tend to maintain a similar level of variability in the future. This assumption is basic in enabling us to predict the probable future price of a commodity.

Probability and statistics can be used to arrive at valuations for commodity options—the determination of which options to buy or sell, and when to buy or sell them. The evaluation of risk is also an important consideration in making buy or sell decisions. While the discussion in this chapter generally will be nontechnical, a few concepts will be explained and some notation that is used throughout the chapter will be defined to guide the reader to an understanding of how mathematical models are developed and utilized in making trading decisions.

WHAT IS A MODEL?

A model is an artificial way of representing events in the real world. A mathematical model assigns and constructs quantitative relationships to the phenomenon being studied in order to explain and predict events in real life. The Black and Scholes model, presented later in the chapter, is used to explain theoretical valuations of options and can be used to derive an expected value for commodity options given certain parameters.

PROBABILITY MODELS

In describing the results of a particular course of action it could be stated that: "If A occurs, then B will occur." This would be a model

188

of certainty. If what will happen is not known, or there are a number of possible results, then the model is uncertain. If there are a number of possible results, and the likelihood of each result is known, then the model is probabilistic.

Commodity futures and options price fluctuations can be reduced to a probabilistic model. Probability is used as the best estimate of what could happen in the future if past price fluctuations are maintained. A model based on probabilities assumes that commodity prices are random variables and, therefore, disregards the fundamental approach to analyzing price fluctuations. With statistical analysis, the degree to which a commodity is expected to fluctuate can be calculated. However, probability theory cannot be used to tell what direction a commodity will move; it can only indicate the probabilities associated with how high or low a commodity price will go. Other mathematical techniques are available to analyze price trends and forecast the direction of commodity prices.

The requirements for a complete probabilistic model are:
1. All possible results are listed as outcomes O_n
2. The probability of each result is known or can be estimated. The probabilities are stated as decimal fractions between the interval 0 and 1.00, where 0 means that the result is impossible and 1.00 means it is certain. $P(O_i) =$ the probability of outcome i.
3. The sum of the probabilities of all events must be 1.00. $P(O_1) + P(O_2) + P(O_3) + \ldots + P(O_n) = 1.00$.

The probability distribution of all possible outcomes of an event is the listing of all possible results that can occur and their expected frequencies, expressed in the period of time they will occur.

All commodity trading programs are basically models under uncertainty. If the possible outcomes and the probability of each outcome are known, then they are probabilistic models. Probabilistic models are the best that can be hoped for in making commodity trading decisions. Decision making of when to buy or sell becomes an endeavor to determine what the probabilities (odds) are, and how they favor the trader.

THE NORMAL PROBABILITY DISTRIBUTION

The normal probability distribution can be represented by a bell-shaped curve. The bell-shaped curve, Figure 10–1, is used to describe many random statistical phenomena. Commodity prices are random phenomena that can be described by the normal distribution (bell-shaped curve). In a random market, a commodity which closed at 100 has a 50–50 chance of advancing or declining from its closing price of 100. The probability that a commodity will close above a

FIGURE 10–1
THE BELL-SHAPED CURVE (normal probability distribution)

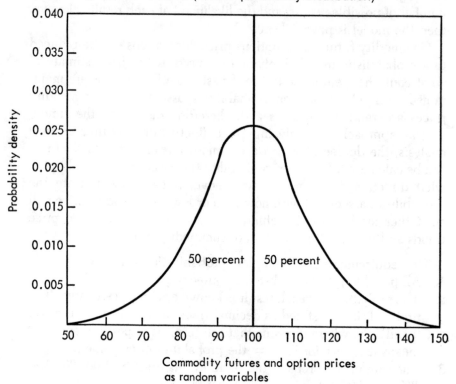

Commodity futures and option prices
as random variables

certain price at the end of the specified period is proportional to the area under the curve beyond that price. Figure 10–2 shows the probability that commodity will end at a particular price, having started at 100. The shaded area, representing 15 percent of the total area under the curve, is beyond the price of 115. Thus, there is a 15-percent chance that the commodity will close above 115. The probability that it will close below 115 is 85 percent.

Figure 10–3 gives the probability that a commodity will close above a particular price. It measures the area under the curve of Figure 10–2 beyond the particular price listed on the horizontal axis. It gives the probability that a commodity will end up beyond that price. For example, there is a 85-percent chance that it will end up less than 115, and a 15-percent chance that it will end up greater than 115.

The variability of a commodity is a measure of the range within which its price will close at the end of a specific period of time. Variability is a measure of the breadth of the curves. It decreases with decreasing time left until expiration. Chances are less that a

190

FIGURE 10–2
PROBABILITY OF A COMMODITY FUTURES ENDING AT A
PARTICULAR PRICE, STARTING FROM A 100

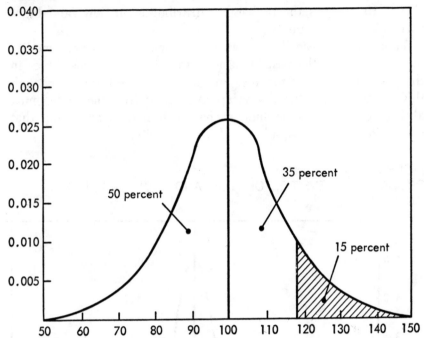

FIGURE 10–3
PROBABILITY THAT A COMMODITY WILL CLOSE ABOVE A
PARTICULAR PRICE

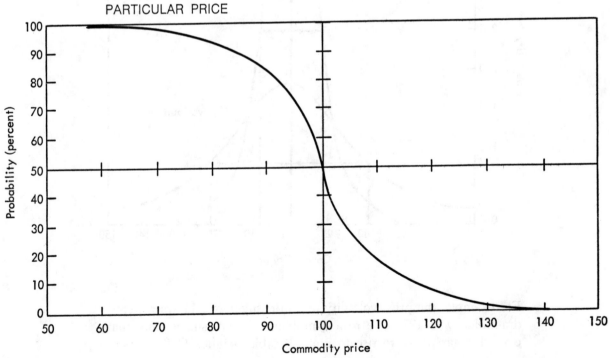

commodity will advance beyond a certain price if it is given less time to do so. Call options with less time left until expiration cost less because the underlying commodity has less time to advance in price. Figure 10–4 shows the probability distributions of low- and high-variability commodities.

Variability is basically a measure of how a particular commodity has fluctuated in the past. A basic assumption is that the forces in the past will continue to cause fluctuations in the future. Although this assumption is generally accepted as being true, the trader must always be aware of fundamental changes in market conditions that could alter the past variability of a commodity.

FIGURE 10–4
PROBABILITY DENSITIES OF HIGH AND LOW VOLATILITY
COMMODITIES

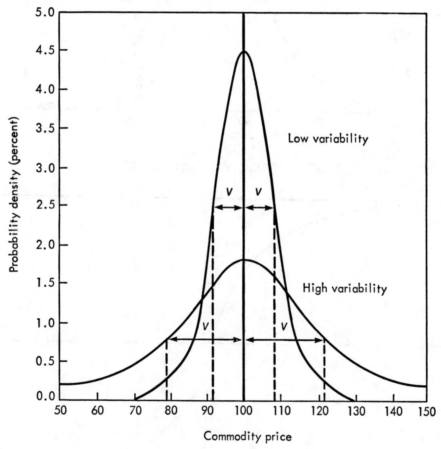

For example, the price volatility of world sugar No. 11 was altered dramatically in 1974 due to a combination of unusual events that caused sugar prices to rise to unpredictable heights. Coffee prices experienced significant changes in volatility early in 1974. The lesson to be learned from these examples is that future events do not have to repeat past events. However, an analysis of historical price variability patterns can provide useful guidelines for formulating a trading strategy, but traders should always be on the lookout for unusual circumstances that can alter these patterns. Failure to become alert to special circumstances or profound changes in the fundamentals of a commodity market can be extremely costly to both speculators and hedgers. Mathematical models are useful only as a quantitative guide to decision making. They cannot predict the impact of "acts of God," unusual weather conditions, or an unstable political environment on market behavior!

EXPECTED VALUE (EV)

With the description of a probabilistic model out of the way, consideration can be given to decision making under probabilistic conditions. Given knowledge of outcomes and a basis for a decision it is relatively easy to make decisions under certainty. For example, given two commodities to choose from and certain outcomes, it is easy to

Action	Outcome
Buy July Copper 70 Call	$ 800 profit
Buy July Silver 450 Call	$1,500 profit

make a choice if profit is the criteria (see accompanying tables). Expanding the notation of probabilistic outcomes to another similar problem such as "Buy July Silver 450 Calls" and "Buy July Copper 70 Calls" (see accompanying tables).

BUY JULY SILVER 450 CALLS

Outcome (O)	Probability $P_{(o)}$	$P_{(o)} \times (O)$
$3,000	0.20	$600
100	0.50	50
(2,000)	0.30	(600)
Total	1.00	
Expected profit		$50

BUY JULY COPPER 70 CALLS

Outcomes (O)	Probability $P_{(o)}$	$P_{(o)} \times (O)$
$2,000	0.30	$600
1,000	0.40	400
(1,000)	0.30	(300)
Total	1.00	
Expected profit		$700

Based upon the computed expected profits for buying July copper 70 versus buying July silver 450 calls, the purchase of the July copper calls yields the higher expected return—$700 versus $50. If all trading decisions were this simple, everyone who understood and traded commodities markets would be a millionaire. Obviously, this is not the case, because the variable of risk enters the picture to confound our judgment and embarrass our trading decisions.

RISK

Risk is the probability of incurring a loss from market action. Trading decisions are never free from at least one outcome that represents a loss. To examine the nature of risk, the probability distribution of three trading opportunities will be studied (see accompanying table). Outcomes are expressed in dollar gain or (loss) on investment. It should be noted that few traders would accept the chance of a loss (risk) without reason. Greater risks are usually accompanied by an opportunity for greater gains.

Action	Outcomes (O)	Probability $P_{(o)}$
Buy July copper 70 call	$1,000	0.30
	2,000	0.40
	(800)	0.30
		1.00
Buy July silver 450 call	$3,000	0.20
	100	0.50
	(2,000)	0.30
		1.00

It is somewhat more difficult to see which decision is best. Actually the method of choosing between buying copper 70 or silver 450 calls depends upon two factors—the average return on investment and the trader's attitude toward risk. The average return or expected profit will be considered first, and risk will be discussed in the next section.

The expected value of the two alternatives is the average expected profit if the decision were made a large number of times. It is calculated by multiplying each outcome (O) by its probability of occurring $P_{(o)}$ and summing the results. In the case of July copper 70 calls versus July silver 450 calls, the results are shown in the accompanying table.

Examining these alternatives we see that decision A involves more risk than decisions B or C, but the potential profitability is also substantially higher (100 percent). It is safe to assume that if potential losses are equal, the choice with the lowest probability of loss in-

194

	Action	Outcome (O)	Probability $P_{(0)}$	$P_{(0)} \times (O)$
A.	Buy July 100 cocoa calls	$10,000	0.30	$3,000
		0	0.40	0
		(10,000)	0.30	(3,000)
	Total		1.00	
	Expected profit			$0
B.	Buy July 450 silver calls	$5,000	0.30	$1,500
		0	0.40	0
		(5,000)	0.30	(1,500)
	Total		1.00	
	Expected profit			$0
C.	Buy July 70 copper calls	$10,000	0.15	$1,500
		0	0.70	0
		(10,000)	0.15	(1,500)
	Total		1.00	
	Expected profit			$0

volves less risk. It can also be assumed that if the probabilities of loss for each alternative is equal, the alternative with the lowest dollar loss has less risk. Therefore, it is not possible to compare the risk of buying July silver 450 calls with July 70 copper calls because the probable dollar loss is equal. The question becomes: "Is a 15-percent chance of losing $10,000 more or less risky than a 30-percent chance of losing $5,000?" The answer depends on the attitude of trader toward risk-taking.

The solution to the last problem is a matter of traders' psychology and the decision maker's utility for money. People are risk preferers, risk neutral, or risk avoiders. If individuals are asked what they would pay for a 50–50 chance of winning a $1,000, the risk neutral person would pay $500 (the Expected Value), the risk avoider would only be willing to pay less than $500, and the risk preferer will pay more than $500. The analysis of risk cannot be discussed further. Suffice it to say, that the assumption of risk in making decisions within certain parameters is possible *only after a trader knows what risk orientation he or she has—risk preferer, risk neutral, or risk avoider.* Self-awareness of risk orientation will come only after an individual has had trading experience with an opportunity to receive feedback regarding his or her attitudes toward the markets and performance in making profitable decisions.

DIVERSIFICATION AND RISK REDUCTION

While traders may react toward risk differently, diversification of market positions can reduce risk because the probabilities for taking large losses are reduced by being spread over a greater number of positions instead of being concentrated into a few. Speculators should diversify their positions in the commodities markets in order to improve risk management and thus preserve trading capital for future profit-making opportunities. The evaluation of risk is subjective. However, if traders know their own attitudes toward taking risks, they can construct a portfolio of commodity positions according to their personal preference—low-risk, medium-risk, or high-risk portfolios. The number of commodities traded in the portfolio and the volatility of each commodity influence the degree of risk exposure. Portfolios trading a large number of commodities will generally exhibit less risk than portfolios trading a small number. A portfolio composed of commodities with low volatility will usually have less risk than a portfolio with highly volatile commodities.

COMPONENT VARIABLES FOR A THEORETICAL OPTIONS PRICING MODEL

Now that readers have labored through a brief discussion of probability and statistics, decision theory, and risk management, we are ready to develop a theoretical model for valuing option prices. Developing a valid procedure for valuing option premiums lies at the heart of a profitable speculative or commercial trading program. Naturally, option buyers want option prices to be undervalued in relationship to their expected return on investment (EROI). Option writers (sellers) want option prices to be overvalued in relation to their risks of holding the underlying commodity futures.

Option premiums are a function of (1) volatility of the underlying commodity, (2) time to expiration of the option contract, (3) strike price of the option, (4) prevailing interest on a riskless investment (such as 90-day U.S. treasury bills), and (5) the current commodity futures price.

Option premiums will also vary among the different contract series. Some contract series are in greater demand than others. For example, a July 80 copper 70 call might command a greater premium compared to a December 80 copper 70 call because option buyers tend to exert a greater demand for the near-month maturity contract dates relative to more distant months, thus causing a relatively higher premium for the near-month maturity contracts.

1. Volatility of the commodity price

Volatility is the degree of price change over time. A commodity that fluctuated 30 percent over a 90-day period is ten times more volatile than one that fluctuates 3 percent during the same period. A simple arithmetic expression can be used to give a crude estimate of volatility over a fixed period of time:

$$\frac{(\text{Highest price} - \text{Lowest price})}{\left(\dfrac{\text{Highest price} + \text{Lowest price}}{2}\right)} = \text{Volatility} = v_i = \frac{75.00 - 65.00}{70.00} = 0.14$$

For example, if July copper futures prices ranged from a high of 75.00 cents to a low of 65.00 cents during a 12-month period, an estimate of its annual volatility would be 0.14. A more accurate estimate of volatility can be computed by taking successively shorter intervals of volatility estimates, summing them, and then dividing by the total number of intervals:

$$\text{Volatility} = \frac{\sum_{1}^{n}(v_1 + v_2 + v_3 \ldots v_n)}{n}$$

where n = number of intervals.

Once traders have a calculated volatility index, they can rank and compare different commodities from lowest to highest volatility. The more volatile commodities command higher option premiums because they stimulate greater speculative buying. Less volatile commodities usually attract the more conservative option writers (sellers) because they want to reduce risks associated with holding an underlying futures contract. Less volatile commodities usually command smaller premiums because speculators are less interested in buying them.

2. Time to expiration of the option

"Time to expiration" is defined as the remaining time left (usually specified in days or weeks) between the purchase or writing of an option and its expiration date. An unsold or unexercised option expires worthless on its expiration date. Therefore, option buyers must take action prior to the expiration date if they are to redeem any value left in the option. The value of an option premium is related to its time value.

The value of a simple option is proportional to the square root of time. That is, a four-month option costs twice as much as a one-month option (the square root of four is two). In other words, the more time remaining in an option prior to expiration, the greater will be its premium. Naturally, a 90-day July 80 silver 490 call offers a greater premium than a 30-day July 80 silver 490 call. The relative value of an option premium drops at an accelerated rate as an option approaches its expiration date. Most speculators are not interested in buying options with only 10 or 20 days left to expiration. They would rather buy an option with greater time value.

3. Strike price of the option

The strike price designates the specific price at which an option writer incurs an obligation to an option holder. A call writer has a potential obligation to sell a futures contract, and a put writer has an obligation to buy a futures contract. The strike price of an option allows us to distinguish between *out-of-the-money* options versus *in-the-money* options. Also we can use the strike price to calculate the *intrinsic value* and *true premium* of an option.

Out-of-the-money call options are defined as those option series with a strike price above that of the current market value of the commodity. Out-of-the-money put options are those series with a strike price below that of the current market price. For example, if the current market price of silver is 447.00, then all contract series with a strike price of 450 or higher would be out-of-the-money call options. All contract series with a strike price of 440 or lower would be out-of-the-money put options. The *intrinsic value* of an option is defined as the difference in dollar amount between market price of the commodity and the strike price of the contract series. For example, if a July 80 silver futures contract was trading at 478.00, and a July 80 silver call with a strike price of 470 had a premium of $1,000 (or 20.00 cents per troy oz.), then the intrinsic value of an in-the-money call option would be as follows:

Current market price — Call option strike price = 478.00 — 470.00 =
8.00 cents per oz. = Intrinsic value

Call option premium = 20.00 — 8.00 =
12.00 cents true option premium

The intrinsic values and premiums for in-the-money puts are calculated as follows:

Put option strike price — Current market price = 490.00 — 478.00 =
12.00 cents per oz. = Intrinsic value

Put option premium = 20.00 — 12.00 =
8.00 cents true put option premium

In-the-money call options are defined as those contract series in which the current market value of the commodity is above the strike price. In-the-money puts have a strike price above the current market price of the commodity. In-the-money puts and calls have intrinsic value due to the favorable market price of the underlying futures contract. Out-of-the-money options have no intrinsic value, only true premium, since it would be unfavorable for option holders to exercise their options and sell futures contracts at a profit. In-the-money options can be exercised and sold at a favorable profit by the option holder.

198

Option buyers usually prefer to purchase out-of-the-money puts or calls because less money is required, whereas some option writers may prefer to sell in-the-money options against futures contracts to reduce risks associated with holding a futures position. The premium paid to the writer can also be applied toward margin requirements for the underlying futures contract.

4. Short-term interest rates

The prevailing interest rate affects the rate of return on any investment because interest rates are a measure of the cost of money. High interest rates indicate a shortage of money in circulation, whereas low interest rates indicate a relative over-supply of money.

If all other variables in an option valuation formula except the short-term interest rate are held constant, an increase in the interest rate always increases the value of an option. To get an idea of why this is so, an increase in the interest rate reduces the present value of the exercise price of the option. Since the exercise price is a potential liability for the option writer, this increases the value of the option. An increase in the interest rate will have a greater effect on an option with a longer maturity than on an option with a shorter maturity. Thus, a change in interest rates will alter the relative values of near- and distant-month options. An increase in the interest rate has the same effect as a reduction in the exercise price of an option. A 1-percent decline in the price of a 90-day treasury bill maturing at the same time as the option has the same effect as a 1-percent reduction in the exercise price. A change in the interest rate will not occur in isolation. During the same period there may be a change in the commodity price as well as a change in the volatility of the commodity. The change in option price will reflect the interaction of all these variables.

5. Current market price of the commodity futures

Commodity prices generally fluctuate over a wide range during a year in response to seasonal changes in supply and demand for the commodity. The adage often quoted in commodity trading "to buy cheap and sell dear" still holds true. The problem is "How cheap is cheap and how dear is dear?" If one looks at a particular commodity's annual price pattern on a bar chart, one will obtain an immediate awareness of which prices are in the low range and which ones are in the high range for the year. (Refer to Chart 46 on October New York sugar.) As the reader can see, prices between October 1976 through March 1977 are relatively low compared to prices between May 1976 through August 1976. If October sugar is

CHART 46
BAR GRAPH OF N.Y. WORLD SUGAR NO. 11 OCTOBER FUTURES PRICES

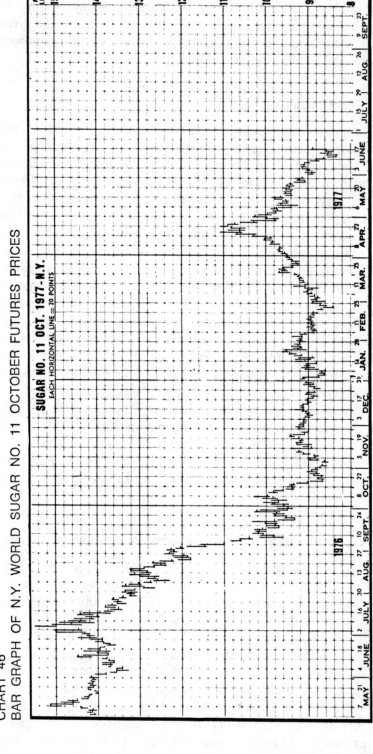

SUGAR NO. 11 OCT. 1977-N.Y.
EACH HORIZONTAL LINE = 20 POINTS

truly in a trading range between 8.50 and 10.00 cents, then the logical thing to do would be to buy call options on sugar when it is trading around 8.5 cents and to buy put options when it is trading around 10.00 cents. An examination of a price chart can stimulate option buying with regard to the current market price of the commodity compared to where it has been during the year.

THE BLACK AND SCHOLES MODEL FOR VALUATION OF OPTION PREMIUMS

The component variables that make up the "value" of a put or call option can be integrated into a mathematical formula to derive expected values for put and call premiums. The Black and Scholes option pricing model was first published in 1970, then revised in 1972. Fischer Black and Myron Scholes, both professors at Massachusetts Institute of Technology, derived the mathematical option pricing model primarily for providing theoretical comparisons for Over-the-Counter and listed securities options traded on the stock options exchange.

The Black and Scholes option pricing model has been used by securities investors to determine when any given stock option is overpriced or underpriced in relation to its expected value. The variables of time, strike price, current stock price, interest rate, and volatility can be fed into a computer to give a prospective option buyer or option writer an expected value that can be compared to the current market price. Once comparisons have been made, a determination can be made as to which options are the best buys and which ones are the best writes. This simply means to write (sell) those options that the Black and Scholes model says are overvalued, and buy those options that the model says are undervalued.

The utility of the Black and Scholes model is that speculators and hedgers have available another tool for analysis of option pricing. Techniques of fundamental and technical analysis, applications of decision theory, and the Black and Scholes valuation formula can be utilized to enhance the profitability of a commodity options trading program to a considerable extent.

For example, when the model shows that the July copper 70 call is undervalued because its expected value is $1,000, even though the market price is still at $800, the trader can assume that "in all probability" the actual call price will move toward its theoretical value. Of course, the price of copper could decline, but the model says that $1,000 is a fair value for the option. Therefore, if traders buy the July copper 70 calls at $800 (which the model says should be offered for $1,000), they have bought a copper call at a 20-percent discount from its theoretically valued price. Investors can utilize other analytic tools, such as technical and fundamental analysis of the underlying commodity, to prove or disprove what the Black and Scholes formula says the expected value of the call premium should be. Refer to Chapter 8 on fundamental and technical analysis for a more complete discussion of how the various analytical tools can be utilized in making trading decisions. No matter what the model says, if other information gleened from fundamental and technical analysis does not confirm that a particular "undervalued option" (according to the model) is the one to buy, then it would be better to look for more attractive situations in which other tools of price analysis confirm the expected option value.

The main feature of the Black and Scholes model is that it attempts to create a rigorous guide to what the expected value of a commodity option should be compared to what the current price is. The Black and Scholes model integrates five variables into a mathematical formula: (1) the price of the underlying commodity futures, (2) time value until expiration of the option, (3) the short-term interest rate on a riskless investment, (4) volatility of the underlying commodity futures price, and (5) the exercise price of the option. Thus, on an option with a fixed exercise price, an increase in one of the other variables will increase the value of the option.

Another feature of the Black and Scholes model is the *hedge ratio*. This ratio recognizes the fact that a 100-point move in the underlying commodity futures price might not be matched by a 100-point move in the options price. A hedge ratio of 0.50 means that two options will make 100 points if the underlying commodity futures price moves up 100 points. On an option with a fixed exercise price, the hedge ratio increases with time to expiration and as the futures price increases. The hedge ratio can be used to maximize ratio writing returns. Ratio writing refers to writing (selling) two or more puts or calls options per futures contract held long or short. Ratio writing is *extremely risky* because a large move in a short period of time in the futures price can alter the hedge ratio significantly. Therefore, ratio writing should only be done by well-financed, sophisticated speculators. Commercial traders who want to earn additional revenues from current inventories could also look at ratio writing as a viable hedging strategy.

The next chapter describes more fully the commercial applications of options as a hedging vehicle for producers, processors, and distributors. The Black and Scholes formula is just one of many useful tools of analysis in making a decision whether to buy or sell options. Whether the trader be a speculator or hedger, it is nevertheless important to develop procedures for evaluating the expected value of an option contract before buying or writing it.

202

Chapter 11

Commercial applications of commodity options

Commercial traders (hedgers) can reduce business risks and receive additional returns on inventory investment through the use of trading futures and options. This chapter will discuss the principal trading strategies which can be employed by commercial traders. It will introduce several new concepts applicable to commercial traders to assist them in making marketing decisions for their products.

When we speak of commercial traders, we are referring to those commodity dealers—processors, consumers, distributors—that can utilize the futures (closely related to the deliverable) grade of commodity traded on futures exchanges. For example, sugar growers, refiners, and soft drink manufacturers can utilize the New York sugar commodity futures and option contracts to their advantage by adopting trading strategies based on their hedging needs and marketing objectives.

In businesses where commodity trading is an important activity, executives are faced with decisions regarding who should assume the responsibility for commodity transactions and where to assign it within the hierarchy of the organizational structure. As financial officers of companies engaged in commodity transactions have experienced, poor supervision and management of this responsibility can have disastrous consequences to a firm's assets. However, properly supervised commodity trading can give a firm a competitive edge over other companies whose management has not been educated to the commercial benefits of commodity futures and options trading. Although this book is about the domestic commodity options markets, a discussion of the role of commodity futures and their relationship to commodity options is fundamental.

Senior executives who have made the decision to embark on the road of commodity trading must establish controls and performance measures over trading activities. This involves placing limitations on the company's participation in the futures and options markets and setting up management information systems (MIS) to monitor and measure the performance of a firm's trading strategies. Most companies, both large and small, have access to data-processing facilities. Computer programs can be written to accomplish a firm's objectives of risk management and performance appraisal of commodity transactions. Generally, most companies set up commodity trading as a separate profit center under the supervision of the purchasing department or financial operations division. Each firm must adopt its own particular organizational structure and performance appraisal measures according to its specific needs, limitations, and marketing objectives.

Businesses must adopt either formal or informal policies and procedures for managing commodity trading before they can begin. These policies should impose constraints of some kind on (1) personnel who may trade for the company, (2) funds committed for trading, (3) quantities contracted for, (4) hedging, (5) spreading, (6) speculating, (7) financing of margin requirements, (8) brokers and brokerage firms to be used, and (9) data-processing resources to be employed. Larger organizations usually place greater degree of restrictions and constraints on commodity trading than smaller, more loosely organized businesses.

Brokerage firms in compliance with new regulations and guidelines of the Commodity Futures Trading Commission (CFTC) require more documentation of a firm's activities in the commodity markets than previously. Brokerage firms impose trading limits on a firm's activities to prevent financial problems arising from over-trading or over-extension of credit. Many commercial positions in the futures market are backed by *Commodity Hedge Loan Agreements* (see Figure 11–1). This agreement is a three-party contract among the bank, the company, and the brokerage firm to ensure adequate credit financing of all hedged commodity transactions. The commodity hedge loan agreement places restrictions upon the activities of a company but also helps to ensure its financial integrity by providing a checks and balances system among the three interested parties.

Compared with trading commodity futures, commercial trading in put and calls options is a relatively unpublicized business activity, primarily because the bulk of commodity option trading has been restricted to London dealers and a few large U.S. commercial metals dealers who make a market for their options. Perhaps the main reason for the relative obscurity of commodity options trading is that most of it is carried on by a comparatively small number of professionals. With the opening of commodity option trading on U.S. exchanges, commercial trading in commodity options should flourish and provide commercial dealers with an opportunity to reduce business risks and to receive additional revenues from inventories.

The motive for commercial participation in the commodity options markets is not speculation but to reduce the risk of sharp changes in raw material costs and to ensure that these materials are available when they are needed. This chapter presents an overview and some background information for trading commodity options for the benefit of business executives and others who have had no previous experience with these markets.

Chief executives, financial officers, purchasing executives, and production managers in companies that do not now participate in the commodity futures markets should find this chapter informative and financially rewarding. Sharp executives who can show their company's top management how to reduce their business risks on commodity purchases and to earn additional revenues on inventories will

FIGURE 11–1

```
┌─────────────────────────────────────────────────────────────┐
│                    LETTERHEAD OF BANK                        │
│                                                              │
│                                    _____ 1977      │
│   Name of Brokerage Firm                                     │
│   (Address)                                                  │
│   Dear Sirs:                                                 │
│       We have entered into arrangements with _____   │
│   (the ''Debtor'') to finance transactions for trading in ___│
│   futures contracts and/or _____ option contracts. │
│   The Debtor has, or intends to open, an account or accounts │
│   with you for such transactions.                            │
│       Under our arrangements with the Debtor we are          │
│   authorized by the Debtor (whose confirmation appears       │
│   below) to instruct you as follows:                         │
│       (1) We are to receive duplicates of confirmations of   │
│   transactions executed in the Debtor's accounts and of      │
│   statements of account periodically sent by you to the      │
│   Debtor.                                                     │
│       (2) No funds are to be withdrawn by the Debtor from    │
│   the Debtor's accounts without our written approval.        │
│       (3) These instructions are to continue in effect until │
│   withdrawn by written notice from us.                       │
│                                                              │
│                              Yours very truly,               │
│                                (NAME OF BANK)                │
│                                                              │
│                                                              │
│   _____     By _____            │
│   Name of brokerage firm                                     │
│   Confirmed:                                                 │
│                                                              │
│                                                              │
│   _____                                        │
│   Debtor                                                     │
└─────────────────────────────────────────────────────────────┘
```

rise faster in the company than the executive who is unknowledgeable on this subject. Students in graduate schools of business ad-
ministration may find this chapter helpful as supplementary reading
in accounting, economics finance, and management courses.

The primary reasons for a firm's engaging in trading commodity
futures and options are (1) protection against possible increases in
costs of raw or processed materials, (2) assurance of an alternate

supply of raw or processed materials in the event of failure of the primary sources, (3) protection against declines in the values of raw or processed materials held in inventories, and (4) speculation for the purpose of earning trading profits.

The economic justification for the commodity futures and options markets is to allow consumers, processors, or dealers of a commodity to pass along some of the risks of ownership to others (speculators). This transfer of risk is referred to as *hedging*. Many popular books on commodity trading discuss concepts of hedging with regard to using the futures contracts, but primary sources for discussing the role of commodity options as a hedging vehicle are meager. The purpose of this chapter is to provide the business executive with a general and working knowledge of how to use a combination of commodity futures and options contracts in developing a hedging program.

In its most elementary form, hedging is the process by which a producer or processor buys or sells futures, or options, contracts to guarantee either future prices or future inventories of a specific commodity. Hedging is based upon the assumption that cash and futures prices tend to move together and will converge during the delivery month. Generally, this is true. Thus at the time that futures contract are sold or repurchased, commercial dealers have assured themselves of a price for their commodity within a range they find acceptable. For example, if sugar producers sell sugar futures to coincide with the expected harvest of a sugar beet crop, and if the prices of cash and futures decrease by harvest time, as the producers forecast, they can buy back the futures contract at a price less than what they sold it for. Their profit on the futures transactions will offset the lower cash price they receive when they sell their sugar crop production. If, on the other hand, they forecast prices going up, they can buy back the futures contract at a small loss that will be offset by a higher cash price they receive on the sale of their sugar crop. In either case, their realized profits on the sale of sugar production is held very close to the expected profit.

Another form of hedge is that used by business executives who intend to purchase future inventories. If the purchase of the commodity at the current price of a futures contract would yield a reasonable profit, and if the users feel that prices have a good chance of increasing later on, they would purchase a futures contract. Then, if the price of the commodity actually does increase, their cost of materials is protected because the futures price most likely will increase along with the cash price. Their profit on the sale of the futures contract offsets the increase in actual cost over that which they originally found acceptable. Should prices decrease, however, users would suffer a loss on the futures contract, but the actual cost of purchasing the commodity would be less than they had planned, and this would result in a greater than expected profit on the use of the commodity.

For some cash commodities that have a futures market, the pricing of the delivered commodity is based upon the futures prices. Parties agree to a future delivery time and to all terms of a contract other than price. The cash price is specified as having a discount or premium to the futures price at the time of delivery. For example, the price of spot cocoa to be delivered in July might be specified as being 2.00 cents under September futures on the day of delivery. In this manner, a forward contract can be made and a contract price quoted based upon the futures price with adjustments for differences in quality and delivery locations.

In each of these situations, a commodity producer and/or processor has succeeded in transferring some of the price risk arising from ownership through the use of the futures market. The transfer of price risk through hedging is not as exact as textbook illustrations would lead the reader to believe because cash and futures prices do not move exactly in the same direction, nor is it generally feasible to hedge all of the physical commodity to be used. Thus the practice of hedging is not an entirely mechanical process which can be achieved profitably without thought to the (a) amounts to be hedged, (b) timing of the hedge, (c) prospective price changes and forecasts, and (d) removing the hedge by offsetting the existing futures position.

The commercial role of hedging has two beneficial effects on a free market economy, which can be briefly described as affecting consumer prices and commercial financing of raw and processed commodity materials. When producers see the costs of doing business or prices subject to large and rapid changes, they must build their profit margins to cover possible cost increases. This would result in higher consumer prices at all levels of consumption and use. Hedging limits the need for price protection built into profit margins. Prices, therefore, need not be set as high as they would if the commodity had not been hedged. However, hedging not only limits the commodity producers or consumers' price risk but also limits profits because once a hedge is placed on, the business executive has guaranteed himself or herself an expected rate of return (profit margin) on inventories. For example, a copper producer in March may hedge (sell futures) on copper inventories that have a cost basis of 55.00 cents per pound for December delivery at the futures price of 65.00 cents per pound. This type of hedge would guarantee a profit on producers' inventories. However, if civil war breaks out in Chile, or if industrial consumption reduces copper stockpiles to below average levels, copper prices by December could be selling at 85.00 cents per pound. Thus the hedge which seemed a good idea in March created a paper loss of 10.00 cents per pound in December. There are no easy solutions to this dilemma—which has soured many business executives from using the futures market as a hedging tool! On the other hand, many thriving businesses during good times have failed when commodity prices have risen or fallen precipitously. In our experience, four guidelines should be followed for using hedging as a profitable financial tool:

1. The business executive must develop a short- and long-term perspective of the market in making price forecasts.
2. He or she must know the break-even points and have an accurate analysis of this basis (difference between futures and cash delivery markets).
3. He or she should formulate an optimistic, pessimistic, and realistic appraisal of present and future profit margins.
4. He or she needs to know what percentage of the inventories can be hedged that will prevent disastrous results and yet allow him or her to participate in additional profits during good times. (This percentage is usually between 30 to 50 percent of the expected inventory commitments; however, it requires detailed financial analysis of the firm's sales, inventory warehousing, profit margins, inventory turnover, and channels of supply and distribution to compute this percentage.)

Volatile commodity prices makes commercial users of these commodities a greater financial risk than most bankers find acceptable. Bankers are more likely to lend money to a business that produces or uses commodities if the commodity commitments are hedged and the firm has a history of successful hedging. Commercial lenders who are knowledgeable about hedging usually give preferential treatment to borrowers whose inventories are hedged.

Actual hedging transactions are considerably more complex than this brief chapter can present. The authors would like to stress the importance of an accurate computation of a firm's basis—difference between the cash and futures delivery markets—in determining the success or failure of any hedging program. Executives must know the price differentials between the specific amounts, grades, and delivery locations of the commodity they deal in versus the contract sizes, grades, and delivery locations of the futures (options) contract in order to calculate their basis exactly. Sometimes the basis may be very small while other times it may be substantial—enough so to wipe out any profits from hedging.

Hedging is a useful tool for more than price protection. It can also be used to ensure a source of supply for scarce materials. By taking a long position in the futures market, and maintaining it throughout the life of the contract, the owner of the contract can expect delivery even though there is a shortage of the commodity in the general market place.

Because put and call options can be exercised for the underlying commodity futures, hedgers who buy or write options may make or receive delivery of the actual commodity.

1. *Call buyers* and *put writers* are potential buyers of actual commodities.
2. *Put buyers* and *call writers* are potential sellers of actual commodities.

Usually, put and call options will be offset without deliveries being made. Occasionally, hedgers might find it to their financial advantages to receive or make delivery against option contracts as a marketing alternative for their business.

WHAT IS THE ROLE OF THE SPECULATOR?

Commercial traders should not discourage the role of the speculator. In the past, speculators have been blamed for wild price movements in commodities that had been previously stable. Speculators provide liquidity in the market, thereby helping it to function as an economic institution. Speculators operate on the belief that they can predict price movements. They buy futures contracts when they think prices will go up and sell futures when they think they will decline. The activity of speculators in the market is important to hedgers because they have someone to trade with. Consequently, the role of the speculator is encouraged by commodity exchanges and brokerage firms who serve the commercial interests. Liquidity is increased even more by speculators known as "scalpers" and "day traders." Day traders are short-term speculators who attempts to close out all their positions by the end of the day. Scalpers trade for small, quick profits and rarely maintain open positions after the close of the trading day. Day traders and scalpers generally take on large positions in the market (25 contracts or more) which assists hedgers in providing a continuous flow of buyer and seller activity for their contracts. Day traders and scalpers usually take on larger positions than position speculators because a greater number of trades are necessary to generate profits and they feel there is less risk in closing out their positions before the end of the day.

Position speculators, on the other hand, hold onto their positions for several days, weeks, and sometimes months because they believe that the fundamental or technical conditions of the market are ripe for a major move. If position speculators are wrong about their forecasts of the market, they generally cut their losses before margin calls consume all their trading capital.

Commodity spreaders constitute another class of speculators that provide liquidity to the market place. A spread is the simultaneous purchase of one futures month and the sale of another, either in the same or different commodity, or exchange. For example, a spread trader might buy 25 contracts of July copper and sell 25 contracts of December copper at a fixed price difference. Experienced commercial as well as speculative traders engage in spreading futures contracts. The economic justification for spreading (other than to generate trading profits) is that this activity substantially increases the liquidity of the market without undue risks inherent in holding net positions.

There is another form of speculation that is frequently not considered as speculation. It is the decision-making process of when or when not to hedge. When a commodity is stored for sale at a later date, the holder of the commodity is speculating on the price of the inventory. The consumers of a commodity who do not purchase their requirements until they are needed are also speculating. In either case, a price change in the commodity could have an adverse consequence upon the profits unless the physical-supply position is hedged.

The timing of the hedge is itself a form of speculation. In that context, all commodity futures trading (and commodity option trading) has elements of speculation. Executives who are maintaining a hedging program for economic purposes still must make a decision about when to put on or lift a hedge. Thus, they are speculators to the extent that they can obtain greater or less protection of their profits as a result of the timing of individual hedging activities.

So far we have discussed the role of hedging in the futures market with little mention of the role of commodity options. Since this book is primarily about commodity options, now is the time to relate the two commercial tools for hedging. A discussion of commodity options would be inseparable from an understanding of the role and applications of futures markets. The same concepts used in describing hedging in the futures markets applies equally well to commodity options.

Some of the major differences in using commodity options versus using futures contracts are:

1. Futures contracts require that the commercial customer place from 3 to 5 percent of the value of the commodity on deposit with the broker (new business margin), and then to deposit additional funds (variation margin) if the hedge goes against the customer because of unfavorable price changes.

2. Commodity options purchases require only a deposit of a fixed premium without additional margin funds being required if the hedge goes against the customer.
3. Option writing against futures contracts or inventories produces premium income to the writer.
4. Not all futures markets will have corresponding option markets.

PUT AND CALL TRADING STRATEGIES FOR HEDGERS

Commercial traders have a different problem than speculators because they desire to reduce business risks associated with commodity trading. Therefore, trading strategies using commodity options must be developed with that perspective in mind. Put and call trading, as outlined here, are the principal ones that commercial traders can utilize in reducing business risks depending upon whether they are producers, processors, or distributors.

Strategy I — Purchase call options

The purchase of call options for commercials is very similar to buying futures contracts as a hedge against rising prices. The primary difference is that call option premiums are fully paid, whereas futures contracts are margined.

This strategy can be utilized by commercials who wish to hedge against a price rise of a commodity needed for a future inventory. For example, if chocolate processors need a monthly inventory of 100,000 pounds of cocoa beans, they may want to purchase cocoa calls today to hedge against rising cocoa prices when they actually purchase their inventories. Calls are a form of price insurance against unsecured rising replacement material costs. It would be a shock to a chocolate processor to pay 90.00 cents per pound for cocoa beans one month, and then pay 140.00 cents per pound for cocoa five months later. The purchase of calls could help reduce some of the price uncertainty of future inventory requirements. Similar situations exist for coffee roasters and precious metal fabricators.

Strategy II — Purchase puts

This strategy can be utilized to protect a surplus inventory of commodities against a price decline until the processor can sell or use up the surplus inventory. For example, a jewelry manufacturer, who has a surplus inventory of silver that will be converted into ring settings, may want to purchase puts to protect against declining silver prices. Puts can be a form of price insurance against declining inventory values. If, in fact, silver prices do decline as the manufacturer suspects they might, the purchase of puts has made the company more competitive in the market because it has preserved profit margins from declining inventory values compared to the manufacturer who took no price protection. Even though many production costs can be passed on to the consumer, business executives who have taken price protection against declining inventory values are still at a distinct advantage over those who had not.

The purchase of put options for commercials is very similar in concept to selling futures contracts as a hedge against falling prices. The primary difference is that put option premiums are fully paid for, whereas futures contracts are margined.

Commercial dealers with a substantial credit line may find the buying or selling of futures contracts more feasible than the purchase of puts and calls because less money is required initially to buy or sell a futures contract than to pay full premiums for option contracts. Put and call options have the distinct advantage over futures contracts in that the potential risk is limited to the option premium, whereas futures contracts may require additional maintenance margin money to maintain the long or short futures hedge positions until the hedge can be lifted. Only judgment and experience can be the guide to executives as to whether they should purchase option contracts or trade futures. Probably a combination of option and futures contracts to meet hedging needs might be an intelligent answer to this problem. (See Examples A and B.)

EXAMPLE A

BUYING A DECEMBER SILVER FUTURES CONTRACT VERSUS BUYING A DECEMBER SILVER 470 CALL*

Opening transactions:
    Buy December futures at 463.00
    Initial margin is $1,000
    Buy December 470 calls at $1,500

Closing transactions: If silver prices rise to 500.00.

Sell December futures at	500.00	Sell December 470 calls at	$2,000
Bought at	463.00	Bought at	1,500
Net profits	37.00		$ 500

37.00¢ × 50.00 = $1,850

Closing transactions: If silver prices decline to 410.00.

Sell December futures at	410.00	December 470 call	
Bought at	463.00	expires worthless	
(Net losses)	53.00	Bought	$1,500

53.00 × $50 = ($2,650.00)

* The call holder's loss was limited to $1,500 at the onset of the transaction, whereas the buyer of the futures contract had to post $1,400 per contract additional margin funds to maintain the hedge.

213

EXAMPLE B

SELLING SHORT A MARCH SUGAR FUTURES VERSUS BUYING A MARCH SUGAR 12.00 PUT IN ANTICIPATION OF A DECLINE IN SUGAR PRICES*

Opening transactions:
Sell short March sugar futures at 12.30¢
Initial margin required is $2,000.00
Buy March 12.00 put at $900

Closing transactions: If price of sugar futures decline to 10.30¢ per lb.

Buy March futures at	10.30¢	Sell March put at	$2,240
Sold at	12.30¢	Bought at	900
Net profits 2.00¢ × $1,120 = $2,240			$1,340

Closing transactions: If price of sugar futures rises to 14.30¢ per lb.

Buy March futures at	14.30¢	March Sugar 12.00 put expires	
Sold at	12.30¢	worthless	($900)
(Net losses)	($2,240)		($900)

* The put holder's loss was limited to $900 at the beginning of the transaction, whereas the short seller of futures contract had to post $1,740 per contract additional margin funds to maintain his hedge.

Strategy III—Covered call option writing (buying futures contracts versus the writing of call options)

This strategy can be utilized by commercials to reduce costs of future replacement inventories. For example, a copper fabricator who purchases copper futures contracts as a hedge against rising replacement inventory costs could write (sell) copper call options against long futures positions in order to receive income premium. The premium received reduces replacement inventory costs. Covered option writing can be a risky trading strategy if the underlying commodity price declines precipitously because the option premium received by the writer will only offset a portion of the price decline of the declining futures price. Covered option writing works best when commodity prices remain stable or rise moderately because under these conditions, business executives have achieved their objectives of reducing replacement inventory costs by the amount of the option premium.

Strategy IV — Covered put option writing (selling short a futures contract versus the writing of a put option)

This strategy can be utilized by commercials to reduce the costs of current inventories. For example, a copper fabricator who sells short copper futures contracts as a hedge against declining inventories values could write (sell) put options against the short futures positions in order to receive income on current inventories. The premium received reduces the costs of storage and insurance on current inventories. For example, if storage and insurance costs for copper is 0.50 cents per pound per month, and a put option premium is 1.50 cents per pound per month, the copper fabricator has covered the costs of holding surplus inventories until the copper is processed into its finished form. Covered put option writing can be risky, especially if the underlying commodity price rises dramatically, since the option premium received by the writer will only offset a portion of the price rise of the underlying short futures position. Covered put option writing works best when commodity prices remain relatively stable or rise moderately because under these conditions the executive has achieved an objective of reducing costs of holding current inventories.

Strategy V — Buying a call option against a short futures contract

This is a defensive strategy in which the purchase of a call option serves as a measure of risk insurance against a rising market when a commercial has a short futures hedge. For example, if a sugar producer has sold short futures contracts as a hedge for protection against declining world sugar prices when the crop is harvested may want to take additional protection against the possibility of a dramatic rise in world sugar prices during the interim. This producer can purchase sugar call options to substantially reduce the risk of incurring additional margin calls on short futures positions if world sugar prices should take a dramatic rise (as they did in 1974 when world sugar prices climbed to 65.00 cents per pound in less than a year).

For commercial traders experienced in futures trading, purchase of call options can enhance the effectiveness of a hedging program by lifting and putting on a short futures hedge several times during the life of an option contract. Place on a short futures hedge when the price trend is down, then lift the hedge when the price trend reverses to the upside. When the price trend reverses to the downside, reinstate the short futures hedge until the trend reverses again. Trading short futures positions against call options in this manner can be very profitable for the commercial trader since call options provide price risk insurance unobtainable in the futures market.

Strategy VI — Buying a put option against a long futures contract

This strategy, like Strategy V, is a defensive maneuver to offer price risk insurance to the commercial trader against a long futures hedge position when commodity prices are declining. For example, if a sugar refiner has a long futures hedge on world sugar contracts for protection against price rises on replacement inventories, he or she may want to buy put options to take additional protection against a dramatic decline in world sugar prices during the interim. The refiner will purchase sugar put options to substantially reduce the risk of incurring additional margin calls on the long futures position if world sugar prices should take a precipitous decline, as they did in 1975 when world sugar prices descended from 45.00 cents per pound to 14.00 cents per pound during a six-month period.

For commercial traders experienced in futures trading, purchase of put options can enhance the effectiveness of a hedging program by trading futures contracts against put options—lifting and placing long futures hedges several times during the life of a put option. Place on a long futures hedge when the price trend is up, then lift the hedge when the price trend reverses to the downside. When the price trend reverses to the upside, reinstate the long futures hedge until the trend changes to the downside. Trading long futures hedge positions against put options in this manner can be very profitable for the commercial trader since put options provide risk insurance unobtainable in the futures market.

Strategy VII — Writing put and call options (not covered by futures positions) against actual or potential inventories of substantially identical commodities as represented by the specifications of the option contract

Strategy VII is very similar to Strategies III and IV except that a commercial trader has written uncovered (naked) put and call options. Uncovered writing strategies should never be done for speculation but for hedging only. If commercial dealers have actual or potential inventories of cocoa, coffee, copper, or silver similar to the delivery specifications of an option contract, then writing options against an inventory position only makes good sense because option premiums received reduces the costs of doing business and gives a commercial trader a competitive edge in the marketing of the products. Uncovered put and call writing (also referred to as naked writing) should never be done for speculation because an uncovered option writer is in the untenable position of having only limited profit potential but exposure to unlimited risks. Commodity markets—unlike securities markets where uncovered option writing is done by sophisticated investors—are much too volatile to make uncovered option writing a viable strategy for speculators.

Strategy VIII — Commercial option spreads

A commercial option spread involves the simultaneous buying and writing of either put or call options in the same month at different strike prices, or in different months at the same strike price. Commercial spreads become potentially profitable only if a trader can purchase undervalued puts or calls and simultaneously write overvalued put or call options. Spreading put or call options in this manner will tend to keep premiums in line with each other because extremely overvalued or undervalued put or call situations will not exist for long, due to the influence of spreading. An additional advantage of spreads is the limited risk and reduced amount of funds required to trade spreads. The premium received from writing an option will be subtracted from the premium required for the purchase side of the spread, thereby reducing the amount of the investment required. In order to qualify as a commercial spread, commercial traders must buy calls or write put options in those months that they need the replacement inventory, and likewise they should buy puts and write calls in those months in which they have inventory on hand in order to qualify as a bona fide hedge against price risk of actual or potential inventory positions.

Strategy IX — Buying or writing commercial straddles and combinations

A commodity straddle is the purchase or sale of an equivalent number of puts and calls on a given underlying commodity or futures contract with the same exercise price and expiration date. A combination is similar to a straddle but differs in that either the exercise price and/or expiration dates are not the same. For example, the purchase or sale of a July cocoa 120 call versus the purchase or sale of a July cocoa 120 put is a straddle. An example of a combination would be the purchase or sale of a July cocoa 120 call versus the purchase or sale of a September cocoa 120 put (expiration date differs), or the purchase or sale of a July 140 cocoa put (exercise price differs).

Commercial traders would purchase a straddle (or combination) only if they anticipate a major move in the price of the commodity but are uncertain of which direction. Buying straddles can only be justified as a hedge if the volatility of the market is so severe as to prevent unsatisfactory forward pricing, such as was the case with sugar prices in 1974 and coffee prices in 1976. The purchase of a straddle has the distinct advantage of providing price insurance on both sides of the market. If the market price declines, the put side makes money. If the market price rises, the call side makes money. The primary advantage of purchasing straddles is to trade futures contracts against them, since both long and short futures positions are covered by the straddle. Developing a trading plan using the straddles (or combinations) as protection for net long or short futures positions could be very profitable since risks are limited with unlimited potential for trading profits throughout the life of the straddle.

Commercial traders could write (sell) straddles, or combinations, on commodities that have relatively low volatility because the premium income received reduces the cost basis for purchasing and holding current inventories. For example, if a copper fabricator wrote a December copper 70 call versus a December copper 70 put, the net result would be the following if the price of December copper futures remained at 70.00 cents per pound.

EXAMPLE C

Sell December copper 70 call at	$1,250
Sell December copper 70 put at	1,250
Premium received	$2,500

As long as the price of December copper futures stays between 65.00 to 75.00 cents, the commercial trader makes money, which can be applied toward reducing the replacement costs of copper inventories. If both sides of the straddle expire unexercised, the cost basis for copper inventories will be reduced by 10.00 cents per pound, or by 14 percent if the cost basis of the inventory were 70.00 cents per pound.

WHAT ABOUT DELIVERY AGAINST OPTION CONTRACTS?

It should be remembered that call option buyers may exercise their option to a long futures contract which can be held until they accept delivery of the actual commodity. Likewise, put buyers may exercise their option to a short futures contract which can be held until they decide to make delivery of the actual commodity.

Although about 95 percent of all option contracts will be offset, and not exercised into futures contracts for delivery, there will be times that it would be advantageous for a hedger to accept or to make delivery—when, for a particular location, accepting or making delivery is the most profitable alternative. At the same time, at another location, it may not be the most advantageous. In deciding whether to exercise put or call options to futures contracts, the commercial trader should calculate all of the costs involved in accomplishing delivery and then compare that to the best price in another market.

HOW TO SELECT A BROKER FOR COMMERCIAL ACCOUNTS

In choosing a broker, the commercial trader should look for someone who is interested and willing to service hedge accounts. Some registered representatives prefer to handle commercial accounts. Others are not willing to spend the time or effort necessary to do a good job. A knowledgeable broker should be able to explain the various aspects of hedging, provide up-to-date commodity research pertinent to hedging needs, aid in calculating price relationships, and be of assistance in accepting or making delivery, if necessary. A good broker should also be able to provide fast and reliable execution of orders.

HOW TO CALCULATE THE BASIS AND PLOT IT ON A GRAPH

The basis is the difference over or under a designated futures price at which a cash commodity of a certain description is sold or quoted. When the futures price is over the price of the cash commodity, it is referred to as a *premium basis*. Likewise, when the futures price is under the cash price, it is called a *discount basis*. The following examples should help to clarify these definitions

EXAMPLE D
PREMIUM BASIS FOR SPOT SILVER
(November 1)

December silver futures price	456.00 cents
Spot silver price in New York	453.00 cents
December futures over spot	3.00 cents

EXAMPLE E
DISCOUNT BASIS FOR SPOT COCOA
(October 20)

March cocoa futures price	166.00 cents
Spot accra cocoa in New York	187.00 cents
March futures discounted to spot	21.00 cents

Since futures and option contracts represent a specific quality, quantity, and location of a commodity, the price difference between the contract market and the market where a hedger actually buys or sells the products can differ significantly. The basis can be calculated daily, weekly, or bimonthly depending upon the marketing needs of a commercial dealer. A period of time greater than bimonthly is not recommended because the wide fluctuations between spot and futures prices can distort the appearance of the basis. Calculation of the basis either daily or weekly (using Friday's closing futures price) presents a more accurate view of the variability between spot and futures price relationships.

Selection of the futures contract delivery month for calculating the basis is very important, and again depends upon the marketing needs of a commercial dealer. For example, if a chocolate manufacturer buys large quantities of cocoa beans for processing in March and September, the basis relationships should be calculated using March and September futures prices, and not July or December futures prices. The price expectations for July and December cocoa prices may be considerably different than for March and September, thus presenting a "wrong" basis relationship for hedging inventory requirements.

Plotting the basis on a graph over a period of a year can assist a commercial dealer in making marketing decisions: When is the best time to buy? When is the best time to sell? Should I buy futures contracts, option contracts, or forward contracts to meet my inventory requirements? Figure 11–2 illustrates an example of basis

FIGURE 11–2
HYPOTHETICAL BASIS CHART OF CASH PRICES VERSUS NEAREST MONTH FUTURES PRICES FOR A COMMODITY

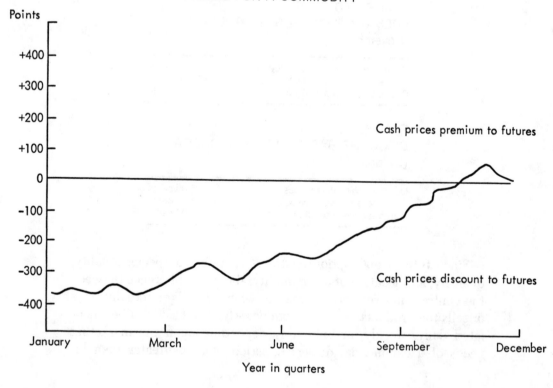

graph. The spot price is plotted as the amount of dollars, cents, or points plus or minus to the futures price, which is represented as a base line. The basis graph can assist the hedger in judging when the best time to place or lift hedges in the futures or options markets because a graph gives a pictorial representation of the variability in premiums and discounts over time.

There are two primary ways of calculating the basis for any local market: (1) historical price relationships and (2) actual cost calculation.

To calculate the basis with the first method, past futures prices are compared to prices obtained at the local spot market. For example, if a commercial silver dealer located in Dallas, Texas, were figuring a basis using the New York COMEX silver contract, he or she would calculate the price differences between the silver futures contract and the actual silver price paid in Dallas. The commercial silver dealer may find that silver prices in Dallas are normally 2.00 cents higher than prices paid at futures delivery points in New York. The basis would, therefore, be 2.00 cents, and any silver dealer who markets silver at Dallas would adjust the futures price by 2.00 cents per troy oz. when figuring the basis.

To determine the basis with the second method, the commercial dealer must obtain the actual cost of delivering silver bullion bars to the specified futures delivery locations (exchange-approved depositories within a 50-mile radius of New York City). To calculate the basis between Dallas and New York City via this method, the commercial dealer must estimate freight costs, interest and insurance charges, and certification costs. This total can then be used to adjust for the actual basis at Dallas, Texas.

PROCEDURES FOR GETTING STARTED TRADING COMMODITY OPTIONS

The following steps are suggested for establishing a commercial trading operation for commodity options. The size of the hedging operation, of course, affects implementation of these procedures.

1. Assign personnel to formulate trading program and authorize all trades, for example, Vice President of Purchasing.
2. Determine which commodities would be appropriate for the business to trade in, for example, sugar and cocoa in the case of a confectioner.
3. Determine the monthly, quarterly, semiannual, and annual inventory positions of each commodity to be traded.
4. Determine the basis relationships of each commodity to hedge for each trading period in which commodity is hedged.

5. Formulate appropriate trading model for hedging inventory commitments.
6. Develop and validate performance criteria for measuring profitability of the trading model; for example, increase profitability by 10, 15, or 20 percent on invested capital.
7. Develop computer programs for utilization of data-processing facility for monitoring commodity positions, market price trends, profitability of trading model, inventory accounting, and basis relationships.
8. Determine the minimum and maximum desirable hedge positions versus inventory requirements to ensure objectives of risk reduction, of price protections, and of trading profitability are adequately satisfied.
9. Open a commercial trade account with a brokerage firm that has commodity specialists and analysts in the commodities to be hedged.

This concludes the chapter on commercial applications of commodity option trading. The authors have described only a few of many possible commercial trading methods available to the processor, distributor, and producer. With imagination and experience, commercial traders can devise trading strategies based upon sound principles to enhance the profitability of their business. Option trading strategies and examples discussed here will provide some insight as to the commercial applications of option contracts. Even though put and call option trading has been done for over 30 years by London merchants, commodity options are a relatively novel endeavor in the United States. The intelligent use of option trading by commercials can reduce business risks associated with the production, consumption, and distribution of commodities. Option trading in combination with futures trading can enhance the effectiveness of the hedging process as a viable means for an executive to receive greater risk capital financing, to lower costs of doing business, and to reduce risks of price volatility in marketing products.

Chapter 12

Special tax considerations in trading commodity futures and options

This chapter will discuss the current rules and regulations regarding taxation of options and futures transactions for both speculative and commercial investors. Readers are forewarned that tax rulings may change after publication of this book and readers should therefore seek assistance from a qualified tax attorney or Certified Public Accountant for individual tax situations. Material presented in this chapter will serve only as guidelines to the current interpretation of the Internal Revenue Codes.

Tax rulings as applied to options and futures trading can be divided into four general categories depending upon the nature of the transaction and its outcome. These categories are (1) short-term capital gains and losses, (2) long-term capital gains and losses, (3) ordinary income, and (4) ordinary losses. All *speculative positions* in options and futures transactions are taxed as either long- or short-term capital gains or losses, whereas all *commercial positions* are taxed as ordinary income, or losses if the positions were taken against either an unsold or unpurchased quantity of inventory of an underlying commodity. A commercial dealer's inventory of a commodity does not have to be of exact deliverable grades as required by a commodity exchange to qualify as a commercial hedge (nonspeculative) position in the futures or options markets. The price basis of the dealer's inventory should be reasonably related to the price behavior of the specified, deliverable grades traded on the exchange.

TAX TREATMENT OF COMMERCIAL (HEDGE) TRANSACTIONS

All profits and losses generated from the purchase or sale of commodity futures and option contracts are subject to be taxed at ordinary income (or loss) rates to the business. Brokerage commissions are also considered to be an ordinary business expense and are deductible from the gross profits of a transaction. This ruling holds true regardless if the business is a sole proprietorship, partnership, or corporation. Examples A and B will illustrate this tax ruling.

For commercial dealers who wish to speculate in the commodities markets as well as use them as hedging vehicles, brokerage firms can designate separate accounts. One type of account can be approved for speculation and another for commercial hedging transactions. Brokers usually designate these different accounts by a number series that identifies the account as either speculative or commercial. Profits and losses generated from the purchase or sale of options and futures contracts in speculative accounts are subject to the same tax treatment as a regular (noncommercial) speculator.

EXAMPLE A
COVERED CALL WRITING: SELLING FUTURES
CONTRACTS VERSUS WRITING CALLS

Opening transactions (August 1979)
    March 80 sugar futures = 9.50 cents per pound
    Buy 10 March sugar futures at 9.50 cents per pound
    Sell 10 March sugar 10.00 calls at $500

Closing transactions (March 1980)
    March 80 sugar futures = 11.50 cents per pound
    Sell 10 March sugar futures at 10.00 cents per pound
    March 80 calls exercised at 10.00 cents per pound

Tax result
    $10 \times 10.00\text{¢} \times \$1,120$ per cent = \$112,000
    $10 \times 9.50\text{¢} \times \$1,120$ per cent = <u>106,400</u>
    Net gain on futures position   = \$ 5,600 ordinary income
    $10 \times \$500$ per call = \$5,000 ordinary income
    Received from the writing of calls against futures
    Net result = \$5,600 + \$5,000 = \$10,600
    Ordinary income to business from covered call option writing

Explanation
    Covered call writing for commercial accounts generates ordinary
income to the business. Profits (or losses) from futures transactions generate ordinary income (or loss) to the business and are
taxed at the usual rates.

EXAMPLE B
STRADDLE PURCHASE: BUYING CALLS VERSUS
BUYING PUTS

Opening transactions (August 1979)
    March 80 sugar futures = 9.50 cents per pound
    Buy 10 March 80 sugar 9.50 calls at \$1,000
    Buy 10 March 80 sugar 9.50 puts at . . . . <u>800</u>
                              \$1,800

Closing transactions (March 1980)
    March 80 sugar futures = 11.50 cents per pound
    Sell 10 March 80 sugar 9.50 calls at \$2,240
    March 80 sugar 9.50 puts expire worthless at . . . . . <u>(800)</u>
                              \$1,440 profit

Tax result
    $10 \times \$2,240$ = \$22,400 ordinary income on calls
    $10 \times$ (\$800) =   (8,000) ordinary loss on puts
    Net profit   = \$14,400 ordinary income to business

Explanation
    Profits (and losses) generated from the purchase and resale of the
different components of a straddle for commercial accounts are
taxed at ordinary income rates to the business. In this example,
the call component produced \$22,400 ordinary income and the
put component generated (\$8,000) in ordinary losses for net profit
of \$14,400.

Tax treatment of profits and losses for speculative traders will be discussed next.

TAX TREATMENT OF SPECULATIVE TRANSACTIONS

Tax treatment of the long futures positions

A holder of a long futures position is subject to long- or short-term capital gain (or loss) upon liquidation depending upon the length of the holding period. Long futures contracts held over nine months are subject to long-term capital gain (or loss), whereas long positions held less than nine months are subject to short-term capital gain (or loss).

Holders of commodity options are subject to the longer holding period of 12 months in order to qualify for long-term capital gains treatment.

Tax treatment of short futures transactions

A holder of a short futures contract is subject to short-term capital gains (or loss) regardless of the length of the holding period upon liquidation. The short seller of a futures contract can never qualify for long-term capital gains treatment, simply because a capital asset has never been owned, but has already been sold to a potential buyer (the holder of a long futures contract).

Tax treatment of commodity option purchases

A commodity option is a capital asset to its holder if he or she is not a dealer in the underlying commodity and if the underlying commodity futures contract is (or would be, if acquired) treated as a capital asset in his or her hands. Profits (and losses) generated from the purchase and sale of puts and calls are subject to short- or long-term capital gains depending upon the holding period of the option. The 1976 Tax Reform Act changed the holding period between short- and long-term to 12 months for option contracts. If the put or call holder liquidates the option contract prior to the 12-month period, profits and losses are taxed at short-term capital gains rates. If held longer than 12 months, they are taxed at long-term capital gains rates. When an option is sold, the resulting capital gain or loss is determined by the difference between the premium originally paid and the proceeds received in the closing sale transaction.

If the option expires unexercised, the resulting loss is treated as long- or short-term capital loss depending upon the holding period.

226

For tax purposes, an expired option is considered to have been sold for no consideration ($0) on the expiration date.

If a put or call holder exercises his or her option to an underlying futures contract, the premium paid to the option writer is added or subtracted from the purchase or sale price of the futures contract. The call buyer who exercises the option to a long futures position adds the premium to the purchase price of the futures contract to give a revised cost basis. Put buyers who exercise their option to a short futures contract subtract the premium paid from the sale price of the futures contract to revise their cost basis. Examples C and D will illustrate this tax ruling.

An easy way to simplify the tax complexities of an exercised option is to always think of a call option buyer as a potential long position, and a put buyer as a potential short position in the futures markets. We will now proceed to a discussion of the tax treatment of written options.

Tax treatment of written put and call options

A written call option is a potential obligation by the writer to sell a long futures contract to the call buyer. A written put option is a potential obligation by the writer to deliver a short futures contract to the put buyer. Premiums paid by put and call buyers to the

---

EXAMPLE C
CALL OPTION HOLDER EXERCISES THE
OPTION FOR A LONG FUTURES POSITION

Opening transactions (March)
  August gold futures = $146 per oz.
  Buy one August gold 150 call
  Premium for call = $3 per oz. × 100 oz. = $300*

Closing transactions (August)
  August gold futures = $168 per oz.
  Exercise one gold 150 call for long futures contract
  Sell one long gold futures at $168 per oz.

Tax result
  Sold one August gold futures $168
  Revised cost basis for call option $153
  $15 per oz. short-term capital gain
  100 oz. × $15 per oz. = $1,500 short-term capital gain

Explanation
  The revised cost basis for the call option exercised for a long futures contract: $3 per oz. premium plus (+) $150 exercise price for the option = $153. The tax result from exercising a profitable call and then selling the futures contract is a $1,500 short-term capital gain. Note: Exercising an option for a futures contract entails additional transaction costs. Generally, it would be less expensive to sell the option and not exercise it.

---

* Assumes 100 oz. gold contract

227

EXAMPLE D
PUT OPTION HOLDER EXERCISES THE
OPTION FOR A SHORT FUTURES
CONTRACT

Opening transactions (May)
  August gold futures = $163 per oz.
  Buy one August gold 160 put
  Premium for put = $5 per oz. × 100 oz. = $500*

Closing transactions (August)
  August gold futures = $151 per oz.
  Exercise one gold 160 put for short futures contract
  Buy back one short gold futures at $151

Tax result
  Buy back one August gold futures $151
  Revised cost basis for put option $155
  $4 per oz. short-term capital gain
  100 oz. × $4 per oz. = $400 short-term capital gain

Explanation
  The revised cost basis for the put option for a short futures contract: $160 minus $5 per oz. premium = $155. The tax result from exercising a profitable put and then buying back the futures contract is a $400 short-term capital gain.

    * Assumes 100 oz. gold contract.

writers are deferred until termination of the transaction (obligation), at which time they are subject to short-term capital gains (or loss) regardless of the length of the holding period. If a put or call option expires unexercised, the capital gain will be equal to the premium received in the opening writing transaction. For a closing purchase transaction (option writer buys back option prior to expiration), the capital gain (or loss) will be the difference between the premium originally received and the price paid in the closing purchase transaction.

If an option is exercised, then the entire transaction is treated as a purchase or sale of an underlying futures contract. The premium is considered to be a part of the purchase or sale price of the futures contract. Call option premiums received by the writer increase the sale price of the futures contract to the buyer. Put option premiums received by the writer reduce the purchase price of the futures contract. Examples E and F will illustrate the tax treatment of written put and call options.

SPREADS AND STRADDLES

Spreads

Spreading is the simultaneous purchase and sale of commodity options of the same class (puts or calls) on the same underlying

EXAMPLE E
COVERED CALL WRITING: BUYING FUTURES
CONTRACTS VERSUS WRITING CALLS

Opening transaction (July)
    December copper futures = 63.00 cents per pound
    Buy 10 December copper futures 63.00 cents per pound
    Sell 10 December copper 70 calls at $500

Closing transactions (December)
    December copper futures = 69.00 cents per pound
    Sell 10 December copper futures 69.00 cents per pound
    December Copper 70 calls expire worthless

Tax result
    Sold December futures 69.00 cents
    Bought December futures 63.00 cents
    Net result = 7.00 cents per pound
    10 × 7.00¢ × $250 per cent = $17,500
    10 × $500.00 premium = $5,000
    $22,500 net short-term capital gain

Explanation
    Covered call writing generates short-term capital gains from
    the sale of calls. Profits (and losses) from futures transac-
    tions generate short-term capital gains (or losses) unless
    futures contracts are held longer than nine months.

EXAMPLE F
COVERED PUT WRITING: SELLING FUTURES
CONTRACTS VERSUS WRITING PUTS

Opening transactions (August)
    December copper futures = 67.00 cents per pound
    Sell 10 December copper futures 67.00 cents per pound
    Sell 10 December copper 60 puts at $250

Closing transactions (December)
    December copper futures = 60.00 cents per pound
    Buy 10 December copper futures 60.00 cents per pound
    December copper 60 puts expire worthless

Tax result
    Sold December futures 67.00 cents
    Bought December futures 60.00 cents
    Net result 7.00 cents per pound
    10 × 7.00¢ × $250 per cent = $17,500
    10 × $250.00 premium = 2,500
    $20,000 net short-term capital gain

Explanation
    The covered put writer receives premium income from the
    sale of put options, which is taxed at short-term capital
    gains rates. Profits (or losses) generated from the futures
    transactions are also taxed at short-term capital gains rates.

commodity (or commodity futures), differing only in maturity date,
strike price, or both. Spreading commodity options is not subject to
any special tax rules. Each component of the spread is treated as an
individual transaction and generally taxed according to the rules
discussed previously.

It is still true that the two components of the spread may be closed in different taxable years, where possible, to time recognition of the gain or loss. If a spreader has other short-term gains, for example, it may be desirable to close a losing component in the earlier taxable year, in order to offset the tax on prior short-term gains, and to defer any gain on the other component of the spread to a later taxable year.

Straddles

A straddle is the simultaneous purchase or sale of an equal number of puts or calls on the same underlying commodity (or commodity futures) with identical maturity dates and striking prices. Each component of a straddle is treated as an individual transaction and generally taxed according to the rules discussed previously. All premium income or loss to straddle writers from a closing transaction or lapse of an option is now taxed as short-term capital gain or loss. There is no special tax significance to the straddle itself. It is taxed according to its separate components. (See Example G.)

EXAMPLE G
STRADDLE PURCHASE: BUYING CALLS VERSUS
BUYING PUTS

Opening transaction (July)
    December gold futures = $169 per oz.
    Buy 10 December 79 gold 170 calls at $400
    Buy 10 December 79 gold 170 puts at $500
                                                    $900

Closing transaction (December)
    December gold futures = $152 per oz.
    Let 10 December gold 170 calls expire worthless
    Sell 10 December gold 170 puts at $1,800

Tax result
    10 × $400 = ($4,000) premium paid
    10 × 0.0 = 0.00 calls expire worthless
    ($4,000) short-term loss on call side of straddle
    10 × $500 = ($5,000) premium paid
    10 × $1,800 = $18,000
    $13,000 short-term gain on put side of straddle
    $13,000 — ($4,000) = $9,000 short-term net gain on straddle

Explanation
    Profits (and losses) generated from the purchase and resale of the different components of a straddle are taxed at short-term capital gains rates unless held longer than 12 months. In this example, the call component produced a $4,000 capital loss, and the put component yielded a $13,000 capital gain for a net short-term gain of $9,000.

Long-term versus short-term capital gains treatment

As most investors are aware, long-term capital gains receive favored tax treatment under the Internal Revenue Code. One half of the excess of net long-term gains over net short-term capital losses of individuals is taxed at ordinary income rates and the balance is exempt from taxation. Under an alternative taxing method useful to investors in higher income brackets, the first $50,000 of this excess is taxed at a 25-percent rate and the balance is taxed as above (that is, one half of the balance is taxed at ordinary income rates).

Corporations are taxed at a rate of 30 percent on the excess of their net long-term capital gains over their net short-term capital losses, if this is less than the tax that would be payable at ordinary rates. Net short-term capital gains, reduced by net long-term capital losses, are taxed in full at ordinary income rates to both individuals and corporations.

The treatment of capital losses, particularly long-term losses, is significantly less favorable to the taxpayer. Both long- and short-term losses of individuals must be first deducted from capital gains of the corresponding type. Any net long-term capital losses must then be deducted from net short-term capital gains, if any, and any net short-term capital losses must be deducted from net long-term gains. The balance of any long-term or short-term capital losses may then be deducted from ordinary income, but only up to specified limits. A balance consisting of net long-term losses will produce only $1 of deduction against ordinary income for every $2 of loss.

A balance consisting of either net long- or short-term capital losses can be deducted against ordinary income in any taxable year up to a maximum of $3,000. Losses that cannot be used in the taxable year in which they are sustained can be carried forward indefinitely but are subject in each carry-forward year to the $3,000 limitation.

Capital losses of corporations are allowed only to the extent of capital gains. Subject to this limitation, unused corporate capital losses may generally be carried back three years and forward five years.

TAX PLANNING FOR COMMODITY OPTIONS TRANSACTIONS

The primary principles of tax planning for commodity investors are (1) realize long-term capital gains and incur only short-term capital losses, (2) always avoid the risk of taking long-term capital losses, and (3) initiate and close out transactions between different taxable years to apply short gains against short-term losses and defer any "surplus" capital gains to another taxable year.

Tax revisions in the 1976 Tax Reform Act could eliminate the possibility of realizing long-term capital gains from trading options unless maturity dates for designated option series become available for periods longer than 12 months. For example, put and call contracts that have a 13-month expiration date could possibly qualify for long-term capital gains treatment if the option buyer has held a profitable put or call longer than 12 months.

Commodity options transactions can still be used to achieve long-term capital gains in an underlying futures contract. Covered call option writing offers an opportunity for the writer to realize long-term capital gains on a long futures contract and short-term capital gains or loss from the sale of a covered call. The covered call option writer initiates a long futures position and writes a call option against it. The premium received from the written call reduces the risk of holding the underlying futures contract during the six-month period.

Holders of option spreads and straddles could achieve tax advantages by closing out the two legs of a spread or two components of a straddle in different taxable years, where possible, to time recog-

---

EXAMPLE H
CALL OPTION SPREADS: BUYING ONE
CALL OPTION SERIES VERSUS SELLING
ANOTHER CALL OPTION SERIES

Opening transactions (August)
  March silver futures = 463.00
  Buy 10 March silver 450 calls at $1,000
  Sell 10 March silver 470 calls at $200

Second transactions (December of same year)
  March silver futures = 469.00
  Buy 10 March silver 470 calls at ($500)
Tax result
  10 × $200 = $2,000 premium received
  10 × $500 = ($5,000) close out position
              ($3,000) short-term loss for the year

Closing transactions (March of following year)
  March silver futures = 490.00
  Sell 10 March silver 450 calls at $2,000
Tax result
  10 × $1,000 = ($10,000) premium paid
  10 × $2,000 = 20,000 close out position
               $10,000 short-term gain

Explanation
  Profits (and losses) generated from option spreads are taxed according to the net result of their separate components. In this example, the March silver 470 calls generated a $3,000 short-term loss for the initial taxable year. The March 450 calls produced a $10,000 capital gain for the next year. Note: Closing out the legs of a spread in different taxable years could yield tax advantages to a trader; however, when one leg of a spread is closed out prior to the other, a spread no longer exists, and additional margin funds may be required by the broker if the customer's equity is less than the margin requirements necessary to maintain the positions.

---

nition of the gain or loss. If the trader has other short-term gains, he or she may wish to close out a losing leg or component in the earlier taxable year in order to offset the tax on prior short-term gains and defer any gain on the other leg or component to a later taxable year. See Example H.

This procedure differs from a commodity tax straddle because the trader assumes market risk in expectation of profit when a leg of a spread or a component of a straddle is closed out without initiating a new position in a substantially similar option contract series. The status of commodity tax straddles has been recently challenged by the Internal Revenue Service because the initiation of a tax straddle is not presumed to be profit-motivated and carries only slight market risk. The primary purpose of a commodity tax straddle is to move income, short-term capital gains, or unfavorable losses to another year in hopes of obtaining more favorable tax treatment with minimum risk to the taxpayer. The recent Internal Revenue rulings on tax straddles have placed them in jeopardy, and straddles should not be entered into without first obtaining professional tax advice.

This concludes the chapter on the tax treatment of commodity futures and options transactions. Investors are strongly urged to obtain the assistance of a qualified tax consultant if in doubt about the tax status of any commodity transactions. Tax rulings in this area are often complex and subject to periodic revision. Tax considerations should be integrated into an overall speculative or commercial trading program in order to derive maximum benefits available under current tax laws. Ignorance of the tax consequences of commodity transactions can lessen the profitability of an otherwise viable trading program.

Chapter 13

Summary and Conclusions

Domestic options trading promises to be one of the most exciting and dynamic investment vehicles made available to the American public. The next three years are critical for the success of U.S. option markets. If U.S. options trading is conducted in an orderly manner—free of abuses and fraud—then option markets will grow in number and in volume of trading.

Foreign commodity exchanges possibly might permit options trading in their countries after U.S. options trading proves to be a viable speculative and hedging vehicle. If this were to happen, the arbitrage opportunities between U.S. options markets and foreign markets would be nearly limitless.

Of course, we must not forget the ultimate purpose of both futures and option contract markets is to provide a free market for hedging price risks incurred by producers and consumers. Options trading is merely an extension of the commercial hedging concept —but a very important one since the role of speculation is encouraged, and hence market liquidity is expanded to provide more efficient markets for speculation and hedging.

We hope that this book does not sit on a bookshelf collecting dust but will be used profitably by both speculators and commercial hedgers as a valuable reference source for options trading methods and strategies.

Appendix A

Basic trading information

on U.S. exchanges

COCOA

New York Cocoa Exchange

Market hours: 9:30 A.M. to 2:30 P.M.
Contract unit: 30,000 pounds (net) of cocoa beans in original shipping bags.
Price quotations: Cents and 1/100 cents per pound.
Minimum fluctuation: 1/100 cent per pound or $3 per contract.
Trading limits: Six cents above or below previous day's settlement price. Not applicable to current delivery month on or after first notice day.
Maximum range per day: Six cents in any one future. Not applicable to current delivery month on or after first notice day.
Growth deliverable at contract price: Standard growths: Ghana main crop; Bahia; Fine or Superior San Thome; Ivory Coast, fermented main crop; Costa Rican, fermented; Panama, fermented; Lagos, Kinds. Delivery from an exchange licensed warehouse in New York or Philadelphia, or by mutual agreement ex-ship or ex-dock.
Other grades: Deliverable at fixed premiums or discounts.

COFFEE "C" CONTRACT

New York Coffee and Sugar Exchange

Market hours: 9:45 A.M to 2:45 P.M.
Contract unit: 37,500 pounds in about 250 bags.
Price quotation and minimum price move: Cents and decimals of a cent per pound. 1/100 cent minimum ($3.75 per contract).
Trading limits: Six cents above or below previous day's settlement price.

Maximum range six cents. On expiring contract no limit on or after first notice day.

Contract months: Current and 12 succeeding months.

Deliverable growths: Mexican, Salvador, Costa Rica, or Guatemalans. Colombian of the kinds known as Medellin, Armenia, Manizales, Bogota, Sevilla, Girardot, Libano, or Tolima deliverable at 100-to-200-point premium. Growth of Nicaragua and Honduras deliverable at 100-point discount.

Basic grades: Coffee sweet in the cup good roasting quality, and as per types established by the Exchange. The delivery is to consist of one growth and in the case of Colombian, one kind only.

Basic grades deliverable: Mexican, Salvador, Guatemalans, Costa Rica, Nicaragua, Honduras, or Colombians according to respective types— ten points deducted for each imperfection below type. No delivery permitted of coffee containing more than ten imperfections below type. There is no premium for coffee grading better than type.

Delivery points: A licensed warehouse in the port of New York. "C" contract also permits delivery at customary commercial coffee dock in the port of New York where the coffee was originally discharged.

COPPER

New York Copper Exchange

Market hours: 9:50 A.M. to 2:00 P.M. EST

Contract unit: 25,000 pounds (2 percent more or less)

Price quotation and minimum price moves: Cents and tenths of a cent per pound.

Trading limits: Three cents above or below previous settling price.

Maximum range: six cents. Limits on delivery month will be removed on the day before first notice day.

Contract months: January, March, May, July, September, and December to 14 months ahead. In addition, the current calendar month and the two succeeding months shall be traded.

Deliverable unit at contract price: Officially listed brands or markings with basis grade Electrolytic Copper in ingot, ingot bars, wirebars, cakes, slabs, or billets.

Fire Refined High Conductivity copper in ingots or ingot bars at the contract price. Like Copper assaying 99.90 percent at the contract price. Electrolytic Cathodes at $\frac{1}{8}$ percent per pound discount. Fire Refined Copper at $\frac{1}{4}$ cent per pound discount. All copper must be of standard weights and size and confirm to specifications of the ASTM.

GOLD

New York Comex Exchange

Market hours: 9:25 A.M. to 2:30 P.M. (Local time).

Contract unit: 100 troy oz. (5 percent tolerance).

Delivery months: February, April, June, August, October, and December[1]

Price fluctuation: Cents per ounce.

Minimum price move: Ten cents minimum ($10 per contract).

Maximum price move: $10 above/below previous close. No limits on or after day before first notice day.

Delivery points: Exchange licensed depositories in borough of Manhattan.

Deliverable grade: Not less than 995 fineness.

Basis for settlement: Payment shall be made on the basis of the weight stamped upon each bar of gold delivered and the fineness of such gold up to 999.9 fine as set forth in the assay certificate.

Last trading day: Fourth last business day.

First notice day: Second last business day of previous month.

Last notice day: Third last business day.

PLATINUM

New York Mercantile Exchange

Market hours: 9:45 A.M. to 2:10 P.M. EST

Contract unit: 50 troy oz. (2 percent more or less).

Price quotations and minimum price moves: Dollars and cents per troy ounce; 10 cent minimum.

Trading limits: $10 above or below previous settling price.

Maximum range: $20. No limit on delivery month on last trading day. (Subject to variable limits.)

Contract months: January, April, July, and October.

Deliverable unit at contract price: Bar or sheet 99.8 percent pure and platinum metals minimum 99.5 percent pure, at an exchange approved depository within a 50-mile radius of Columbus Circle, New York.

PLYWOOD

Chicago Board of Trade Plywood

Market hours: 10:00 A.M. to 1:00 P.M. CST.

Contract unit: A 50-foot boxcar with a nine foot or wider door containing 36 banded units of 60 pieces each (2,376 pieces, 76,032 square feet), each sheet measuring 48 × 96 × ½ inches. Effective with July 1976 and forward, futures units will contain 66 pieces each for a total of 76,032 square feet. $3\frac{2}{16}$, 4 and/or 5 ply, ½ inch thick CD, Exterior Glue.

Grade standards: U.S. Products Standards as certified by the American Plywood Association, Timber Engineering Company, or Pittsburgh Testing Laboratories, and all panels must be appropriately and legibly marked.

Price quotations and fluctuations: Prices shall be basis f.o.b. Portland, Oregon, in dollars and cents per 1,000 square feet. Minimum price move

---

[1] In addition to said months, trading may be conducted in every calendar month as it becomes the current month and the immediately following two calendar months.

10 cents per 1,000 square feet. Daily fluctuations are limited to $7 per square foot above or below the previous day's settlement price except in the delivery month.

Termination of trading: Trading in the current delivery month ceases 12:15 P.M. on the eighth last business day of the month.

Contract months: Current and any subsequent months. Practice has been contracts one year into the future in January, March, May, July, September, and November.

Notice of delivery. Delivery notice may be given by seller on any business day of the delivery month, except no deliveries permitted during last five business days of delivery month. (Tender is made one business day prior to delivery.)

SILVER

New York COMEX

Market hours: 9:40 A.M. to 2:15 P.M. EST

Contract unit: 5,000 troy oz. (6 percent more or less).

Price quotations and minimum price moves: Cents and hundredths of a cent per troy oz. 10/100 cents minimum.

Trading limits: 20 cents above or below previous settling price.

Maximum range: 40 cents. No limit on delivery month beginning on the day before first notice day.

Contract months: January, March, May, July, September, December, to 17 months, but the three consecutive near months shall always be traded. For example, when January is nearby, February will be traded as it is needed to ensure that the three consecutive calendar months are traded.

Deliverable unit at contract price: Officially listed brands or markings, minimum 0.999 fineness, in bars, cast in bars of 1,000 or 1,100 troy oz. of customarily acceptable in the trade. Delivered in exchange licensed warehouse or vault in the city of New York.

London Cocoa Terminal Market Association

Market hours: 10:00–13:00; 14:30–17:00
Contract unit: 10 metric tons.
Price quotations: Pound sterling per metric ton.
Minimum fluctuation: £0.5 per ton or £5.00 per contract.
Trading limits: £30 per ton up or down from previous close. Market then
   closes for 15 minutes. On re-opening, no further limit is established.
Maximum range per day: None.
Growths deliverable at contract price: Good Fermented Ghana main crop.
   Delivery in bond at approved wharf or bonded warehouse in London,
   Liverpool, and Avonmouth at contract price; in Hull at £1 discount
   per ton, or in Amsterdam or Hamburg at £3 discount per ton.
Other grades: Deliverable at fixed premiums or discounts.
Commission rates round turn:

	Member	Nonmember
Regular	£20	£32
Day trade	£10	£16
Straddle	£20	£32

Delivery months: March, May, July, September, and December.

London Coffee Terminal Market Association

Market hours: 10:30–12:30; 14:30–17:00.
Contract unit: 5 metric tons.
Price quotation: £ per ton.
Minimum price moves: £1 per ton.
Trading limits: None.

Maximum range: None.

Growths deliverable at contract price: Uganda, Tanzania, India, Ghana, Sierra Leone, Nigeria, Angola, Cameroons, Zaire, Ivory Coast, Madagascar, Central African Republic, Togo, and Guinea.

Commission rates nonmember: £19 each trade.

Delivery months: January, March, May, July, September, and November.

London Metal Exchange (Copper)

Market hours: 12:00–12:05; 12:35–12:45; 15:40–15:45; 16:15–16:25 (Kerbs: 13:05–13:30; 16:35–16:50). Trading may take place outside of official hours.

Contract unit: 25 metric tons.

Price quotations and minimum prive moves: £ per ton; £0.5 per ton.

Trading limits: None.

Maximum range per day: None.

Deliverable grade: Wirebars-approved brands-weigth range 90–125 kg. of electrolytic copper at par of High Conductivity Fire Refined at £20 per ton discount. Cathodes–Electrolytic Copper assaying not less than 99.90 percent copper of approved brands.

Commission rates nonmember: 0.5 percent of value of initial transaction.

Delivery months: Cash through three months from initiation of contract.

London Metal Exchange (Lead)

Market hours: Rings, 12:15–12:20, 12:50–12:55, 15:30–15:35, 16:05–16:10; Kerbs, 13:05–13:30, 16:35–16:50.

Contract unit: 25 metric tons.

Price quotations and minimum price moves: £ per metric ton; £0.25 minimum.

Trading limits: None.

Contract months: Spot through three calendar months from initiation of contract.

Deliverable unit at contract price: Refined Pig Lead minimum 99.97 percent pure, in pigs weighing not more than 50 kg. of a brand approved by the exchange in one warehouse in London, Liverpool, Birkenhead, Manchester, Swansea, Birmingham, Hull, Newcastle-on-Tyne, Glasgow, or Avonmouth.

Nonmember commission rates round turn: 1 percent of value of initial transaction.

London Rubber Terminal Market Association

Market hours: 9:45–17:05. Kerb trading permissible.

Contract unit: 5 metric tons per month.

Price quotations and minimum price moves: Pence per kilo; 0.05 per kilo.

Trading limits: 2 pence above or below previous close. Market will close for 30 minutes and then reopen without limits.

242

Maximum range per day: None.
Deliverable grade: International ribbed smoked sheets certified quality #1.
Commission rates: £13 per 5 metric tons—R. T. nonmember; £6.50—Day
   Trade.

London Metal Exchange (Silver)

Market hours: Rings, 12:05–12:10, 13:00–13:05, 15:55–16:00, 16:30–16:35,
   Kerbs, 13:05–13:30, 16:35–16:50. Trading may take place outside of
   official market hours.
Contract unit: 10,000 troy oz. (5 percent more or less).
Price quotations and minimum price moves: Pence and decimals of a pence
   per troy ounce, £0–01.
Trading limits: None.
Contract months: Cash through seven months from contract initiation.
Deliverable unit at contract price: Officially listed brands, minimum 0.999
   fineness, in bars, each weighing 450–1,250 ounces in an approved
   vault/warehouse in London, Hamburg, or Amsterdam at seller's option.
Commission rates round turn: 0.5 percent of value of initial transaction.

United Terminal Sugar Market Association (London)

Market hours: 10:40–12:45, 14:30–17:00, *Kerb,* 17:00–20:00. N.Y.—6 hours
   earlier EST—5 hours EDT.
Contract unit: 50 long tons.(March 1977 forward: 50 metric tons.)
Price quotations and minimum price moves maximum daily move: Pounds
   Sterling per ton, £0.5 per ton, £20 above or below previous 12:30 P.M.
   close £40 range. No limit on second quoted month on and after first
   notice day of the then current spot contract.
Contract months: March, May, August, October, and December.
Deliverable unit at contract price: Bulk raw cane sugar of basis 96° polar-
   ization, produced in a country which is a signatory to Commonwealth
   Sugar Agreement C.I.F.; U.K.
Commission rates round turn: Nonmember £36.

London Metal Exchange (Tin)

Market hours: 12:10–12:15, 12:45–12:50, 15:45–15:55, 16:25–16:30; *Kerbs:*
   13:05–13:30, 16:35–16:50.
Contract unit: 5 metric tons.
Price quotations and minimum price moves: £ per ton, £1 per ton.
Trading limits: None.
Maximum range per day: None.
Deliverable grade: Refined tin assaying not less than 99:75 percent SN of
   approved brands either in ingots or slabs each weighing not less than
   12 kg. nor more than 50 kg.
Nonmember commission rates: 0.5 percent of value of initial transaction.
Delivery months: Cash through three months from contract initiation.

London Metal Exchange (Zinc)

Market hours: 12:20–12:25, 12:55–13:00, 15:35–15:40, 16:10–16:15; Kerbs: 13:05–13:30, 16:35–16:50.

Contract unit: 25 metric tons.

Price quotation and minimum price moves: £ per ton, £0.25 per ton.

Trading limits: None.

Maximum range per day: None.

Deliverable grade: Distillation or electrolysis produced virgin zinc minimum 98 percent pure of approved brands in slabs, plates, or ingots of not more than 50 kg. each.

Commission rates: 1 percent of value of initial transaction—nonmember rate.

Delivery months: Cash through three calendar months from contract initiation.

Glossary

of commodity terms

Actuals   The physical or *cash commodity*, as distinguished from *futures contracts* based upon the commodity.

Basis   1. The relationship of a *cash price* to the price of a particular *futures contract*. 2. In certain other uses, "basis" is understood as a concise expression of what might more completely be expressed as "is based upon the following conditions." For example, "price basis delivered New York, registered in owner's name . . ." means that the price being quoted is based upon those conditions being met.

Bona fide hedger   A classification or definition which may be established by the Commodity Futures Trading Commission for regulation purposes. The definition typically includes the industries which are viewed as having a bona fide hedging potential in their use of futures contracts; the uses of futures contracts which can be classified as bona fide hedging by some or all of those industries; and the size or degree of position that would be classified as bona fide hedging for some or all such industries. All market positions except those falling under the definition of bona fide hedging are classified as speculative and are subject to *margins* and *position limits* established by the CFTC and the exchange. Anyone unsure of his or her status under such a definition should consult a *broker*.

Broker   1. A person paid a fee or commission for acting as an agent in making sales or purchases. 2. When used as floor broker, it means a person who actually executes someone else's trading orders on the trading floor of an exchange. 3. When used to mean account executive, it means the person who deals with customers and their orders in commission house offices. See also *Registered Commodity Representative*.

Call option   The right, but not the obligation, to buy a futures contract through exercising option at its strike price.

Cash (commodity)   The physical commodity, as distinguished from *futures contracts*. The commodity as acquired through a cash market.

Cash market   A market in which transactions for purchase and sale of the physical commodity are made, under whatever terms are agreeable to buyer and seller and are legal under law and the rules of the market organization, if such exists.

Cash price A price quotation obtained in a *cash market*.

Charting The use of graphs and charts in analysis of market behavior so as to plot trends of price movements, average movements of price, volume, and open interest, in the hope that such graphs and charts will help one to anticipate and profit from price trends.

Clearing house An agency connected with a commodity exchange through which all futures contracts are made, *offset*, or fulfilled through *delivery* of the commodity and through which financial settlement is made. It may be a fully chartered separate corporation rather than division of the exchange itself.

Commodity Futures Trading Commission (CFTC) A federal regulatory agency charged and empowered under the Commodity Futures Trading Commission Act of 1974 with regulation of futures trading in all commodities. The commission is comprised of five commissioners, one of who is designated as a chairperson, all appointed by the President subject to Senate confirmation, and it is independent of all cabinet departments.

Day Traders *Speculators,* usually members of an exchange, who take positions in commodity futures and then offset them prior to the close of the same trading day.

Deferred months The more distant *delivery months* in which futures trading is taking place.

Delivery This common word has unique connotations when used in connection with *futures contracts*. Basically, in such usage, delivery refers to the changing of ownership or control of a commodity under very specific terms and procedures established by the exchange upon which the contract is traded. Typically, the commodity must be placed in an approved warehouse, on-track boxcar, or bank and inspected by approved personnel, after which the facility issues a warehouse receipt, shipping certificate, or due bill, which becomes a transferable delivery instrument. Delivery of the delivery instrument typically must be preceded by *delivery notice*. After receipt of the delivery instrument, the new owner typically can arrange with the storage facility to take possession of the physical commodity, can deliver the delivery instrument into the futures market in satisfaction of a *short position,* or can sell the delivery instrument to another market participant who can use it for delivery into the futures market in satisfaction of a short position or for cash.

Delivery month A calendar month during which delivery against a futures contract can be made.

Delivery notice A notice that must be presented by the seller to the *clearing house*. The clearing house then assigns the notice, and the subsequent delivery instrument to the longest-standing buyer on record. Under Chicago Board of Trade rules, such notices must be presented by 8 P.M. of the second business day prior to the day on which delivery is to be made.

Delivery points   Those locations and facilities designated by a commodity exchange at which stocks of a commodity may be delivered in fulfillment of a contract, under procedures established by the exchange.

Discretionary account   An arrangement by which the holder of the account gives written power of attorney to another, often a broker, to make buying and selling decisions without notification to the holder; often referred to as a "managed account" or "controlled account."

First notice day   The first day on which *Notices of Intent to Deliver* the commodity in fulfillment of a given month's futures contract can be made by the seller to the *clearing house* and by the clearing house to a buyer.

Forward contract   A cash market transaction in which two parties agree to the purchase and sale of a commodity at some future time under such conditions as the two agree. In contrast to a *futures contract,* the terms of a forward contract are not standardized; a forward contract is not transferable and usually can be cancelled only with the consent of the other party, which often must be obtained for consideration and under penalty; and forward contracts are not traded in federally designated contract markets. Essentially, forward contract refers to any cash market purchase or sale agreement for which delivery is not made "on the *spot.*"

Fundamental analysis   An approach to market behavior which stresses the study of underlying factors of supply and demand in the commodity in the belief that such analysis will enable one to profit from being able to anticipate price trends.

Futures contract   A transferable agreement to make or take delivery of a standardized amount of a commodity, of standardized minimum quality grades, during a specific month, under terms and conditions established by the federally designated contract market upon which trading is conducted.

Hedging   The initiation of a position in a futures market which is intended as a temporary substitute for the sale or purchase of the actual commodity.

Intrinsic value   For call options, the amount that the market price is *above* the strike price. For put options, the amount that the market price is *below* the strike price. Put or call options with intrinsic value are in-the-money options.

Liquid market   A market where selling and buying can be accomplished with ease due to the presence of a large number of interested buyers and sellers willing and able to trade substantial quantities at small price differences.

Long   As a noun, one who has bought *futures contracts* (or the *cash commodity,* depending upon the market under discussion) and has not yet *offset* that position. As a verb, the action of taking a position in which one has bought futures contracts (or the cash commodity) without taking the offsetting action. For example, if you had no position and you bought five contracts, you would be a "long." However, if your previous position was one of having sold five contracts (that is, "being *short* five"), and you then bought five contracts to offset that position, your second action would not be referred to as "going long" because your position when the second action is concluded would be zero. Long also is used with similar meanings as an adjective or adverb.

Margin An amount of money deposited by both buyers and sellers of futures contracts to ensure performance of the terms of the contract, that is, the *delivery* or taking of delivery of the commodity or the cancellation of the position by a subsequent offsetting trade at such price as can be attained. Margin in commodities is not a payment of equity or downpayment on the commodity itself but rather is in the nature of a performance bond or security deposit.

Margin call A call from a clearing house to a clearing member, or from a brokerage firm to a customer, to bring margin deposits up to a minimum level required by clearing house regulations.

Nearby A *delivery month* of a futures contract that is in the near future, as contrasted with a *deferred* month which is farther into the future.

Net position The number of contracts a trader has bought or sold but not *offset* by opposite trades. For example, if a trader bought 10 December and then sold 15 December, the net position would be five *short*. If the trader then bought ten more, he or she would then be five *long*. Similarly, the net position of a brokerage firm or clearing member can be calculated by determining the total it has bought and sold for its customers.

Offset The liquidation of a purchase of futures or option contracts through sale of an equal number of contracts of the same delivery month, or the covering of a *short* sale of futures through the purchase of an equal number of contracts of the same delivery month. Either action cancels the obligation to make or take delivery of the commodity.

Open interest The total number of futures contracts of a given commodity wihch have not yet been *offset* by opposite futures transactions nor fulfilled by *delivery* of the commodity; the total number of open transactions. Each open transaction has a buyer and a seller, but for calculation of open interest, only one side of the contract is counted.

Option writer An investor who sells (writes) options against futures contracts or against commodity inventories and is paid a premium by a option buyer.

Position A market commitment. For example, one who has bought futures contracts is said to have a *long* position, and conversely, a seller of futures contracts is said to have a *short* position.

Position limit The maximum number of speculative futures contracts one can hold as determined by the *Commodity Futures Trading Commission* and/or the exchange upon which the contract is traded. See also *bona fide hedger, speculator.*

Position trading An approach to trading in which the trader either buys or sells contracts and holds them for an extended period of time, as distinguished from the *day trader,* who will normally initiate and offset his or her position within a single trading session.

Premium The price of the option minus its intrinsic value.

Price limits The maximum price advance or decline from the previous day's *settlement price* permitted for a contract in one trading session by the rules of the exchange. See also *Variable limits.*

Put option The right, but not the obligation, to sell a futures contract through exercising an option at its strike price.

Registered Commodity Representative (RCR) A member or nonmember of an exchange who is registered with the exchange to solicit and handle commodity customer business for a firm.

Reporting limit, reportable position The number of futures contracts, as determined by the exchange and/or the *Commodity Futures Trading Commission,* above which one must report to the exchange and/or the CFTC with regard to the size of one's position by commodity, by delivery month, and by purpose of the trading (that is, *bona fide hedging* or *speculating*).

Scalper A *speculator* who trades a large volume of contracts at small price differences in the hope of being able to earn an acceptable overall profit at minimal risk.

Settlement price The price established by a clearing house at the close of each trading session as the official price to be used in determining net gains or losses, *margin* requirements, and the next day's *price limits,* and for other purposes. The term settlement price is also often used as an approximate equivalent to the term "closing price."

Short As a noun, one who has sold *futures contracts* (or the cash commodity, depending upon the market under discussion) and has not yet *offset* that position. As a verb, the action of taking a position in which one has sold futures contracts (or made a *forward contract* for sale of the cash commodity) without taking the offsetting action. For example, if you had no position and you sold five contracts, your action would be "shorting the futures," and you would then be a "short." However, if your previous position was one of having bought five contracts (that is, "being *long* five"), and you then sold five contracts to offset that position, your second action would not be referred to as "shorting" because your position when the second action was concluded would be zero.

Speculator One who attempts to anticipate commodity price changes and to profit through the sale and purchase or purchase and sale of commodity futures contracts or of the physical commodity.

Spot Refers to the characteristic of being available for immediate (or nearly immediate) delivery. An outgrowth of the phrase "on the spot," it usually refers to a *cash market* price for stocks of the physical commodity that are available for immediate delivery, or vice versa, and depending upon the noun it modifies, the stocks themselves that are available for delivery if an acceptable price is quoted. Thus, cash market transactions are usually grouped into two kinds: *spot* and *forward contracts*. However, "spot" is also sometimes used in reference to the *futures contract* of the current month, in which case trading is still "futures" trading but *delivery* is possible at any time.

Spreading   The simultaneous purchase of one futures contract and sale of another in the expectation that the price relationships between the two will change, at which time one can sell the first and buy back the second at a profit. Examples include the purchase of one *delivery month* and the sale of another in the same commodity on the same exchange, or the purchase and sale of the same delivery month and the same commodity but on different exchanges.

Straddle   A combination of put and call options on the same commodity with the same strike price and expiration date.

Strike price   The price at which a put or call option can be exercised for a short or long futures contract.

Technical analysis   An approach to analysis of futures markets and future trends of commodity prices which examines the technical factors of market activity. Technical analysts normally examine patterns of price change, rates of change, and changes in volume of trading and *open interest*, often by *charting*, in the hope of being able to predict and profit from future trends.

Trading limit   The maximum number of contracts, as determined by an exchange and/or the *Commodity Futures Trading Commission*, that one may trade in a given trading day.

Tender   The act on the part of the seller of a futures contract of giving *notice* to the *clearing house* that he or she intends to deliver the commodity in satisfaction of the futures contract.

Variation call   A call for additional margin deposits made by a *clearing house* to a clearing member while trading is in progress when current price trends have substantially reduced the protective value of the clearing member's margin deposits. Variation calls are payable at the close of the business day.

Variable limits   A Chicago Board of Trade *price limit* system which allows for larger than normally allowable price movements under certain circumstances. Those circumstances are as follows: If a commodity's price closes up or down limit for three consecutive days in three or more contract months during a business year, or all contracts in a business year if there are less than three open, the variable limits policy increases daily price limits to 150 percent of the normal levels for the next three consecutive business days. Those limits remain in effect until at least three contracts in the commodity, or all contracts in a business year if there are less than three open, fail to close up or down the limit during that period. Limits then revert to their original levels.

Books

Arthur, H. B. *Commodity Futures as a Business Management Tool.* Boston: Harvard Business School, 1971.

Chicago Board of Trade. *Commodity Futures Trading: A Bibliography 1967–1973.* Chicago: Chicago Board of Trade, 1974.

Dominguez, J. R. *Devaluation and Futures Markets.* Lexington, Mass.: Lexington Books, 1972.

Gould, Bruce G. *The Dow Jones-Irwin Guide to Commodities Trading.* Homewood, Ill.: Dow Jones-Irwin, 1973.

Granger, C. W. J. *Getting Started in London Commodities.* New York: Investors Intelligence, 1973.

Labys, W. C., and Granger, C. W. J. *Speculation, Hedging and Commodity Price Forecasts.* Lexington, Mass.: Lexington Books, 1971.

Maxwell, J. R., Sr. *Commodity Futures Trading with Moving Averages.* Port Angeles, Wash.: Speer Books, 1976.

Powers, Mark J. *Getting Started in Commodity Futures Trading.* Columbia, Md.: Investor Publications, 1973.

Sanders, Donald H. *Computers and Management.* New York: McGraw-Hill Book Company, 1974.

Teweles, R. J. et al. *The Commodity Futures Game: Who Wins? Who Loses?* New York: McGraw-Hill Book Co., 1974.

Zieg, K. C., and Kaufman, P. J. *Point and Figure Commodity Trading Techniques.* Larchmont, N.Y.: Investors Intelligence, 1975.

Zieg, Kermit C., Jr., and Zieg, Susannah H. *Commodity Options.* New York: Investors Intelligence, 1974.

Articles and Pamphlets

Berton, Lee. "Is the heyday over for the commodities speculator?" *Financial World*, September 5, 1973, pp. 20–24.

Black, F., and Scholes, M. "Valuation of option contracts and a test of market efficiency." *Journal of Finance* 27 (May 1972): 399–417.

Commodity Futures Trading Commission. "News," Release No. 228–76, December 8, 1976, Washington, D.C., pp. 1–6.

Commodity Futures Trading Commission. "News," Release No. 228–77, March 24, 1977, Washington, D.C., pp. 1–8.

"Commodity options: Interim rules and amendments." *Federal Register* 41, 197 (October 8, 1976), pp. 44560–68.

"Commodity options transactions: Proposed amendment of interim regulations." *Federal Register* 42, 65 (April 5, 1977), pp. 18246–64.

Fink, R., and Turner, D. "Computers and commodity price forecasting." *Commodity Year Book 1973.* New York: Commodity Research Bureau, Inc., 1973, pp. 24–30.

Greenspan, W. "Understanding the money futures market." *Commodity Year Book 1973.* New York: Commodity Research Bureau, Inc., pp. 48–54.

Harris, E. B., and Powers, Mark J. "Role of commodity futures and relationship to stock market." *Commercial and Financial Chronicle* 214 (December 23, 1971), pp. 1861–65.

Israel, A. C. "Phenomenal growth of commodity futures trading." *Commercial and Financial Chronicle* 215 (March 23, 1972), pp. 949–54.

Jarecki, H. "Mocatta options: Forerunner of a boom market?" *Commodities* 4 (April 1977), pp. 31–35.

Jobman, Darrell. "How to evaluate a commodity options firm." *Commodities* 5 (December 1976), pp. 20–24.

Jones, Donald L. "The misbehavior of commodity prices." *Commodities* 4 (August 1975), pp. 20–24.

Most, Nathan, and Steur, Lee. "A different approach to commodity options." *Commodities* 6 (February 1977), pp. 32–34.

Murray, T. J. "Furor over commodity options." *Dun's* 101 (March 1973), pp. 69–72.

Almedo, J. P., Jr. "Understanding the lumber and plywood futures market." *Commodity Year Book 1973.* New York: Commodity Research Bureau, Inc., 1973, pp. 6–15.

Olmedo, J. P., Jr. "How to trade and hedge in the lumber and plywood futures markets." *Commodity Year Book 1975.* New York: Commodity Research Bureau, Inc., pp. 24–35.

Parker, George B. "Understanding the London Futures Market." *Commodity Year Book 1971.* New York: Commodity Research Bureau, Inc., 1971, pp. 36–47.

Rainbolt, John. "What the new Commodity Futures Trading Commission means to you." *Commodities* 4 (February 1975), pp. 23–27.

"Regulation and fraud in connection with commodity and commodity option transactions." *Federal Register* 41, 228 (November 24, 1976), pp. 51808–17.

Reinach, A. M. "Commodity futures as a hedge against inflation." *Commodity Year Book 1975.* New York: Commodity Research Bureau, Inc. 1975, pp. 6–12.

Riess, Michael. "Trading London commodity options." *Commodities* 1 (June 1972), pp. 10–15.

Riess, Michael. "Arbitrage as a trading medium." *Commodities* 2 (March 1973), pp. 24–27.

Riess, Michael. "London commodity markets." *Commodities* 3 (February 1974), pp. 17–20.

Schneider, H. "Another step toward domestic options trading." *Commodities* 6 (May 1977), pp. 44–46.

Stevenson, R. A., and Bear, R. M. "Commodities futures: Trends or random walks?" *Journal of Finance* 25 (March 1970), pp. 65–81.

Teweles, R. J.; Harlow, C. V.; and Stone, H. L. "The management of risk." *Commodity Year Book 1975.* New York: Commodity Research Bureau, Inc., 1975, pp. 50–55.

Teweles, R. J. et al. "The behavior of commodity prices." *Commodities* 4 (June 1975), pp. 14–17.

Department of the Treasury, Internal Revenue Service, "Sales and Other Dispositions of Assets," Publication No. 544, 1977 Edition, Washington, D.C.

Department of the Treasury, Internal Revenue Service, "Tax Information on Investment Income and Expenses," Publication No. 550, 1977 Edition, Washington, D.C.

Charts are reproduced with the permission of Commodity Chart Service, Commodity Research Bureau, Inc., New York.

Periodicals and newspapers

American Gold News, P.O. Box 457, Ione, Calif. 95640 (M).

American Metal Market, 7 E. 12th St., New York, N.Y. 10003 (D x. Sat. and Sun.).

Commodities, 1000 Century Plaza, Columbia, Md. 21044.

Consensus, Inc., National Commodity Futures Weekly, 30 W. Pershing Rd., Kansas City, Mo. 64108.

Economist, The, U.S. Address: 527 Madison Ave., New York, N.Y. 10022 (W).

Euromoney, Euromoney Publications, Ltd., 14 Finsbury Circus, London, EC 2 (M).

Financial Executive, 633 Third Ave., New York, N.Y. 10017 (M).

Financial Times of Canada, 1885 Leslie St., Don Mills, Ontario, Canada (W).

Institutional Investor, 488 Madison Ave., New York, N.Y. 10022 (M).

International Management, 1221 Avenue of the Americas, New York, N.Y. 10020 (M).

Investor, 611 N. Broadway, Milwaukee Wis. 53202 (M).

Iron Age, The, Chilton Way, Radnor, Penn. 19089 (W).

Light Metal Age, 693 Mission St., Penthouse, San Francisco, Calif. 94105 (B).

Metal/Center News, 7 E. 12th St., New York, N.Y. 10003 (M).

Metals Week, 1221 Ave. of the Americas, New York, N.Y. 10020 (W).

Mining Record, The, 290 Fillmore St., Denver, Colo. 80206 (W).

Modern Metals, 919 N. Michigan Ave., Chicago, Ill. 60611 (M).

Money Manager, The, The Bond Buyer, 1 State St. Plz., New York, N.Y. 10004 (W).

New York Times, The, 229 E. 43d St., New York, N.Y. 10036 (D).

Times of London, The, U. S. Address: 201 E. 43d St., New York, N.Y. 10017 (D).

World Mining, 500 Howard St., San Francisco, Calif. 94105 (M).

Statistical sources

Canadian Statistical Review (Weekly Supplements) The Ministry of Industry, Trade and Commerce, Ottawa, Ontario K1A 0H5 Canada (M).

Monthly Digest of Statistics, Her Majesty's Stationery Office, P.O. Box 569, London SE1 9NH (M).

Economic Statistics Monthly, Publications Dept., The Credit Information Company of Japan, LTD, 2–8, 1 Chrome, Uchi-Kanda, Chiyoda-ku, Tokyo 101 (M).

International Financial Statistics, International Monetary Fund, 19th and H Sts., NW, Washington, D.C. 20431 (M).

Federal Reserve Bulletin, Federal Reserve Bank, New York, N.Y. (M).

Balance of Payments Yearbook, International Monetary Fund, 19th and H Sts., NW, Washington, D.C. 20431 (A).

Canadian Statistical Review, The Ministry of Industry, Trade and Commerce, Ottawa, Ontario, K1A 0H5, Canada, (M, Weekly Supplement).

The Yearbook of the American Bureau of Metal Statistics, 50 Broadway, New York, N.Y. 10004 (A).

Metal Statistics, 1974, American Metal Market, 7 E. 12th St. New York, N.Y. 10003 (A).

Commodity Yearbook, Commodity Research Bureau, Inc. One Liberty Plz. New York, N.Y. 10006 (A).

Minerals Yearbook, U. S. Bureau of Mines, Dept. of the Interior, Washington, D.C. 20240 (A).

Index